Critical Think

Critical Thinking and Language

The Challenge of Generic Skills and Disciplinary Discourses

Tim John Moore

BLOOMSBURY

LONDON · NEW DELHI · NEW YORK · SYDNEY

Bloomsbury Academic

An imprint of Bloomsbury Publishing Plc

50 Bedford Square   175 Fifth Avenue
London   New York
WC1B 3DP   NY 10010
UK   USA

www.bloomsbury.com

First published by Continuum International Publishing Group 2011
Paperback edition first published 2013

British Library Cataloguing-in-Publication Data
A catalogue record for this book is available from the British Library.

ISBN: HB: 978-1-4411-5750-8
       PB: 978-0-5671-5773-7

Library of Congress Cataloging-in-Publication Data
A catalog record for this book is available from the Library of Congress

Typeset by Amnet International, Dublin, Ireland

For my parents — Bo and June

Contents

Acknowledgements

Many good friends and colleagues have encouraged and supported me in the writing of this book, and also in completing the research upon which it is based. First of all, I owe a great debt to the supervisors of the research: Joanna Tapper and Tim McNamara from the University of Melbourne. Joanna has been a permanent joy to work with, and done much to keep me interested and on track with the project; Tim, whose linguistic and other intellectual interests seem to know no bounds nowadays, has been a great mentor, pushing me into areas of inquiry where I would not otherwise have ventured.

In the conduct of the research itself, I am most grateful to the esteemed historians, philosophers, and cultural studies folk who took part in the study. Not only did they give up valuable time to allow themselves be subjected to my persistent interrogations, but it is their words and ideas about critical thinking – always interesting and often inspiring – that constitute much of the content of this book.

Other colleagues have provided me with much intellectual and moral support along the way. I am especially grateful to my colleague and comrade Rosemary Clerehan, who gave me my first job in the language and learning field 20 years ago, with whom I have shared the changing fortunes of university life, and who remains a great 'critical' friend. Gordon Taylor, over the same period, has been a huge influence, giving me and my colleagues a sense of the infinite possibilities of language and learning work, and of work in the academy generally. Steve Price, Helen Marriot and Andrew Johnson from this period have also helped me in different ways to see the work through. Another colleague, Martin Davies, has been a permanent critic of my ideas, but one who has always pursued this critique in an open and thoughtful way. I am also grateful to my colleagues at Swinburne University – Kay Lipson, Sue Kokonis and Debbi Weaver – who, through their support, have given me the opportunity to explore some of the practical applications of the work.

The book has benefited from the advice of several exceptional scholars. John Swales was a reviewer of the original research, and someone who encouraged me to take the project further; and Ken Hyland gave up his time to provide a thoughtful assessment of an earlier draft of the book. The ideas of both these writers are strongly present in the work. I am also grateful to Sue Starfield for her careful reading of the original manuscript.

I would also like to thank Continuum Books, and especially my two editors Gurdeep Mattu and Colleen Coalter, who have been a pleasure to work with, and who have made the process an entirely painless one.

Finally and most of all, there is my family – my wife Janne Morton, and two boys, Roy and Victor – who sustain me in all ways, and who have expressed barely a 'critical thought' during the long period of this project.

Chapter 1

Introduction: The Problem of Critical Thinking

To purify the dialect of the tribe ...

—*T. S. Eliot*
Four Quartets

For the learning of every virtue, there is an appropriate discipline.
—*Bertrand Russell*
A History of Western Philosophy

1.1 Introduction: Words and Worlds

In his famous book of terms, *Keywords*, Raymond Williams discusses the disorienting effect that language can have on an individual when they enter a new realm of experience. Williams felt this effect himself upon his return to Cambridge University in 1945, after an interruption to his studies during the war years. Although his time away was relatively short, he was sure that in this intervening period the language of the university had somehow changed. In contemplating what for him was 'a new and strange world' around him, Williams remarked to a colleague: 'The fact is that they just don't seem to speak the same language'. (Williams 1976: p. 9)

For Williams, the most noticeable new word in the argot of the postwar campus was the term 'culture'. He said that not only was he hearing the term much more often, but that it also seemed to have acquired new and different senses, which, at the time, he 'could not get clear'. This experience was the motivation for his writing *Keywords*, which he describes as his 'record of inquiry into a shared body of words and meanings in our most general discussions ... of practices and institutions' (p.13). Williams' hope in writing the book was to make some sense – both for himself and for others – of a vocabulary that we all use, and which we seek 'to find our way in'. (p. 22)

The present book is motivated by a similar interest in a particular word and also by a similar difficulty in 'getting its meaning clear'. The word – or rather expression – I have in mind is *critical thinking*. As it was for Williams, my first encounter with this term, along with a sense of its manifold importance in the academy, also coincided with an experience of returning to a university. In the early 1990s, after a period of living abroad, I re-entered the university system both to take up studies in applied linguistics, and also to commence work as a study skills tutor at a large Australian university. The tutoring position, which involved the teaching of academic and language skills, was a relatively new type of work in Australian universities, having emerged out of the many changes that were occurring in the higher education sector around this time (Chanock 2005). These changes – which saw not only large increases in the number of students participating in higher education, but also changes in the types of social, cultural and linguistic backgrounds they came from – meant there was a need for universities to devote themselves in dedicated ways to assisting certain cohorts of students to adapt to the demands of tertiary study.

In the work that my colleagues and I did with students over the ensuing decade – consisting mainly of academic writing classes, and advice sessions for individual students – a notion that was never far away in our discussions and deliberations was the idea of being *critical*. The term, for example, was frequently present in the assignment tasks set for students, the discussion of which formed the basis of many of the writing classes we conducted (e.g. *Critically discuss X. In this assignment, you need to show your critical understanding of Y*, etc.). More tellingly, the term was often present as a key element in much of the written feedback provided to students on their completed assignments – often, sadly, when a piece of work had, in the lecturer's judgement, fallen short of the expected standard (e.g. *This work is too descriptive and not sufficiently critical*, etc.). In many of the academic skills manuals that began to be published at the time, and which slowly filled our office shelves, the idea of students needing to be critical was also a recurring theme.

It seemed, from these experiences, that in the practical domain of helping students to adapt to this new learning environment, the idea of being successful at university was understood increasingly in terms of the degree of 'criticalness' that students could bring to their studies. This, for me, was an interesting development, partly because I could not recall the term being used much at all in the days of my own undergraduate study some 15 years earlier in the 1970s. My growing awareness of the term was also sharpened by the difficulties that both my students and I had in 'getting the term's meaning clear' – both as some general capacity that needed to be adopted, and also, at times, as some specialist form of engagement seemingly demanded by particular contexts of study.

It also became apparent around this time that the term 'critical' was not only being used in the everyday domain of study in the disciplines, but was also gaining currency in a larger rhetorical arena – in the area of national higher education policy. In the 1990s, in Australia and elsewhere, a new agenda began to emerge in the sector, one that saw a shift from an 'inputs' approach to policy, with an emphasis on efficiency and productivity, to a focus on 'outcomes' and 'quality' (Ballard and Clanchy 1995). Central to this project was the imperative for universities 'to describe the attributes that graduates should acquire through their exposure to a high quality education system' (Australian Higher Education Council 1992: p. 32). Thus, in the ensuing years, university administrators applied themselves energetically to 'auditing' the many academic programmes offered by institutions to try to come up with an account of what it was that students would possess, or what it was hoped they would possess, at the end of their degrees. In such processes, which have continued unabated into the new millennium, one of the attributes that it is universally agreed students should develop is the ability to think critically. (Barnett 2004)

1.2 Issues of Critical Thinking

The notion of being critical thus seems to have assumed a reified position in our universities; and indeed the phrase 'critical thinking' has become, as Williams might describe, a keyword 'in our most general discussions of practices and institutions' (1976: p. 13). For John Swales, the term has become a surrogate for one of the defining characteristics of the academic world (Swales, personal communication). However, while many accept the term as a fundamental way of characterizing contemporary higher education, there are many questions and problems that seem to surround its use. The first of these is the basic definitional question – what do we mean precisely when we speak of 'critical thinking'? I indicated earlier my own difficulties in coming to some understanding of the term; the same difficulties are reported widely in the literature (Fox 1994; Atkinson 1997; Chanock 2000; Candlin 1998). Dwight Atkinson, for example, suggests that even though critical thinking has become such a widely discussed concept, many in the university find the term an elusive one:

> academics normally considered masters of precise definition seem almost unwilling or unable to define critical thinking. Rather they often appear to take the concept on faith, perhaps as a self-evident foundation of Western thought – such as freedom of speech. (1997: p. 74)

Along with questions concerning the meaning of critical thinking, there are other issues one must confront. For example, does the term refer to some kind of universal 'generic skill' that is readily transferable to a multiplicity of situations, or is it better understood as only a loose category, taking in a number of diverse modes of thought dependent on specific contexts. Related to these basic epistemological questions are questions of pedagogy. If we wish our students to

become critical thinkers, how is this best achieved? Should there be, for example, dedicated generalist courses in 'thinking', or is it best to teach this ability to
students within the context of their studies in the disciplines. Indeed, is it necessary to teach critical thinking at all? These are all important questions, and the
answers that are proposed for them have the potential to have a major bearing
on the way that university curricula are understood and developed.

1.3 The Critical Thinking Movement and its Critics

All this uncertainty is not to suggest, however, that the idea of 'critical thinking'
has remained an unexamined one, and that it has somehow entered our institutions without some effort to properly interrogate and understand it. Indeed,
the years since the term's 'coming of age' in the late 1980s (Paul 1989) have
seen the emergence of a burgeoning literature on the subject. Much of this has
emanated from a group of scholars known collectively as the 'critical thinking
movement' (Barnett 2000). This group, mainly based in the US, but also increasingly active in the UK and Australia, has devoted itself conscientiously to the
definitional question, producing a variety of accounts of critical thinking – both
in the form of kernel definitions (e.g. Ennis 1987; Paul 1989; van Gelder 2001),
and as taxonomies of constituent skills (e.g. Ennis 1987; Facione 1990). Definitional work of this type has provided a solid educational foundation for the
concept, and has opened the way to the development of a great variety of critical thinking courses and materials, and also a variety of methods for testing
students' acquisition of these skills.

While scholars in the movement have done much to advance the cause of
thinking within contemporary education, it needs to be noted that their ideas
have not been fully embraced by all; indeed, many of the ideas they advance
have become the object of the same kind of critical scrutiny that they typically
advocate for all other fields of inquiry. A number of criticisms have been made.
One of these concerns the multiplicity of definitions that have emerged from
the movement's ranks. While considerable intellectual effort has gone into this
enterprise (Facione 1990), it is not altogether clear that out of these processes,
the concept has ended up being a substantially clearer one. Some critics have
gone so far as to suggest that all this definitional work from within the movement has only managed to make the idea of critical thinking more confusing
than it once was. (e.g. Capossela 1993: p. 1)

Another problem is that the definitional debates conducted by the movement have tended to be somewhat detached from the domains in which critical
thinking actually needs to be applied – that is, in the disciplines of students'
study. It has thus been suggested that there is a tendency to treat the concept as
an abstract and philosophical one, and to rely mainly on methods of introspection and intuition to develop and refine its meanings (Norris 1992). Some critics

have suggested that what is produced ultimately out of such processes are definitions of a more normative nature than ones based in any actual reality, thus casting some doubt on the validity of many of the ideas proposed (Atkinson 1997). Indeed, it is questioned whether such generic concepts represent an accurate description of the critical thinking that goes on in various fields of study, or whether they amount more to some idealized – and possibly even misleading – version of it. (Atkinson 1997)

The types of problems identified here are sometimes characterized as metaphysical ones. Writing in an earlier period about the problems of definitions generally, Ludwig Wittgenstein argued that the difficulties philosophers often find themselves faced with stem from an urge to take some concept and to define it in an abstract way. Inevitably, out of such processes, he argues, many different and alternative meanings are generated leading unavoidably to a 'state of puzzlement' (Wittgenstein 1958a). But for Wittgenstein (at least in his later incarnations), it is folly to imagine that words have some independent, metaphysical meaning; the only solid semantic basis they can be said to have is that which emerges from the way they are used in everyday discourse – hence Wittgenstein's famous dictum: 'the meaning of a word is its use in the language' (1958a: p. 20). For Wittgenstein then, the solution to any difficulties concerning words and their meaning is not to 'think' about them on some abstract plane, but rather to observe how they are used in the 'rough ground' of human activity.

1.4 In Search of Critical Thinking: An Investigation

The preceding ideas provided the basis for the present work. In the case of our term 'critical thinking', it may be that 'to get some clarity' about its meaning, we need to go to the 'rough ground' of the places where it is actually practiced in the university – that is to say, in the disciplines, and to explore the term in its everyday uses. The present work has sought to do this by investigating conceptions of critical thinking as they are understood and taught about by academics from a range of disciplines. The investigation has specifically sought answers to the following questions:

i.   What does 'critical thinking' mean to individual academics teaching in different disciplines within the university?
ii.   In what ways, and to what extent, can we say that there are disciplinary variations in these meanings of critical thinking?
iii. What implications might the answers to questions i and ii have for the teaching of critical thinking in the university?

The disciplines chosen for investigation were ones that had particular relevance to my teaching work – philosophy, history and the literary/cultural studies – all humanities disciplines based at the university at which I was working at the time, hereon referred to as 'University X'. The investigation was carried out using a combination of interview and textual analysis methods, with a focus on how the concept of critical thinking is talked about by academics, and how it is constructed in a range of texts used by them on their teaching programmes. Broadly, the method of investigation fitted with John Swales' now famous methodological portmanteau, 'textography' – an approach described by him as 'something more than a disembodied textual or discoursal analysis, but something less than a full ethnographic account'. (1998: p. 1)

In outlining the questions that informed the investigation, it is also important to indicate what is not covered in the work. The recounting of my teaching experiences earlier would suggest that the question of how students apprehend the idea of being critical is a most pressing one. While this is certainly true, the work does not actually consider critical thinking from the point of view of students. It is instead limited to investigating the perspective of teaching academics – or rather, those of a particular group of academics working in a particular range of disciplines. In this respect, the scope of the study is deliberately narrow. This is partly because students' understandings of notions of criticality have been investigated in a number of studies (e.g. Tsui 2000, 2002; Gellin 2003; Phillips and Bond 2004; Tapper 2004; Waite and Davis 2006), but also because the uncertainty surrounding the notion suggests the need for clarity from those who rely on the term in the everyday contexts of their work, and whose particular apprehensions of it would seem to be somehow crucial to the meanings it assumes.

Another limitation of scope is the study's focus on the idea of understandings and conceptions of critical thinking. Although this book is at heart interested in issues of teaching and learning in the academy, the focus is not on pedagogical matters as such; that is to say, the book does not consider such questions as how exactly critical thinking is taught to students on academic programmes, nor indeed whether it seems to be taught effectively or not. The interest rather is less pedagogical and more epistemological – though, as is suggested above, to have some resolution of these epistemological questions is arguably a necessary first step towards working out what can and should be done in the area of teaching.

The book follows a conventional structure. Following on from this introduction, a review of relevant literature is presented in Chapter 2, covering a history of the idea of critical thought in education, and an elaboration of current debates surrounding the concept. Chapter 3 provides an account of the study's methodology, as well as background about the disciplines studied. The findings of the investigation, which make up the main part of the book, are divided into two sections: Chapter 4 describes the findings from the interview component of the study, and Chapter 5 presents the findings from the textual analysis. In Chapter 6, the study's findings are summarized, and some cautious answers to the questions above are proposed. In the concluding chapter a final definition of the idea of critical thinking is offered.

Chapter 2

Critical Thinking: History, Definitions, Issues

2.1 Introduction

Included in Raymond Williams' *Keywords* is an entry for the term 'critical', or rather a variant of it – 'criticism'. Williams confirms the impressions one has of the problems associated with the term by commencing his account thus: 'criticism has become a very difficult word' (1976: p. 74). He goes on to suggest a range of meanings, including 'its predominant general sense of fault finding', 'an underlying sense of judgement', and also what he calls a 'very confusing specialized sense' the term has acquired in relation to art and literature. Williams speaks of the difficulties in understanding the term's various developments, with some meanings having only emerged recently, and others which appear to be 'breaking down'. (p. 74)

In this chapter, I begin an initial exploration of the idea of critical thinking, and seek 'some understanding of its developments' by referring to the extensive literature that has been written on the subject. The chapter begins with a potted history of the concept – including its importance in higher education – before looking into the major question of definitions. The chapter also considers the related issue of how much we might think of critical thinking as some generic quality, and how much as one shaped by specific domains of inquiry.

2.2 Critical Thinking and Education – A Brief History

The idea of critical thinking having a key role in education goes back perhaps as far as the idea of education itself. It can be dated back to at least the time of the Greeks, especially to Socrates and his desire to show his Athenian pupils what it meant to lead a wise and virtuous life. For Socrates, the key to such wisdom and virtue is critical thought: 'The unexamined life is one not worth living', he famously declared *(The Apology)*. Socrates believed himself to be a teacher at heart – 'a midwife of ideas' was his description – whose role was to encourage his students to interrogate received wisdoms, and moral standards of the day in a spirit of untrammeled inquiry, and 'to follow the argument where it leads'. The Socratic method, one of dialogue and questioning, was to lay the foundations of education in the classical world, including arguably the first Western university – Plato's Academy – and has continued as a kind of pedagogical ideal right through to the present. (Bowen 1972a)

In the Renaissance, which saw a revival of interest in the humanism of the Greeks and a corresponding loosening of the church's hold over the intellectual life of Europe, there was a re-emergence of a belief in the inquiring mind. The challenge to accepted wisdom and knowledge in this period was eventually to culminate in the mass-scale critique that was the Protestant Reformation. A number of Renaissance writers wrote specifically about the implications of the new intellectual spirit for education. Michel de Montaigne, the sixteenth century French writer, who – among other things – bequeathed to modern education that most pedagogical of written genres, the *essai*, believed strongly in the importance of a critical frame. In perhaps his best known work, "Of the Education of Children", Montaigne is dismissive of the educational practices of the time – what he called a humanistic pedantry – declaring that: 'We labour, and toil and plod to fill the memory, and leave both understanding and judgement empty' (*Complete works of Montaigne*, p.125). In his ideas about what a good education might entail, Montaigne, it must be acknowledged, thought little beyond the needs of male members of the aristocratic class. Nevertheless, what he believed young noble boys should be taught was an attitude to accepted wisdom that a modern educator would find exemplary. Even the classical canon, Montaigne insisted, should be fair game.

> I would have the tutor make the child examine and thoroughly sift every thing he reads and lodge nothing in his fancy upon simple authority and trust. Aristotle's principles will then be no more principles to him than those of Epicuris and the stoics. Let this diversity of opinions be propounded to and laid before him, he will himself choose, if he is able; if not he will remain in doubt. (*Complete Works of Montaigne*, p. 131)

To be in a state of doubt, which in the pre-renaissance period amounted to an act of heresy, was to become in the ensuing period a hallowed method in the emerging human sciences, and no more so than in the philosophical position of Descartes. Descartes was perhaps Western thought's ultimate critical thinker, believing that in any contemplation of the world one should begin from a position of extreme scepticism and assume that everything in the world – including something as fundamental as one's own existence in it – is mere illusion. Describing his approach, he wrote: 'I was determined to accept nothing as true which I did not clearly recognize to be so' (*Discourse on Method*: p. 9). Out of Descartes' ontological project, as described in his *Meditations*, God is recovered – but only just, some would say. What emerges with a good deal more certainty, however, is individual human consciousness – made substantial in his famous dictum: 'I think therefore I am'. Not only does man exist, but in the Cartesian view, he is fundamentally a thinking, rational being. Although Descartes did not specifically address issues of education in his writings, it is fair to say that the combined Cartesian values of scepticism and rationalism have provided a powerful image of the type of thinking to which a learned person should aspire. As Stephen Toulmin said of this impact: 'The Cartesian programme was to go on and define the fundamental issues and agenda of epistemology and human sciences for the next 300 years'. (1995: p. ix)

The beginnings of a modern view of education can be traced to the rise of the individual as well as a firm belief in the principle of human betterment during the Enlightenment. The Enlightenment thinker most associated with education – a major Enlightenment project – was Rousseau, whose pedagogical work *Emile* distinguished itself as a piece of critical thinking *par excellence* by becoming 'the most censored, banned and therefore sought-after book of the eighteenth century' (Bowen 1972b). In *Emile*, Rousseau outlines his programme of 'natural education' based on the three latent capacities implanted by the maker – 'conscience, free will and reason'. But while these qualities are what God has conferred on us, Rousseau was sure that the church's educational practices at the time were devoted absolutely to their suppression. An individual's capacity for 'reason' was perhaps at the apex of Rousseau's trinity; but, significantly, he believed that the methods of reason were of their nature always bound up with the pursuit of social justice – an idea, which as we shall see, has been a continuing motif in one type of theorizing about critical thinking.

In any historical survey of critical thinking and education, the figure of John Dewey looms large. Dewey, who had a major influence at the beginning of the twentieth century in the development of the progressive education movement, saw the encouraging of a critical outlook – or what he termed 'reflective thinking' – as fundamental to the pedagogical enterprise. Dewey rejected educational processes that consisted of little more than the 'piling up of information' and strongly believed that children's education should be based primarily on having experience of the world. Also important was learning the capacity to reflect in a thoughtful way on this experience.

> There is such a thing as a readiness to consider in a thoughtful way the subjects that do come within the range of experience – a readiness that contrasts strongly with a disposition to pass judgement on the basis of mere custom, tradition, prejudice etc., and thus shun the task of thinking. (1933: p. 34)

Finally, the beginning of the formal institutionalizing of critical thinking into modern education systems has been associated with the famous report of the Harvard Committee in 1945, which established a blueprint for postwar US education. The document, the outcome of three years of deliberations by a panel of Harvard professors from a range of disciplines, sought to lay out a theory of general education appropriate for a modern democracy like the US. Significant among the educational principles enunciated was the need to provide all citizens with a 'broad critical sense'. In the following passage, the authors lay out in a language surprisingly jargon-free for a university committee, the practical social rationale for their view.

> Since no one can become an expert in all fields, everyone is compelled to trust the judgement of other people pretty thoroughly in most areas of activity. … Therefore I am in peculiar need of a kind of sagacity by which to distinguish the expert from the quack, and the better from the worse expert. From this point of view, the aim of a general education may be defined as that of providing the broad critical sense by which to recognize competence in any field. (p. 54)

2.3 The Importance of Critical Thinking in Contemporary Education

In the preceding discussion, we have seen a number of terms used to denote the broad concept of a critical outlook – Socrates' 'examined life'; Montaigne's 'understanding and judgement'; Dewey's 'reflective thinking'. This terminological variation is an issue that will be taken up in some detail in later chapters of this book. It is fair to say though, that the specific term we have opted for – 'critical thinking' – has achieved a kind of canonical position in recent educational debates around these issues. Indeed critical thinking – or CT, as it is often referred to (e.g. Facione 1990)[1] – has in the last two decades formed the foundation of a broadly-based philosophical and educational movement dedicated to raising the level of thinking in the community, or as Sternberg sees it, to arrest the 'clear decline' in students' abilities 'to achieve higher order skills' (1987: p. x). Richard Paul, the chairman of an august body – The National Council for Excellence in Critical Thinking – refers to this recent focus as a kind of 'coming-out' of the concept:

> For the majority of the idea's history … critical thinking has been 'buried', a conception in practice without an explicit name. Most recently it has undergone something of an awakening, a coming-out, a first major social expression, signaling perhaps a turning point in its history. (Paul 1996: p. 52)

The critical thinking movement has been particularly active in the US, with the convening of numerous conferences on the subject, as well as a proliferation of related journals and publications. Another important manifestation has been the implementation of a multitude of critical thinking courses and programmes at different levels of the US education system (Baron and Sternberg 1987). Commenting on all this activity, Dwight Atkinson describes critical thinking as 'one of the most widely discussed concepts in education and education reform these days'. (1997: p. 71)

In the specific area of higher education, the notion of critical thinking has been used as a way of identifying what is distinctive about the nature of learning in the academy. In his famous treatise, *The Idea of a University*, written in the mid-1800s as part of his role in establishing University College, Dublin, Cardinal Newman saw the exposing of knowledge to critical scrutiny as the fundamental task of the new institution:

> I may take for granted that the true and adequate end of intellectual training of a University is not Learning or Acquirement, but rather is Thought or Reason exercised upon Knowledge. (1980: p.101)

A hundred years later, academics in the modern university were expressing a similar view. In a survey of staff in Britain's expanding tertiary sector in 1970, lecturers were asked to identify what they believed to be the most important teaching objective of their institutions (Entwistle, Pery and Nisbett 1971). The most common response was 'to promote critical thinking'; although a number of staff also noted that their institutions were not always very effective in bringing about this outcome.

In higher education, in Australia and elsewhere, the ideal of critical thinking has in recent times achieved a kind of reified status, particularly in discussions about what qualities and skills a university graduate can be expected to acquire in the course of their studies – so-called 'graduate attributes'. In an influential Australian Government report, *Achieving Quality* (Australian Higher Education Council 1992), which effectively launched the graduate attributes idea in that country, a list of desirable skills is presented. Significantly, the first of these skills mentioned in the report's proposed list is 'the quality of critical thinking' (p. 22), seen as 'an enabling characteristic', which will provide graduates with the 'tools necessary for a constantly changing professional and intellectual environment' (p. 23).

As part of the 'quality' agenda in higher education, universities in Australia, Britain and elsewhere have been engaged over the past decade in a continual process of describing and refining the generic attributes that they believe inform – or ought to inform – their course offerings. Critical thinking remains a perennial in the various lists of putative attributes that have been produced. At the university at which the present investigation was conducted, for example, it is stated that the institution's programmes will enable graduates, *inter alia*, 'to have a broad and critical understanding of knowledge' (University X 2001). At the disciplinary level, critical thinking also figures prominently as a key skill to be taught. For example, in the School of Historical Studies at the same university, it is asserted that graduating students majoring in the school will have acquired 'a developed capacity for critical thinking'.

It needs to be acknowledged that these kinds of statements of educational purpose have been conceived, in part, to satisfy various governmental agencies – who in recent times have become increasingly involved in the monitoring and regulating of university programmes. However, the concept also appears regularly in documents directed at a student audience. For example, in a randomly selected subject in the historical studies programme at the site university – *Nationalism and Revolution in South East Asia* – the term 'critical' can be found in three of the eight unit objectives outlined for students. The term also figures prominently in assignment instructions and in the lists of assessment criteria designed to guide students in their approaches to their academic work. For example, in the first assignment set in the subject above – a document review – students are told that it is important that '[they] organize [their] thoughts into a well argued essay ... by thinking carefully and *critically* about the document to be reviewed' (emphasis added).

The evident importance of 'critical thinking' in higher education can also be observed in the way that the university system is often explained to those who enter it from other cultures. Two prominent writers on this issue, Brigid Ballard and John Clanchy, insist in their advice to Asian background students who are commencing studies at Australian universities, that it is this critical element that distinguishes the Western academic tradition from those they have been reared in. In the anglophone university, Ballard and Clanchy say, there is a progressive shift towards a 'more analytical and *critical* approach', where students come to see knowledge not as fixed and absolute, but as open to 'criticism and development' (1991: p. 14). In contrast, they suggest that other traditions tend to place an emphasis not on an 'extending' attitude to knowledge, but a more 'conserving' one. In such accounts, the words of various ancients from the Eastern tradition are invoked to show up this fundamentally different epistemological outlook. Thus, in Ballard and Clanchy, Confucius is quoted as saying: 'I do not invent, but transmit' (p.15). A number of writers have been justifiably 'critical' of such one-dimensional comparisons between these great and complex traditions (e.g. Zamel 1997) and the generally 'orientalist' nature of the contrasts drawn. Nevertheless, this simple binary of critical and non-critical educational cultures persists as a powerful image in our universities.

2.4 Critical Thinking – But What Is It?

Critical thinking is considered to be fundamental to higher education and, as we have seen, is presented to students as an integral part of their learning at university. Indeed, the term is used to characterize the type of person they are expected to be at the end of their studies – a critical thinker. It has been noted, however, that many academics are unable (or unwilling) to provide precise definitions of the term. Instead, as Atkinson suggests, academics have a tendency to take the concept 'on faith, perhaps as a self-evident foundation of Western thought – such as freedom of speech' (1997: p. 74). Such an observation is also made by Lauren Resnick, who suggests that:

> Thinking skills resist the precise forms of definition we have come to associate with the setting of specified objectives for schooling ... we become aware that although we cannot define it exactly, we can recognize higher order thinking when we see it. (1987: pp. 2–3)

Helen Fox suggests that even when academics do seek to clarify matters, they 'find critical thinking hard to talk about'. This is because the practice, she says, is 'learned intuitively', and so we do not readily have a vocabulary to describe it, especially to 'those who have been brought up differently' (1994: p.125).

Critical thinking can thus be thought of as an instance of what Bourdieu has called *habitus* – that is, a set of cultural norms and practices particular to a social group, that have been unconsciously internalized in the process of socialization, and which are therefore inexpressed and ineffable (1977: p. 95). Significantly for this investigation, Bourdieu's idea of *habitus* is intimately related to notions of judgement. Eschewing the Kantian belief in a universal aesthetic, Bourdieu argues that all preferences, tastes and judgements are shaped by people's *habitus* (1984). One of the tasks for sociological inquiry, he suggests, is to identify in any *habitus* the principles by which these judgements are made:

> When we speak of the aristocratic asceticism of teachers, or the pretensions of the petit bourgeoisie, one is not only describing these people one by one, or even the most important of their properties, but also endeavouring to name the principle which generates all the properties, and all the judgements of their properties, or of other people's properties. (1984: p. 110)

However, for Bourdieu, *habitus* is not a simple and neutral account of group cultural practices – rather it is seen by him as a differentiated 'system of dispositions', which are at the root of class and power 'distinctions' within a culture. Thus, in the context of higher education, we can think of the *habitus* of critical thinking not only as a defining cultural norm, but also as one that serves to distinguish and separate certain groups within the academy. Certainly, the possession of this skill is one way in which we might distinguish the two great classes of the university – the 'expert' teacher and 'novice' student. However, it can also be seen as a significant way in which the student group itself is divided – between those who come to 'internalize' this 'disposition' and who are successful in the system, and those who do not, and who are therefore deemed to be lacking in some way. Perhaps, the potentially alienating quality of 'critical thinking' is nowhere more apparent than in the situation where a student is told on the one hand that they must be a 'critical thinker', but on the other that nowhere in their work should they refer to themselves in such a role – by relying on that most proscribed of collocations – 'I think'. A significant task in the modern university would therefore seem to be to develop the pedagogical means by which the concept of critical thinking, and its associated practices, can be made articulate to students – or as Bourdieu might recommend, for 'its principles to be named'.

2.5 Defining Critical Thinking

The idea of defining and clarifying critical thinking will be a fundamental task in this book, so we will begin by considering some of the ways that this might be done – as well as some of the definitions that have been proposed so far in the literature. It is fair to say that any useful definition of 'critical thinking' – or any characterizing of a person whom we would want to identify as a 'critical thinker' – hinges on the term 'critical'. This is because, after Saussure, we can say that the notion of critical thinking takes its sense from being distinguishable in some way from that kind of thinking we would deem to be *non*-critical. Perhaps the first logical place to look for a definition of the term 'critical' is in the dictionary – although in doing this we are opting for only one type of defining methodology – referred to as 'lexical definition' or 'definition by synonym' (Audi 1999). In consulting the dictionary, one finds reference to a broad array of qualities, and is immediately confronted by the difficulty of pinning the term down.

The *Oxford English Dictionary* provides three main definitions. One type of meaning of 'critical' takes in the notion of a 'decisive moment' or 'turning point'. The *OED* traces this meaning to usages in a number of domains – in medical discourses ('You may reckon it [the headache] *critical*, if in a fever it fall on a critical day' – *Bonet's Merc. Compit* 1684); in military discourses ('That month by producing new prospects has been *critical*' – Thomas Jefferson: *Writings* 1786); and in natural scientific discourses ('This angle is called the limiting or *critical* angle of refraction' – W. Lees: *Acoustics* 1873). A second meaning, quite unrelated to the first, it would seem, is 'critical' as a human disposition; namely, 'given to adverse or unfavourable judgement', 'fault-finding', 'censorious'. The *OED* cites Iago's famous words to Desdemona in *Othello* to illustrate this particular meaning: 'I am nothing if not critical.' This, as Ralph Johnson (1992) suggests, is probably the term's most popular usage. A final meaning is critical not as a particular slant on things, but as a general intellectual method; namely, 'the exercise of careful judgement or observation'. This meaning is traced to an early judicial usage: 'Exact and critical trial should be made …whereby determination might be made' (Sir Thomas Browne: *Pseud. Ep.* 1650). It is perhaps this final meaning that resonates most with the way the term is used in the academy, although for some students it can seem that in some contexts of study, the second and third meanings are almost indistinguishable.

To add to the confusion, the *OED* touches briefly on another distinctive usage – one also commonly heard in certain areas of academe. This is that form of 'criticality' which is associated with a certain liberationist outlook, and which is linked to Marx's distinctively activist take on critique – 'not to interpret the world, but to change it'. This form of 'critical' thinking can be characterized as one involving a mainly negative stance towards extant social practices, ones that are generally seen as oppressive of the broad mass of people. The term is known most famously in the name given to the distinctive mode of inquiry associated with the Frankfurt school – 'critical theory', and also that given to the educational philosophy of Paulo Freire – 'critical pedagogy' (1970). More recently in applied linguistics, it has been invoked to describe activist approaches to the analysis of language – e.g. Norman Fairclough's 'critical discourse analysis' (Fairclough 1985), as well as to the teaching of language – e.g. Sarah Benesch's 'critical English for academic purposes' (Benesch 2001). Martyn Hammersley's account of this critical tradition in the university seems a fair summary:

> What the term 'critical' generally refers to ... is forms of research which assume that we can only understand society as a totality and that in producing knowledge of society, critical research reveals what is obscured by ideology, such ideology being pervasive, and playing an essential role in the status quo. (1996: p. 4–5)

Commenting on these two 'academic' meanings of 'critical', (i.e. denoting a general intellectual disposition, and denoting a socially critical stance), Atkinson argues that the use of the same term in these different contexts seems 'largely coincidental' (1997; p. 74)[2]. One has its origins, Atkinson suggests, in the classic Marxist concept of 'critical consciousness', and the other in non-Marxist traditions of Western rationalism. Thus, Atkinson is suggesting that we should think of the term as homonymous in this instance – with a single signifier denoting two distinct signifieds. This may indeed be the case, although from the perspective of an undergraduate student trying to make sense of the 'critical' stance they are being enjoined to adopt, it is unlikely that they will readily distinguish two traditions of meaning here, and by extension, two distinct modes of thinking. Some commentators also suggest that there is a particular way of thinking about the modern university – what Gerard Delanty (2001: p. 210) characterizes as 'the university as institutionalized critique' – which deliberately recognizes no such distinction. According to this view, universities have a role 'not simply to reproduce social or cultural values, but also to problematize the cultural models of society with which they contend', and academics (and, one assumes, those they teach) are seen not as 'reproducers', but as 'transformers of society's cognitive structures'. (2001: p.10)

A more serious problem however, than this one of definitional vagueness, is the one mentioned earlier – that many academics typically take the concept of critical thinking 'on faith' (Atkinson 1997) and fail in their teaching to make explicit what it is they mean when they want their students to be critical thinkers. But while this may be true of the disciplines in general, there is one group of scholars who, amid all this apparent inarticulateness, have embraced fully the definitional task – the aforementioned educationists, philosophers, psychologists and others who make up the critical thinking movement. Indeed, there are some within this movement who have devoted almost whole careers to trying to pin the term down. As Johnson notes, the issue of defining critical thinking has become 'such a hot topic [for these scholars] that almost no-one can keep clear of it' (1992: p. 39). There is a reason for all this attention – those involved in the movement are convinced that understanding and properly teaching the skill of critical thinking are both fundamental tasks in a modern democratic society. As Stephen Norris explains, the aim of the movement is to make students and citizens 'better critical thinkers', and so to 'bring about change in the world'. (1992: p. 13)

2.6 Definitions within the 'Critical Thinking Movement'

Broadly speaking, the definitions that have been offered within the critical thinking movement have been of two kinds: brief statements that try to capture the essence of critical thinking in a sentence or two; and longer taxonomic lists that seek to characterize the concept by outlining a range of skills and sub-skills which together constitute the broader thinking activity. In the first category, a range of statements have been proposed by different theorists including the following – referred to as the 'group of five' and regarded by Johnson (1992) as the more influential and 'theoretically grounded':

i.   Robert Ennis' (1962) early formulation: 'the correct assessing of statements' and his later reworking – 'reasonable, reflective thinking that is focused on deciding what to believe or do' (1987: p.10);
ii.   John McPeck's 'appropriate use of reflective scepticism within the problem area under consideration' (1981: p. 7);
iii. Matthew Lipman's 'skillful, responsible thinking that facilitates good judgement' (1988: p. 39);
iv.   Richard Paul's 'disciplined, self-directed thinking which exemplifies the perfection of thinking appropriate to a particular domain of thinking' (1989: p. 214);
v.   Harvey Siegel's 'educational cognate of rationality', and definition of a critical thinker as 'the individual who is appropriately moved by reasons' (1988: p. 127).

On one level, these kernel definitions seem to offer fairly similar conceptions of the skill in question – despite some authors insisting on the uniqueness of their particular formulation. What is common to all is the idea that critical thinking involves judgement of some kind. Thus, in each definition, we see a central term that denotes some cognate thinking activity – 'assessing', 'deciding', 'being sceptical', 'judging', and so on. Also common to each is a sense of this judgement having some distinctive quality about it, which presumably for each of the various writers is what distinguishes it from other, less critical forms of judgement. Thus, we find a range of qualifying adjectives used to describe the activity – 'correct', 'reasonable', 'reflective', 'skillful', 'responsible', 'disciplined', 'self-directed', and so forth. While this is a mixed collection of terms, it is possible to discern among them several key themes, which together give a picture of what is broadly consensual among the various positions. The first of these is that the desired kind of judgement is seen as basically a rational one – thus the use of terms like 'reasonable', 'correct', 'disciplined', 'reasoned' and Siegel's 'rationality'. The second is that these judgements are understood to arise from some kind of intentional thinking activity – or what is described in the education literature as 'metacognitive' thinking (thus the terms 'reflective' and 'self-directed'). A final theme is the suggestion that the judgements need to be basically ethical ones (thus the term 'responsible').

It can be seen that most of the definitions above contain elements of the first two themes – that is, critical thinking as both rational and self-aware ('thought evaluating thought', as Johnson [1992] describes it). The third theme – the ethical element – is perhaps a little less clear cut than the other two. Among the five definitions listed, the notion of 'responsibility' only appears explicitly in Lipman's. However, it is noted that in some of the more expanded accounts provided elsewhere by these thinkers, an ethical approach to thinking seems to be regarded as criterial. Robert Ennis (1985), for example, has suggested that critical thinking has a 'dispositional' dimension to it, which includes, among other things, the importance of 'presenting a position clearly and *honestly*' (my emphasis). Similarly, Richard Paul (1996), in a more extended account, says that students instructed in the ways of critical thinking will be led progressively to 'a life of intellectual and moral integrity'.

Among these various accounts, a fair degree of consensus seems to exist, even if together they provide perhaps a less than illuminating view of the activity in question. There is one issue however, on which one finds clear divergence – this is whether the type of judgements that a thinker makes are dependent, in some way, on what specifically their thinking is being directed at; in other words, whether critical thinking should be thought of as a 'generalized' skill (or set of skills) which can be applied to any subject matter, or whether the form it takes varies according to different contexts. In McPeck's definition, for example, we can see an allegiance to the latter position – with his suggestion that the way one applies a 'sceptical' frame of mind will be contingent on the 'particular problem area under consideration' (1981: p. 7). Paul also recognizes a contextual element when he refers to types of 'thinking appropriate to a particular mode or domain' (1989: p. 24). For the others, domain-specificity is significantly absent in their definitions. This difference constitutes a major parting of the ways among critical thinking theorists, one which will be discussed in more detail in the next section, and which, as we shall see, has important implications for the way these writers believe critical thinking should be taught.

The other type of defining that has gone on within the movement – perhaps because of the lack of utility ultimately of the kernel definitions above – has involved identifying in the broad critical thinking activity a range of specific constitutive thinking skills; for example, 'thinking inductively' or 'providing explanations' or 'identifying assumptions' (e.g. D'Angelo 1971). The various lists that have been produced have had the aim of not only clarifying the concept theoretically, but also of establishing a framework for the teaching and assessing of critical thinking. Arguably the most influential of these has been Robert Ennis's (1987) paper 'A taxonomy of critical thinking dispositions and abilities' (Norris 1992). As Ennis's title suggests, there is classifying here according to two broad divisions – 'dispositions' and 'abilities'. Among Ennis's fourteen putative dispositions are such affective qualities as 'trying to be well-informed', 'looking for alternatives', 'being open-minded', 'taking a position when the evidence and reasons are sufficient to do so', and so on. This list is followed by a range of more specific cognitive 'abilities', which are provided in full below:

1. grasping the meaning of statements
2. judging whether there is ambiguity in a line of reasoning
3. judging whether certain statements contradict one another
4. judging whether a conclusion necessarily follows
5. judging whether a statements is specific enough
6. judging whether a statement is actually the application of a certain principle
7. judging whether an observation statement is reliable
8. judging whether an inductive conclusion is warranted
9. judging whether the problem has been identified
10. judging whether something is an assumption
11. judging whether a definition is adequate
12. judging whether a statement by an alleged authority is acceptable

While Ennis's first list – his dispositions – is designed to capture a general spirit of critical thinking, his second list attempts to provide a systematic list of discrete cognitive operations which, for him, not only describe what an accomplished critical thinker does, but also suggest what it is exactly that a novice thinker needs to be taught. Indeed, Ennis suggests that the order in which these abilities are listed in his taxonomy is the one in which 'they might appear in a critical thinking course at college level' (1987: p. 11).

Taxonomies like Ennis's certainly provide a fuller picture of critical thinking and, for some educationists, have proved helpful both in establishing the need for critical thinking programmes in universities as well as suggesting how they might be organized. But there has been some disquiet within the movement about the basis on which such lists have been assembled. One problem is that they represent only a single theorist's particular take on the concept. Thus, what has emerged in the literature is a growing number of competing classifications, and inevitably a fair amount of disputation between proponents about what exactly should be covered in a critical thinking programme. This rivalry has led some to call for a 'moratorium on critical thinking definitions' (Johnson 1992: p. 53), and for others to call for an examination of extant conceptions to find out if some agreement might be reached. (Norris 1992)

Interestingly, in the early 1990s, a concerted attempt was made to build such a consensus within the movement, with the convening of a panel of 'critical thinking experts' under the auspices of the American Philosophical Association (Facione 1990). Included in this panel were three of the 'group of five' referred to earlier – Ennis, Paul and Lipman. Peter Facione reports some success in the panel's 'systematic inquiry into the current state of CT'. Out of their deliberations, a single list of specific skills was assembled (namely, 'interpretation', 'analysis', 'evaluation', 'inference', 'explanation' and 'self-regulation'). Facione does acknowledge, however, that the position reached was some way off being a consensual one – an unsurprising outcome perhaps at a 'critical thinking' convention – with a number of experts insisting on alternative lists, and at least one asking to be excluded from the reports findings. (1990: p. 3)

For many educationists, especially those outside the critical thinking movement, a degree of impatience and frustration has been expressed at the almost interminable discussions and disputes that have gone on about the elusive critical thinking grail. Toni-Lee Capossela, for example, suggests that all this definitional work has only served to make the concept more obscure:

> It seems reasonable to suppose that a concept so frequently invoked would long ago have acquired a clear-cut definition, but in fact the opposite is true: with each new appearance, critical thinking becomes less, rather than more, clearly defined. (1993: p.1)

For Norris, the problem underlying the multiplicity of views and resultant blurring of the concept is the lack of an empirical basis in the various attempts at characterizing critical thinking. Norris points out, rightly in my view, that for many theorists, critical thinking has really been conceived in the first instance as a desirable 'educational value' rather than an actual psychological reality and thus, the defining that has gone on has been within a framework of how one might 'best promote [their] educational goals' (1992: p. 4). Atkinson expresses the same view when he deems most extant definitions to be essentially 'desiderative or polemical'. (1997: p. 74)

Another problem outlined by Norris is that the definitional work has taken place mainly within the domain of philosophy, with an attempt to resolve issues largely through methods of 'conceptual analysis' and introspection. He notes with disdain, for example, how Ennis – and by implication others – have produced the items on their lists:

> I remember Ennis answering, to a question about how he decided to stop adding to his list, that he included all that came to mind. The implication is that if he thought of more he would add them. (p. 10)

For Norris, it is not sufficient to base a definition on such intuitive judgements, noting, as he does, that 'virtually all major theories of meaning assume that empirical research is necessary for determining denotation'. (p. 12)

The type of empirical research Norris has in mind is one of a psychological, behavioural kind. The way forward, he suggests, is to study how people think when faced with different kinds of tasks – as a way of finding out the underlying traits of a critical thinker. It is all well and good, Norris says, to be attached to certain abilities and dispositions of critical thinking, but if we want to be sure that this is actually what people do, then 'the psychology of human beings', he insists, 'must be taken into account' (1992: p.13). While Norris's suggested programme is commendable for at least wishing to root notions of critical thinking within actual human experience and within some educational reality, there is a problem of circularity in his proposal. On the one hand, one investigates the activities of critical thinkers to establish the underlying traits of this type of person, but on the other, one needs some *a priori* understanding of these traits in the first place in order to identify who qualifies as a critical thinker. As Ennis says in response to Norris, empirical research like this can do important things – like establishing how many people do and do not satisfy the criteria for critical thinking – but it 'cannot by itself identify the referents of the concept of critical thinking'. (1992b: p. 3)

Norris's behavioural empiricism thus seems problematic. There is, however, another type of empirical project that might be pursued. This is not to consider critical thinking as some kind of psychological quality, but rather as an institutional and discursive one – as an *habitus*. As mentioned earlier, Wittgenstein has suggested that many of the problems that beset philosophy arise from an assumption that one of the primary tasks of the discipline is to define concepts in some abstract way. For him, there are no such abstract meanings. Instead, words and expressions only take on meanings from the way they are used 'in the stream of life'. As he famously declared in his later opus *Philosophical Investigations*:

> For a large class of cases in which we employ the word 'meaning' it can be defined thus: the meaning of a word is its use in the language. (1958a: p. 20)

Wittgenstein believed that many philosophical problems stem from looking at words in isolation, in a static way. 'The confusions which occupy us', he declared, 'arise when language is like an engine idling, not when it is doing work' (1958a: p. 51). Indeed, this may be a way of understanding the definitional impasse that the critical thinking movement seems to have found itself in; that is, there has been a tendency to detach the concept from its actual uses, and then to attach to it either notions that are thought to be somehow intrinsic to it, or else notions that one desires it to have. A concept treated in this way will inevitably yield many different meanings, and will lead us into what Wittgenstein called a state of 'puzzlement'.

For Wittgenstein, the task of philosophy – and indeed of the human sciences generally – is to lead our understanding out of such impasses: 'to shew the fly the way out of the fly bottle' as he famously described it (1958a: p. 103). To do this involves a special type of empiricism, not one that examines people's behaviours as such, but rather a linguistic empiricism that is concerned with examining 'the workings of our language, in such a way as to make us recognize those workings … in spite of an urge to misunderstand them' (1958a: p.47). In order to recognize these 'workings', according to Wittgenstein, one needs to see how different terms function within different contexts – or what he called 'language games'. He uses the example of the meaning of the word 'question' to illustrate this point. If we do not think of the different contexts in which the term 'question' is used, he says, we will miss out on recognizing its multiplicity of meanings – for example, 'questions' as requests for information, or as requests for assistance, or as descriptions of a state of uncertainty, or even in some contexts, paradoxically, declarations of a state of certainty – as in the rhetorical question (p. 12). Thus, one must not rely on what one thinks the word 'question' means, but instead observe those situations in which it is being used. 'Don't think, but look', was his blunt instruction to his fellow philosophers (p. 31).

In relation to the problem before us – to understand better what is meant by the term critical thinking – it would seem that the project that Wittgenstein outlines may be one worth pursuing. Characteristically, in a work as abstruse as *Philosophical Investigations*, Wittgenstein does not elaborate in any systematic way on how one might proceed methodologically in conducting an investigation into the 'workings of a word'. The following sketch, however, from his companion *Brown Book* is perhaps the beginnings of such a method:

> Let us see what use we make of … an expression. What the situations are in which we use this expression, what sentences would precede or follow it (what kind of conversation it is a part of). (1958b: p. 179)

In the context of university study, one therefore needs to explore the 'situations' in which the term 'critical thinking' is used (its contexts), and 'what sentences precede and follow it' (its co-texts) – in short, what is needed is a discourse approach. As mentioned previously, Norris is sure that in determining the denotation of a word, some kind of empirical process is usually necessary. For Wittgenstein, the only valid form of empiricism is one that takes notions that we live by as 'forms of life'.

2.7 How General is Critical Thinking?

Students undertaking a degree at university are usually involved in studies in a range of subjects and disciplines, and in each of these areas they are typically enjoined to adopt a critical approach to their studies. However, as noted earlier, there is a question about whether being 'critical' in these different domains involves essentially the same general type of cognitive activity. Thus, is it the case that a student can learn about critical thinking in one domain of study and then apply it unproblematically to another? Does the history student, for example, over the course of their studies develop a critical outlook which will then assist them in their studies in philosophy (and vice versa)? Along with its interest in the 'definition' question, the critical thinking movement has devoted a good deal of attention to this issue of generalizability. As Norris explains, this is an important issue because the stance one adopts 'affects how critical thinking is taught, how it is tested, and how research is conducted' (1992: p. x). As we shall see, the critical thinking movement has more often than not fallen in behind the generalist line, but that is not to say that there have not been serious voices of dissent from several quarters.

In educational debates, the issue of generalizability can be traced back at least to Dewey. Norris (1992), in a volume that explicitly addresses the generalizability issue, notes Dewey's view that 'the various ways in which men do think can be told, and can be described in their *general* features' (Dewey, 1933: p.4, emphasis added). However, Max Black, another early advocate for the teaching of critical thinking, lays out a rival specifist position by asserting that 'the critic's judgement of the value of a piece of music (or an omelet or a piece of reasoning) is grounded in knowledge of principles and standards appropriate to the subject matter' (1946: p. 7). Norris also notes that within a single pedagogical position, ambivalence can often be expressed about the issue. Thus, in the Harvard Committee's report into the objectives of a general education, cited earlier, there is mention of effective thinking comprising 'certain broad mental skills' (1945: p. 66). Elsewhere, however, the committee claims, rather reductively one would say, that 'the three phases of effective thinking – logical, relational and imaginative – correspond roughly to three divisions of learning – the natural sciences, the social studies and the humanities respectively'. (p. 67)

These discussions in educational circles about the generalizabilty of 'the ways that men think' recapitulate a more basic debate conducted around the same time within European analytical philosophy. The quest for a general heuristics of thinking recalls the Vienna Circle's objective to find a straightforward and universal method for evaluating the truthfulness of propositions. The members of this group – which included Moritz Schlick, Rudolph Carnap and others – would ultimately admit only two types of propositions as capable of being verified and therefore as meaningful: those which are analytically true (or true by definition, such as 'all bachelors are unmarried men'), and those which are empirically true (like 'water boils at 100 degrees Celsius'). All other statements – including ethical propositions like 'murder is wrong', or aesthetic judgements like 'Picasso is a great artist' – were dismissed by the Circle as statements of personal preference and were considered to be quite literally meaningless (Edmonds and Eidinow 2001). The 'logical positivist' position was encapsulated in the well-known maxim: 'The meaning of a statement is the method by which it is verified' (cited in Gardner 1985: p. 63), an idea which is subsequently echoed in Robert Ennis's (1962) earlier account of critical thinking as the 'correct assessing of statements'.

Logical positivism drew much of its inspiration from the early work of Wittgenstein – in particular the *Tractatus Logicus-Philosophicus*, whose famous opening words – 'The world is all that is the case' – suggest a strong affinity with the logical positivist view (1961: p.1). However, the later Wittgenstein of the *Philosophical Investigations* was dismissive of the possibilities of any universal method for getting at the truthfulness of statements. Instead, for Wittgenstein II (as his later position has been described) a statement cannot be analysed semantically on its own terms, but can only be understood in relation to the 'language game' (or discourse) of which it is a part. The implications of Wittgenstein's relativism for the field of epistemology were subsequently explored by one his students, Stephen Toulmin, in his work on the nature of argument. Toulmin concluded that an argument, like a proposition, assumes different forms in different contexts of knowledge, and that what counts as a valid argument in one field may not necessarily be seen as such in others:

What has to be recognized first is that validity is an intra-field, not an inter-field notion. Arguments within any field can be judged by standards appropriate within that field and some will fall short; but it must be expected that the standards will be field-dependent, and that the merits to be demanded of an argument in one field will be found to be absent (in the nature of things) from entirely meritorious arguments in another. (1958: p.32)

In contemporary discussions within the critical thinking movement about the generalizability of thinking skills, we can see a lineage with these earlier mid-century debates. Arguably, the modern version has two different, though related strands to it – the issue of epistemological generalizability (how general are these skills?) and another psychological dimension (how readily can these learned skills be transferred across domains?). The position that one adopts in relation to these issues has important implications for the question of how critical thinking is best taught, particularly whether it should be treated as a separate subject in its own right. Thus, as Norris explains, 'whether or not critical thinking should be taught as a separate school subject depends upon whether there are aspects of critical thinking that apply to all or most subjects, and upon whether separate instruction in critical thinking proves useful for subjects in areas in which they did not receive instruction'. (1992: p. 2)

It is fair to say that in educational debates in recent years – especially in the US – the generalist position has been very much in the ascendance. Much of the original impetus for this approach came from a succession of tests and reports in the US in the 1980s that suggested serious declines in the literacy and thinking abilities of American high school students. The names of some of these reports indicate well the pessimistic conclusions contained within them – *A Nation at Risk* (National Commission on Excellence in Education 1983); *An Imperiled Generation: Saving Urban Schools* (1988). In the findings of one particularly influential study, the National Assessment of Educational Progress (NAEP 1981), it was suggested, for example, that only about half of school leavers could write a satisfactory piece of explanatory prose, and only about 15% could defend a point of view effectively with argument. (cited in Nickerson 1994)

The generalist approach was borne out of this sense of crisis, and – as some have suggested (Capossela 1993) – has found its continuing rationale by holding to a generally gloomy view of the education system and the abilities of students. Deanna Kuhn, for example, a strong generalist advocate in the US, spoke two decades ago of the widespread agreement 'that education is failing in its most central mission – to teach students to think' (1991: p. 62); and Tim van Gelder, an Australian 'critical thinking expert', has recently commented on the very poor reasoning skills of Australian higher education students, noting in his own informal study that 'almost none' of his 95 students could adequately perform a simple task of analysing and evaluating the main argument of a book chapter. (van Gelder 2000)

For advocates of the generalist position the only way to arrest this decline is to have dedicated programmes designed to develop students' thinking abilities. As Nickerson (1994) suggests: 'Improving the quality of [students' thinking] appears to require, at least, an effort aimed explicitly at that objective' (1994: p. 416). One outcome of this situation, as mentioned, has been the proliferation of thinking skills courses across all levels of the education system. At the tertiary level, dedicated programmes have been especially common in the US. For example, since the 1980s, the California State University system has specified the study of critical thinking as a requirement for graduation. Facione's report for the American Philosophical Association – cited earlier – urges universities to make general critical thinking courses available to all students, though stressing that all such courses need to be as broadly relevant as possible:

> ... no academic unit should be restricted in principle from participating in an institution's CT programme, provided that the overall institutional programme in CT equips students in applying CT to a broad range of educational, personal and civic subjects, issues and problems. (1990: p.16)

At Australian universities, generalist thinking skills courses have been slow to take off – although recently there have been signs of a growing interest (Davies, 2006). One programme that has received a good deal of publicity is the *Reasonable!* project at the University of Melbourne, which provides 'quality practice' in the form of a software programme bringing about, as the author claims, 'substantial gains' in students' thinking skills. (van Gelder 2000)

However, despite widespread support for these types of thinking programmes, the generalists have been under some pressure to show that such offerings do have broad applicability, and that there are in fact 'a set of critical thinking skills which cut across subject boundaries' (McPeck 1992: p.198). The case for epistemological generalizability has been made in a variety of ways. Anthony Blair, for example, highlights the importance of a particular thinking ability – 'the evaluating of information sources' – which he takes to be what critical thinking is mainly about. The type of teaching programme Blair suggests needs to be focused on appreciating our fundamental dependence on the beliefs of others, and this means 'recognizing the roles of various sources, making the appropriate evaluative judgements of their reliability, and continuously adjusting our beliefs accordingly' (1992: p. 126–27). Thus, students need to be engaged in activities that get them to objectively consider such issues as whether sources are credible, whether they have appropriate expertise, whether they were competent at the time of making their assessment, whether their judgements are disinterested, and so on. (p. 127)

For Blair, the type of thinking that students crucially need to learn about ('the evaluation of sources') is analogous with much of what goes on in many judicial processes – typically the examining and cross-examining of testimony as a way of arriving at some approximation of the truth. Interestingly, it is in this legal domain that Robert Ennis (1987) also sees the justification for a generalist thinking approach. In his influential paper 'A taxonomy of critical thinking dispositions and abilities', referred to earlier, Ennis seeks to show how all the various skills of critical thinking that he opts for in his list – 'induction', 'deduction', 'identification of assumptions', and so on – were precisely those that he needed in order to 'operationalize' when he acted as a jury member in a murder trial. As an example, he points out how the jury in its deliberations constantly relied on the skills of 'inductive inference' – like establishing the generalized principle that hearsay is often unreliable – to manage its negotiations and work towards a verdict. In using the jury example, Ennis seeks to establish the generalizability of these skills, but wishes also to assert their transferability. As he notes, 'obviously there was no subject that I studied in school called juries or killing', yet there was an expectation that jury members would call upon certain general critical faculties to complete the task before them. They were able to do this, Ennis suggests, with varying degrees of success. (1987: p. 17)

Ennis's and Blair's accounts of epistemological generalizability refer, it must be said, to rather specific instances; that is, the application of critical thinking in legal domains. Perhaps the most forceful general account is that offered by Siegel (1988). He argues against any relativist position, asserting that there is a single common epistemological principle which unites all that we would call critical thinking, and which distinguishes it from non-critical thinking – this is the idea that all knowledge claims in any field of inquiry must be supported by reasons. It is the identification and assessment of these reasons that any thinking programme needs to be fundamentally concerned with, and one is guided here, Seigel suggests, by the simple maxim: 'a good reason is that which warrants a conclusion' (1988: p. 100). For Siegel, this principle cuts across all disciplines. Thus, to take the field of science as an example, he suggests that:

.... it does not have principles of reason unique to itself since what counts as a good reason in science (for example, that the putative reason in question provides the best explanation of the phenomenon under consideration; or that it significantly increases the probability of the hypothesis being considered) often counts as a good reason both in other fields and in countless, everyday life contexts. (p. 99)

Along with having to establish that the principles underlying these general programmes do have broad application, the critical thinking movement has also been required to show that once these principles have been learnt, students can in fact readily apply them to a range of new contexts – the transfer question. This, however, has been difficult to demonstrate in any conclusive way. As Nickerson (1994) concedes, the difficulties in establishing associations between those behaviours that students engage in within and without classroom settings are indeed 'formidable'. One clear problem, for example, is matching the discrete and clearly delineated problems presented on a critical thinking programme with the less predictable and unstructured way that cognate problems are encountered and dealt with in reality.

To investigate the impacts of their efforts in any thorough way, the critical thinking movement has been forced to rely on a more manageable methodology – critical thinking testing. Indeed the development of the 'critical thinking test' has been almost as active an endeavour as the running of programmes. The first well-known example, the *Watson-Glaser Critical Thinking Appraisal*, devised in the US in 1980, uses a multiple choice format to test two putative skills – the ability to recognize assumptions, and the ability to make inferences. This test has functioned as a model for a multitude of other similar instruments, developed subsequently, including one devised and promoted by Robert Ennis – the *Cornell Critical Thinking Test* – which purports to independently measure each of the various skills outlined in his taxonomy. In Australia, mass-scale testing of critical thinking has been mooted in the form of the *Graduate Skills Assessment*, which some favour as a way of assessing the critical thinking 'attributes' of Australian university graduates. (Australian Council of Education Research 2001)

All such testing is premised on the idea that critical thinking is a general, non field-specific ability; thus, the claim is that it is possible to produce a uniform standardized measure of ability, irrespective of a testee's background of study. Conceived in this way, these tests have come to be used for a range of purposes – to make assessments of the critical thinking abilities of various cohorts of students, to identify the effect of different types of educational programmes (including dedicated critical thinking courses), to make claims about the relative efficacies of such programmes, and so on. However, some are sceptical about the validity of these types of assessment. Charles Blatz, echoing the views of a number of writers, questions whether performance on a multiple choice critical thinking test is really able to tell us whether a particular individual qualifies as a critical thinker, or whether ultimately it can only tell us about their ability to perform on this type of test. It is noted that this latter quality may or may not be quite the same thing as being a critical thinker (Blatz 1992). Indeed, given the lack of clarity around the notion of critical thinking – as discussed at length in the previous section – it is fair to assume that the construct of critical thinking as it operates in these tests probably reflects, more than anything, the particular and variable way that each test designer has come to understand the concept.

All the busy activity of the generalists in the critical thinking movement – or 'industry' as Ronald Barnett (2000) has dubbed it – has come under the critical scrutiny of a number of writers who take a specifist position in relation to these issues (Glaser 1984; Hirsch 1987; McPeck 1990; Blatz 1992; Moore 2004). One serious matter for this group concerns the question of the epistemic content of courses. Because generalist programmes are focused on the development of skills, the content on which these skills are hung tends to be largely incidental in the various critical thinking curricula that have been devised. However, as Glaser suggests, familiarity and active engagement with content seems to be crucial in the application and development of critical thinking. In an influential article 'Education and thinking: The role of knowledge', which reviews extensive psychological work done in the area of schema theory, Glaser concludes that an individual's capacity to solve problems is conditional to a large extent on the extant knowledge they have of the subject matter. As he explains:

Much recent work emphasizes a new dimension of difference between individuals who display more or less ability in thinking and problem solving.

This dimension is the possession and utilization of an organized body of conceptual and procedural knowledge and a major component of thinking is seen to be the possession of accessible and useable knowledge. (1984: p. 97)

Robert Siegler and Dean Richards draw a similar conclusion when they point out that 'knowledge of specific content domains [seems to be] a crucial dimension of development in its own right' (1982: p. 93). They suggest further that 'changes in such knowledge may underlie other changes previously attributed to the growth of capabilities and strategies' (p. 93). Such conclusions suggest that, in terms of the psychological processes involved in becoming a critical thinker, the idea of the content-weak, generalist skills-development course may be a flawed one.

Perhaps the thinker who has challenged the generalist position more than anyone else has been John McPeck, mentioned earlier as a member of the 'group of five', but a notably dissident one. McPeck's definition of critical thinking, it will be recalled, was 'the appropriate use of reflective scepticism *within the problem area under consideration*' (1981: p. 7, original emphasis). In his insistence on this contextual element, we can see in McPeck's position a rejection of the idea that any principles of critical thinking can be applied in some automatic, heuristic way. Thus, for McPeck, the content at which the thinking activity is directed is crucial. It is nonsense, he says, for someone to claim that they teach thinking *simpliciter*. This is because thinking, by definition, is 'always thinking about something, and that something can never be "everything in general" but must always be something in particular'. (1981: p. 4)

On the issue of epistemological generalizability, McPeck is a clear relativist. In his work he acknowledges Stephen Toulmin as an influence, and in the following passage he deliberately draws on the terminology of Wittgenstein:

> Just as the rules of a particular game do not necessarily apply to other games, so certain principles of reason may apply within certain spheres of human experience, but not in others. A principle in business or law may be fallacious in science or ethics. (1981: p.72)

While acknowledging that there are some very limited general thinking skills, McPeck insists that 'they offer little to get excited about' (1992: p. 202). This is because, he suggests, the more general the skill, the more trivially obvious it seems to be – like 'not contradicting one's self, or not believing everything one hears' (p. 202). For McPeck, the truly useful thinking skills tend to be limited to specific domains or narrower areas of application.

The teaching implications of McPeck's position are that the development of students' critical abilities should always be pursued within the context of their study within the respective disciplines. The two different approaches are summarized by McPeck thus:

If I were to put my disagreement with the [general thinking] movement into one bold-relief sentence it is this: in their attempt to develop critical thinking, they have the order of cause and effect reversed. They believe that if you train students in certain logical skills (e.g. the fallacies, etc.) the result will be general improvement in each of the disciplines or qualities of mind. Whereas I contend that if we improve the quality of understanding through the disciplines (which may have little to do with 'logic' directly), you will then get a concomitant improvement in the thinking capacity. (1990, p. 21)

At the heart of all exchanges between these adversaries is the basic epistemological question – that is, whether different fields of knowledge depend on variable principles of critical thinking. McPeck insists on differences – 'the crucial epistemic questions', he says 'tend to vary among domains and subjects' (1992: p. 204). Robert Ennis insists, as we have seen, on similarities, although he concedes that 'the extent of interfield commonalities is a topic that does require extensive research' (1992a: p.31). What are needed to resolve the deadlock, Ennis suggests, are studies of the textual instantiations of critical thinking – 'the careful comparative analysis of articles and arguments [from a range of disciplines]' (p. 31). This is an interesting research agenda for someone with Ennis's background to set. This is because it takes the inquiry out of his and McPeck's fields of educational philosophy and into text-based areas of inquiry. So far, however, it seems that Ennis's agenda has not really been pursued systematically by anyone within the critical thinking movement.

In the investigation carried out for this book, it was my intention to take up the issue of interfield comparisons in a comprehensive way. Thus, along with trying to find out what academics mean when they say that they want their students to be critical thinkers, the investigation also sought to discover how these meanings compared both within and across different disciplinary settings. It was hoped that such an analysis would offer some insights into the interfield issue, and would in turn provide some basis for judging the relevance of the generalist and discipline-specific approaches we have considered.

2.8 Critiquing Critical Thinking

In these preliminary discussions of critical thinking and the disciplines, it would be remiss to leave off without considering, at least briefly, how a critical outlook has been applied to the concept of critical thinking itself. As we have seen, the ideal of seeing knowledge through the critical frame of reason has been a powerful theme in the traditions of Western thought and also in the ways that the modern university has been conceived (Newman 1980). But alongside this current is an alternative strand that has been – at best – sceptical about the possibilities of a critical rationality. Such a view has always been strong in the

Romantic tradition – 'the sleep of reason produces monsters' declared William Blake. In recent times, important critiques of rationality have emerged from several philosophical positions – notably hermeneutics and postmodernism – including the latter's various feminist incarnations. These critiques have perhaps one element in common: the desire to establish a place for 'multiple subjectivities' in the acts of seeing and engaging with knowledge – not a defence of the necessary 'relativism' that such a position implies, but a wholehearted embrace of it.

For Hans-Georg Gadamer, a more recent thinker in the hermeneutic tradition, acts of understanding and of judgement are intimately tied to one's own individual pre-understandings of knowledge, or 'prejudices', as he calls them (1975). These prejudices, according to Gadamer, not only condition our understanding, but also provide the conditions without which understanding could not take place. This idea is a powerful challenge to the paradigm of critical thinking, which in many of its versions sees 'prejudicial thinking' as something like its opposite, and is thought to be fundamentally what students need to overcome. Thus, as we noted in Dewey's account above, a contrast is made between 'a readiness to consider [subjects] in a thoughtful way' and 'a disposition to pass judgement on the basis of mere tradition and prejudice' (1933: p. 34). However, for Gadamer, such a view is also the outcome of *mere* tradition and prejudice, one which he associates with the particular outlook of the Enlightenment. As he neatly puts it:

> The fundamental prejudice of the Enlightenment is the prejudice against prejudice itself, which denies tradition its power. (1975: p.270)

A more comprehensive assault on the Enlightenment view – and for many, a more lethal one – has come from within the ranks of postmodernist thought, especially in the works of Foucault and Derrida. For Foucualt, there are no universal ways of knowing, only particular 'discursive formations' or *epistemes* of which the Enlightenment (or modern episteme) is but one (1970). Also significant, for Foucault, is that what drives the formation and practices of such epistemes is not some fundamental epistemological yearning – such as a rational search for truth – but rather the operations of power: 'It is in discourse', he says, 'that power and knowledge are joined together'. (1980: p. 100)

In Derrida's work, the modernist episteme is scrutinized and critiqued further. Derrida uses the term 'logocentrism' to characterize this dominant paradigm of thought, one which, he suggests, always seeks to look beyond the signs and representations of knowledge to concepts and things in some pure and unmediated form (1967). The system of the *logos*, whose origins can be traced back to Descartes, Derrida suggests, is committed to the view that truth, knowledge, being and reality can all be known in some 'clear and distinct' way, quite separate from the way they are represented. But for Derrida there is nothing epistemologically neutral in the knowledge of the logos; in fact, it has at its centre an elaborated system of binary opposites – good/bad, presence/absence, identity/difference, the reasoned/unreasoned (and for this work – the critical and non-critical). Significantly, for Derrida, in each of these binaries there is always one term that is structurally dominant and which is given the privilege of defining itself and of relegating to the other all that is not it (1967).

In postmodern feminist critiques of epistemology, Derrida's 'logocentrism' is characterized specifically as 'masculinist' (or 'phallocentric') ways of knowing (Grosz 1989). Writers in this tradition, including Julia Kristeva, Luce Irigiray and Michele Le Doeuff, have been interested in deconstructing these dominant discourses, and as Grosz describes it: 'to contest singular concepts of truth, and to encourage a proliferation of voices and a plurality of perspectives' (1989: p. 25). Michele Le Doeuff, to take just one example of a theorist in this tradition, has concentrated her efforts specifically on philosophical discourse, noting that in all philosophical writing there is unavoidably an 'imaginary' element ('fables, myths and poetry') often evoked by writers as a way of exemplifying certain philosophical principles. As she 'imaginatively' characterizes these elements:

> ... statues that breath the scent of roses, comedies, tragedies, architects, foundations, dwellings, doors and windows, sand, navigators, various musical instruments, islands, clocks, horses, donkeys, and even a lion ... in short a whole pictorial world capable of brightening up even the most cut and dry 'History of Philosophy'. (1980: p.10)

But philosophy, according to Le Doeuff, in all its rationalist guises, shows no interest in this 'imaginary' element, 'inscribing itself – labelling itself as philosophical – by means of a deviation from ... all that is image-making in it' (p. 9). However, for Le Doeuff, the imaginary in philosophical texts, which functions as a kind of alternative epistemology, needs to be better understood and also given a legitimacy alongside the more overtly rationalist discourse of 'concepts, procedures and systems':

> If anyone attempted to write a history of philosophical imagery, would this history ever be recognised as a history of philosophy, by the same rights as a history of concepts, procedures, systems? The images that appear in theoretical works are normally conceived as being outside the work, so that an interest in them is considered as philosophy only from a strictly anecdotal viewpoint. (p.10)

These epistemological critiques from within recent continental theory provide a backdrop for a number of educationists who have challenged the version of critical thinking as they believe it to be taught within the modern university. Kerry Walters (1994), for example, is critical of the 'generic accounts' in the US for being highly 'logistic' in nature, and for their tendency to take detached and impersonal thinking as some ideal form – personified, Walters suggests, in the clinically logical character of Spock in the original *Star Trek*. Walters argues further that while some claim this 'logicism' to be a universal form, in fact it serves only to marginalize alternative forms of thinking. For Blythe Clinchy (1994), a feminist critic, these marginalized forms are inevitably those types of thinking that can be associated with certain, more 'feminine' engagements with knowledge. Clinchy draws a distinction between, on the one hand, a 'separate knowing' which has the qualities of 'detachment', 'impersonality', 'procedural rigidity'; and on the other a 'connected knowing' which is concerned more with an empathic understanding – that is, trying to 'get into the heads' of those one wishes to understand. This latter form, which Clinchy believes is less valued in the university, is most centrally 'a *non*-critical thinking' (p. 38, my emphasis).

While Walters and Clinchy are critical of the 'generic' versions of critical thinking, Ronald Barnett, a prolific writer on higher education in Britain, believes there is a similar restrictiveness within disciplinary modes of thought. Thus, he notes that students are all too often required to fall in with the established critical routines of the subjects they are studying:

> Disciplines are frameworks, albeit not entirely of a rigid construction. They provide security and identity for those who live and work in them. Accordingly, while in principle a framework can be left and another entered, such a move will happen rarely. The framework is a normative structure, exerting a strong pull. (2000: p. 121)

Barnett suggests that a genuine higher education would be one that encourages students to recognize the limits of critique within the framework of a single discipline and to draw on – in some personal and idiosyncratic way – the perspectives they have picked up from a range of other learning contexts. As an example, he points to the educational possibilities of a scientific claim being situated and evaluated within a range of alternative disciplinary frameworks such as history, sociology, philosophy – or even aesthetics where unlikely criteria such as 'elegance, élan, daring, insightfulness, riskiness, profundity, and wit' might come into play (p.120). Thus, for Barnett, the ideal form of critical thinking is a kind of 'metacritique', wherein the evaluation is directed less at knowledge *per se*, and more at the structures in which knowledge resides. In a view quite at odds with the aims of many in the critical thinking movement, Barnett sees the desired form of intellectual development in students as a shift towards an 'increasingly sophisticated relativism'. (p. 122)

In the investigation conducted for this book, it was taken as given that there is something called 'critical thinking' that academics are engaged in teaching to their students. However, the preceding discussion suggests that, along with exploring how academics understand and teach critical thinking, there is a need also to find out whether, within the pedagogical routines of the university, these academics were generally content with the critical frame in which they and their students must operate – or whether there was another, better version of the 'examined life' they could imagine.

2.9 An Alternative School of Thought – Disciplinary Discourses

It was noted above that, within the critical thinking movement, there has to date been no take up of the discourse agenda suggested by Ennis – 'the careful comparative analysis of articles and arguments [from a range of disciplines]' (1992: p.31). There is, however, a school of research – one quite unrelated to the psychological and philosophical concerns of the movement – that has pursued this kind of study with great enthusiasm. This is the field of 'disciplinary discourses'. Because this latter group takes as its main point of departure the outcomes of thinking (discursive practices) rather than the movement's focus on the processes of thinking (cognition), the two areas have effectively operated as parallel universes – and there has been virtually no interaction between them.

The field of disciplinary discourses arguably has its origins in cultural anthropology, especially in the work of Clifford Geertz (1973, 1983). In his fine collection of essays, *Local Knowledge*, whose title is suggestive of the relativist position advanced, Geertz lays out his central thesis: that the ideas one associates with a discipline are inseparable from the social and literary practices out of which they are produced. As he evocatively explains:

> ...to an ethnographer sorting through the machinery of distant ideas, the shapes of knowledge are always ineluctably local, indivisible from their instruments and encasements. (1983: p. 4)

This idea of a discipline's social and communicative norms being distinctive in some way is the premise of another influential anthropological work – Tony Becher's (1989) *Academic Tribes and Territories*. Becher's is a full blown ethnography which seeks to characterize the 'life-world' of practicing academics in a variety of disciplinary specialisms. The work covers a range of issues: how academics define their disciplines – including how they seek to delimit them from other related disciplines; what the discipline's central intellectual and epistemological concerns are thought to be; the nature of communication patterns in the discipline; methods and rituals for inducting new scholars and so on. His conclusions point to a diversity of beliefs, practices and values – those of a differentiated community of 'tribes' – which Becher relates to the highly distinctive intellectual tasks with which each individual discipline is fundamentally engaged.

Out of this anthropological view has emerged a firm belief in the idea of boundaries in academic knowledge and practice – ones which the sojourning undergraduate student has to negotiate as they move in their studies from subject to subject, and from department to department. Ballard and Clanchy, in an interesting case study – arguably one more credible than their better known work on the experiences of international students at Australian universities – report on the difficulties faced by one local Australian student in his negotiating of one such disciplinary divide between literature and anthropology. In their careful analysis of essays written in the two subject areas, the authors show how the student, whose writing was normally of a generally high standard, struggled to achieve adequate grades in literature 'essentially because his anthropological concerns and perspectives appeared to intrude unwittingly into his literary studies' (1988: p. 16). As evidence of this 'intrusion', Ballard and Clanchy note that certain key lexis used by the student (like *image* and *symbol*) were employed in his literature essays not to denote textual constructions of reality, but instead to denote certain social constructions; that is, an anthropological as opposed to a literary use of terms. (p.16)

Observations from case studies like this have led many educators to believe that familiarity with a discipline's distinctive modes of thinking and writing is crucial to a student's success in the academy. As Ballard and Clanchy go on to explain:

> The key to improving students' standards of literacy lies we think in ... exploring the fundamental relationship between the culture [and sub-cultures] of knowledge and the language by which it is maintained and expressed. (p.7)

In recent years, the exploring of this relationship has been the spur for a burgeoning body of research within the fields of rhetorical studies and discourse analysis – with the aim of both describing and explicating what is salient about the discursive forms of various disciplines – or Geertz's distinctive 'instruments and encasements' (see, for example Bazerman 1988; McDonald 1994; Berkenkotter and Huckin 1995; Candlin 1998; Hyland 2000). As these studies show, there has been a range of linguistic entrees into exploring the ways in which these discursive differences inhere. Susan McDonald (1994), for example, is able to illustrate interesting differences between the disciplines of psychology, history and literary history by focusing on the nature of *sentence subjects*, which are for her suggestive of quite different modes of argumentation.

Perhaps the most substantive contribution in this field to date has been Ken Hyland's *Disciplinary Discourses* – written from within the pedagogical traditions of English for specific purposes. In his study of academic texts across a range of disciplines and genres, Hyland's main interest is in the socially interactive dimensions of published academic writing – to see writing as a process of situated rhetorical action. As he explains, by examining a range of pragmatic features, it is possible 'to identify how writers from different disciplines typically position themselves and their work in relation to other members of their professional communities'. (2000: p. x)

As far as I know, no disciplinary discourse studies conducted so far have specifically taken up the idea of critical thinking *per se*, though one chapter in Hyland's book – an investigation into the textual dynamics of the book review genre – does indeed come close. Focusing on the semantic units of 'praise' and 'criticism' in his corpus of reviews, Hyland recognizes broad differences in the distribution of these units between the humanities and social sciences on the one hand (philosophy, sociology, applied linguistics, marketing), and the science and technology disciplines on the other (engineering, physics, biology). He notes, for example, that the so-called 'soft' disciplines of the humanities and social sciences can be rather 'harder' in their reviewing practices than their 'hard' scientific counterparts:

> Reviews in science and engineering ... were much shorter and assessments more compressed and more dense, averaging 15.6 per 1,000 words compared to 8.5 for the soft reviews. Praise tended to be more fulsome and criticism more acerbic in the soft knowledge papers. The hard knowledge reviews, on the other hand, were dominated by praise. (2000: p. 50)

Hyland also investigated the general content of these evaluations in his reviews and again noticed certain differences – with some disciplines focusing more on issues of writing style, others on textual attributes (such as use of visual material), and others again on publishing issues (such as price and printing standards). Finally, in the section of his work most relevant to the proposed project, Hyland seeks to identify the most frequent evaluative terms in the different samples – what he calls 'contrasting vocabularies' of critique. He noted, for example, the frequency of such positive epithets as *useful, important,* and *interesting* across all disciplines, but with a clustering of other evaluative terms around certain disciplines – *detailed* in philosophy, *up-to-date* in the hard sciences, and *practical* in engineering.

Investigation of variation in textual practices in different disciplinary cultures has proved to be a productive field of inquiry. However, one cannot help noticing in the findings of such research, an ever-increasing commitment to the idea of disparity, disjunction and even incommensurability between the cultures of the disciplines. For example, a belief in 'strong disciplinary boundaries' is clearly stated in the following conclusion drawn by some of the field's more prominent researchers:

> [In disciplinary cultures] there are strong boundaries defining membership and initiation, variations in knowledge, structures and norms of inquiry, different vocabularies and discourses, differing standards of rhetorical intimacy

modes of expression and distinctions in typical approaches to teaching. (Candlin, Bhatia and Hyland 1997: p. 25)

Candlin perhaps puts the case even more forcefully when he states elsewhere that: 'Disciplinary cultures are extraordinarily differentiated in almost any respect one might name' (1998: p. 5). In such a mapping of the disciplinary landscape, there is little consolation, it must be said, for the border-crossing undergraduate. Hyland, for example, is quite pessimistic about students being able to draw on understandings they might acquire from studies in other fields, suggesting instead that they need to learn from scratch the particular academic style of each new discipline they enter. 'Each [disciplinary] discourse', he declares 'has unique ways of identifying issues, asking questions, ... presenting arguments, and these make the possibility of transferable skills unlikely'. (2000: p.145)

But, there is a need for caution in these matters, one that was sounded early by Geertz. While acknowledging that there are undeniable differences in disciplinary styles, Geertz warns against too firm a belief in reductive categories, and impermeable borders:

> Grand rubrics like Natural Sciences, Biological Sciences, Social Science and the Humanities have their uses in organizing curricula, in sorting scholars into cliques and professional communities and in distinguishing broad traditions of intellectual style. And of course the sorts of work conducted under any one of them do show some general resemblances to one another and some genuine differences from the sorts that are conducted under the others. ... But when these rubrics are taken to be a borders-and-territories map of modern intellectual life. Or worse, a Linnean catalogue into which to classify scholarly species, they merely block from view what is really going on out there where men and women are thinking about things and writing down what it is they think. (1983: p. 7)

For educationists trying to make these matters comprehensible for their students, an insistence on the idea of discrete categories of knowledge is thought ultimately to be unhelpful. Barnett suggests that amid the fragmentation of disciplinary cultures, there is a need to try to recover what he calls 'a discourse of the universal' (2001: p.15). In a similar vein, Gordon Taylor argues that in any attempt to outline a coherent view of modern university education, the starting point must always be the specifics of disciplinary knowledge; but there is equally a need, he says, to try to identify whatever overarching patterns might inhere these knowledges.

> The attempt to articulate what transcends particular discipline-specific knowledge and technique is one that cannot be shirked. Indeed given the nature

of human language and thought, which rely upon generalisation, it is inevitable. But there are considerable complications. (2000: p. 158)

The 'complications' to which Taylor refers arise from the difficulty in finding ways out of the binary oppositions of same and difference. As we have seen in the preceding discussion about the varying conceptions of critical thinking, generalists like Ennis and Siegel are committed to the idea of the similar and the general, whereas adversaries in the movement like McPeck are drawn to the different and the particular. Like the critical thinking specifists, researchers in the fields of disciplinary discourses have also been inclined to notions of difference. However, it is possible that the two distinct cases argued for arise in the first instance from a basic pre-disposition to view one's data from one of either perspective. Perhaps it is in relation to this issue that the fundamental incommensurability lies.

And so, as Wittgenstein might ask, 'how is the fly to find its way out of the fly bottle?' Taylor (2000) asserts that the common thread in all discourses is language, and indeed it is in understandings of language that Wittgenstein would suggest the solutions to problems like this lie. In *Philosophical Investigations*, Wittgenstein proposes a very different way of seeing resemblance – not as a choice between polarities, nor even as a continuum, but as a network in which similarities overlap and criss-cross in complex and interesting ways. He demonstrates this notion of resemblance through his now famous account of the meanings of the word 'game', quoted at length here:

You talk about all sorts of language games, but have nowhere said what the essence of a language game and hence of language is: what is common to all these activities, and what makes them into language or parts of language.

I am saying that these phenomena have no one thing in common which makes us use the same word for all, - but that they are related to one another in many different ways. And it is because of the relationship that we call them all 'language'. I will try to explain.

Consider for example the proceedings that we call 'games'. I mean board-games, card-games, ball-games, Olympic games, and so on. What is common to them all? – Don't say: 'There *must* be something in common, or they could not be called "games"'- but *look* and *see*. Whether there is anything common to all. – For if you look at them you will see something that is common to *all*, but similarities, relationships, and a whole series of them at that. To repeat: don't think but look! - Look for example, at board games, with their multifarious relationships. Now pass to card games; here you may find correspondences with the first group, but many common features drop-out, and others appear. When we pass next to ball games, much that is common is retained, but much is lost. Are they all amusing? Compare chess with noughts and crosses. Or is there always winning or losing, or competition between players? Think of patience. In ball games there is winning and losing; but when a child throws his ball at a wall and catches it again, this feature has disappeared ... we can go through the many, many groups of games in the same way; we can see how similarities crop up and disappear.

And the result of this examination is: we see a complicated network of similarities overlapping and criss-crossing: sometimes overall similarities, sometimes similarities of detail. (1958a: p. 31)

In the present investigation, which looked at notions of critical thinking across a range of disciplines, the intention was to approach data neither from assumptions of sameness nor of difference – that is to imagine that the critical thinking in Discipline A was at heart of a similar or of a different kind to that in Discipline B. On this point Wittgenstein says we cannot hope to find a single, unitary meaning of a term (some essential property which it denotes), but nor should we ever assume that there is incoherence – for without some underlying coherence there would be a need, presumably, for other distinctly different terms. Unlike many of his fellow philosophers, Wittgenstein (1961), even as far back as the *Tractatus*, is committed to the idea that wisdom about these matters resides in language as it is used:

All the propositions of our everyday language, just as they stand, are in perfect logical order. (1961: p. 83)

It is the search for networks of 'coherence', and 'logic' around the various usages of the term 'critical thinking' that is the principal concern of the study described in the ensuing pages.

2.10 The Problem Restated

The investigation was conceived in the light of the preceding discussion. Its main aim, as mentioned, was to explore conceptions of critical thinking as they are understood and taught by academics from a range of disciplines at an Australian university. Specifically, the intention was to seek answers to the following questions:

i.   What does 'critical thinking' seem to mean to individual academics teaching in different disciplines within the university?
ii. In what ways, and to what extent, can we say that there are disciplinary variations in these meanings of critical thinking?
iii. What implications might the answers to i) and ii) have for the teaching of critical thinking in the university?

Chapter 3

In Search of Critical Thinking

3.1 Introduction

The present study was conducted in the Faculty of Arts at a large Australian university – the place of my work from 1996–2006. As already mentioned, the three disciplines selected for investigation were: history, philosophy and literary/cultural studies. Two types of data were collected for the study: 1) spoken data obtained from interviews with academics from the three discipline areas, and 2) textual data, which were a range of teaching documents used by these academics on their courses. The data for the study were collected from 2005–2006.

The present chapter is divided into two main sections. The first part deals with the idea of disciplinarity, including a description of the disciplines selected for the investigation – both in their general sense, and in their particular incarnations at University X. The remainder of the chapter describes the method used in the study.

3.2 Disciplines and Disciplinarity

As stated at the end of the previous chapter, the study was interested, in part, in finding out whether conceptions of critical thinking appear to vary in different discipline settings. In such a design, the construct of 'critical thinking' can be thought of as the study's dependent variable (y), and the idea of disciplinarity as an independent variable (x). A difficulty, however, is that disciplinarity as a concept is not at all a clear-cut one, and on the face of it, appears to pose the same kind of definitional problems we have seen for the study's key term – 'critical thinking'.

In more conventional accounts, an academic discipline is usually defined and identified by the distinct knowledge domains and intellectual problems with which a particular group of scholars is concerned. Such a view is expressed in the following account by Nelson, Treichler and Grossberg:

Disciplines stake out their territories ... by claiming a *particular* domain of objects, and by developing a *unique* set of methodological practices, and by carrying forward a founding tradition and lexicon (1992: p. 1, my emphasis).

Toulmin expresses a similar view when he suggests that each discipline is 'charac-terised by its own body of concepts, methods and fundamental aims' (1972: p.25).

Such definitions, which emphasize the 'particularity', even 'uniqueness', of different areas of study, suggest that disciplines of their nature can be thought of as relatively fixed and discrete entities; that is to say, for example, that studies in philosophy can be clearly delineated from say, studies in history or in literature. The interdisciplinary nature of a good deal of academic work, however, makes such a conception problematic. The fluidity of these fields can be seen, for example, in the many sub-disciplinary specializations that combine elements from several areas. Thus, drawing on the examples above, portmanteaus such as philosophy of history, or history of philosophy, or literary history and so on, are all legitimate areas of study in their own right, and are often not readily assign-able to any single, parent discipline. The evident overlapping of the intellectual territories of the disciplines, as well as the regular shifting and redrawing of their boundaries, have thus lead many to challenge the idea of disciplines as discrete, pre-existing categories (e.g. Prior 1998).

In the light of these difficulties, an alternative approach is to distinguish dis-ciplines not on the basis of what they study, but by the 'the different modes in which arguments are generated, developed, expressed and reported' (Becher 1989: p. 23). Thus, rather than seeing a discipline (variable x) as producing certain types of cognitive and textual forms (variable y), in such an account, the direction of causality is in fact reversed – and it is the collective expression of different modes of thought that go to produce the discipline. While there is an intuitive appeal in this type of discursive explanation, for the present study there is some circularity in the argument here. The study was interested in find-ing out if there is a disciplinary basis in critical thinking, but according to this latter view, it is these different modes of thinking that ultimately define the discipline.

To avoid these difficulties and conundrums, and to get some fix on the vari-able of discipline for the study, the approach adopted has been a pragmatic one, borrowing from Paul Prior's notion of 'discipline as social fact' (1998). In explaining this idea, Prior draws an analogy between academic disciplines and political parties. He suggests that just as a political system is made up of a variety of political parties whose particular designations (e.g. the Democratic Party in the US) have both institutional and ideological meanings for the citizens of a polity, so it is that faculties are made up of disciplines whose denotations have a similar pragmatic significance for those who teach and learn within them (1998: p. 26). Thus, for example, to be an academic or a student working in a part of the university that is designated 'history' is, according to Prior, 'a social fact of some consequence', one from which a variety of beliefs, purposes, practices and the like might be extrapolated.

In the present investigation, each of the disciplines was thus identified through the way in which it is institutionally named and allocated. For two of the disciplines considered – history and philosophy – each, as a realm of knowledge, was identified for the purposes of the study as *that* which is taught within the particular unit bearing its name – namely the School of Historical Studies, and the School of Philosophy. As we shall see, the situation was a little more complicated for the area of literature, where the term 'literature' was used in the designations of two different academic units – the Department of English Literature, and the Centre for Comparative Literature and Cultural Studies. For this discipline area, data were collected from both sites, and the particular designation chosen to denote the field was literary/cultural studies. The complex history of this area, both as an academic discipline and as an administrative entity within University X, is discussed in detail later in this chapter.

3.3 The Disciplines Investigated

The growing literature on disciplinary cultures and discourses has seen attention being given to a wide range of disciplines. Some of the studies in the field have been large-scale surveys, covering multiple and diverse discipline areas, usually selected on the basis of some generative taxonomy, for example 'pure-applied' or 'hard-soft' knowledge fields (Becher 1989). Within this broad brush approach, the studies of Tony Becher and Ken Hyland, referred to in the previous chapter, are perhaps the most well known. More common, however, have been studies that have focused more on disciplinary depth, rather than breadth, with investigations into smaller sets of disciplines. Examples of the latter approach have been Charles Bazerman's (1988) groundbreaking study on the differing rhetorics of science, sociology of science, and literature; and Susan Peck MacDonald's (1994) study of a range of sub-disciplinary specializations from the social sciences and humanities – namely, attachment research in psychology, colonial New England social history, and new historicism in literary studies.

An interesting variant on the select discipline approach is that adopted by John Swales (1998) in his study *Other floors, other voices: A textography of a small university building*. As the title of this work suggests, the basis for selection was not some abstract rubric under which the different disciplines are conventionally categorized, but in fact the range of disciplines that happened to be housed in a particular university building. (Swales himself was an occupant of the building, and also a participant in the study.) The disciplines in Swales's study thus took in the somewhat eccentric combination of systematic botany, computing, and English language teaching – a grouping that perhaps reflects more than anything else the sometimes random and arbitrary ways in which physical resources in universities are organized and allocated.

The present investigation, taking in the humanities disciplines of history, philosophy, and literary/cultural studies, fits with the 'cognate discipline' studies such as those by Bazerman and MacDonald, but also has the same 'site study' character of Swales's work – with the three disciplines selected located on adjoining floors in the one faculty building. As was the case in Swales's study, the design of the present study was motivated in part by the researcher's desire, also an occupant of the site building, to make some sense of these various discourse worlds operating in such close proximity to one another.

Most importantly, however, the disciplines investigated were selected as a configuration that had clear relevance to students' study on university programmes. As discussed previously, critical thinking's potential for confusion appears to arise not only from a general sense of vagueness surrounding the concept, but also from the possibility that the notion may mean slightly different things in different disciplinary contexts (Ballard and Clanchy 1988). Thus, the study sought to investigate a range of disciplines that were cognate in an educational sense; that is, ones that students in the structure of their undergraduate studies may find themselves having to engage with concurrently, and where any such differences might have some bearing on their experience of study. The disciplines selected were ones that, while facing some difficulties in an increasingly vocationally-oriented climate in Australian higher education, have managed to maintain their levels of enrolments over the last decade (Pascoe 2002).

3.4 History, Philosophy, Literary/Cultural Studies

In what follows, a brief sketch is provided of each of the discipline areas covered in the study, both in their general sense, and in their particular institutional manifestations at University X. The intention here is to offer some account of the main intellectual concerns of each, along with their recent histories and controversies. Before doing this, however, some preliminary remarks are offered about the broader academic context of which they are a part.

The disciplines of history, philosophy, and literary/cultural studies all fall conventionally within the larger category of the humanities, defined by one professional body dedicated to the field's advancement as:

> that area of study devoted to the creation, maintenance and transmission of knowledge about humans as self-conscious individuals, and about human culture in all its manifestations. (Australian Academy of the Humanities 1999: p. 1)

While the humanities have always occupied a central place in the modern university, many are of the view that the field's best days were experienced some time ago, particularly over the period spanning from the 1960s to the 1980s (Pascoe, MacIntyre and Ainley 2003). In Australia, for example, this was a time when government commissions could insist, without reservation, that a key responsibility for all universities was to provide a 'full and true education' in the humanities in order 'to produce rounded human beings' (Murray Committee, cited in Pascoe et al. 2003: p. 22). In recent times, the situation for the field has been far less certain, characterized by some as being a period of 'dramatic change' (Pascoe 2002), and by others – those of a less sanguine outlook – as being one of almost 'permanent crisis' (Coady 1998; Nightingale 1998).

Two developments are often cited as factors contributing to this uncertainty. One has been the emergence of a particular type of scholarship in the humanities known collectively as the 'new humanities' (Ruthven 1992). There are different ways in which this broad movement might be characterized, but it is often understood to involve a consciously theoretical approach to scholarship in general, and of the ideas and theories associated with post-structuralism and postmodernism in particular. As Andrew Milner and Jeff Browitt suggest, the influence of this movement has been all encompassing – even if its ideas and approaches have not been wholeheartedly embraced by all those who have come within its sphere:

> Almost everyone who has worked in humanities and social sciences, whether in Western Europe, the Americas or Australasia at any time in the last three decades … would have encountered transdisciplinary 'theory' … Whether appalled by its poverty, like [E.P] Thompson or attracted by its glamour like Terry Eagleton there is no doubting its cultural salience. (2002: p. 11–12)

A number of scholars acknowledge the destabilizing effects that these 'paradigmatic shifts' (Kuhn 1962) have had on the field's sense of identity and collective purpose (Frow 1992; Hodge 1995). John Frow, an important figure in the emergence of cultural studies in Australia, and normally a partisan of the 'new humanities' paradigm, describes the situation thus:

> The increased complexity of theory … and the anti-systemic impetus of post-structuralism have [unavoidably] undermined our sense [in the humanities] of the cumulative nature of knowledge and so of a common continuous project in which local research would be integrated, sooner or later, into a coherent whole. (1992: p. 25)

The other factor, a development which has its origins quite outside the humanities, has been the application of neo-liberal principles to virtually all areas of public life, including the academy. For many, the hard and unforgiving utilitarianism of the neo-liberal creed have been wholly antithetical to the old 'liberal' values of the humanities. Thus, Frow, who shows some ambivalence about the impact of 'theory' on the field, has no doubts at all about the malign effect these latter philosophies have had on the humanities, contributing more than anything else, he suggests, to their abject loss of 'prestige and authority':

> The [chief] antagonist of the humanities is that set of utilitarian discourses, from economics to competency evaluation, which have come to occupy a privileged place in our education system and in our polity. (1992: p. 25)

It is in this environment of change, and apparent uncertainty, that we can understand some of the dynamics at work in each of the disciplines considered in the present study.

3.4.1 History

While no simple synopsis of the discipline of history is possible, practitioners in the field generally agree that it is united not only by a fundamental interest in the past – many other disciplines have this same interest – but also by a drive to 'interpret' and 'explain' this past in some reasoned and considered way (Evans 2005). In a recent volume, *What is history now?*, an update of E. H. Carr's classic work, the contributors generally agreed that while historians are always prey to the perceptions and understandings of their particular age, the discipline's overriding concern, nevertheless, is to somehow 'unravel the meanings of the past' in the ways that one's sources will allow (Cannadine 2001: p. xii).

History, like all other disciplines, has been touched over the last decades by the spirit of the new humanities (Swain 2005). Questions about how much and how well an historian can know the past – ones raised by Benedetto Croce and R. G. Collingwood a century earlier – have become more acute under the influence of the relativist perspective of much contemporary theory (Swain 2005). Notwithstanding the view of some – that such an influence has served only to undermine the integrity of historical studies (e.g. Windschuttle 1994) – many see the postmodernist outlook opening up many new fields of inquiry. Thus, some observers note an overall shift in recent decades away from 'grand narratives' of nation, politics and the economy towards smaller-scale cultural analyses, especially ones devoted to once-ignored sub-cultural groups and movements (Cannadine 2001). The approach, it is suggested, has also led to work of a more interdisciplinary nature, with influences felt from such areas as textual analysis, performance and cinema studies, and psychology (Swain 2005; Pascoe 2002).

Arguably, the most intense debate in the field in recent years has been felt not so much in relation to questions about the best ways to study and know the past, but rather to the particular conclusions that certain historians have drawn about this past. In Australian historical studies, for example, this has been particularly evident in the differing and often adversative ways that historians have sought to characterize the nation's past – whether to see it mainly as a chronicle of progress and achievement, or as one beset by currents of violence and oppression, manifested especially in the treatment of the nation's indigenous people since white settlement. This debate, which has been conducted in most robust terms in recent times, is known in Australia as the 'History Wars' (MacIntyre 2003), and has been dubbed abroad as 'the Culture Wars down under' (Rubinstein 2006).

While historians will argue about the nature of different historical periods and episodes, it is fair to say that the discipline has been less prone than other fields to major theoretical and methodological debates and conflicts (Macintyre 2003). Even Hayden White, one of the discipline's more contentious theoreticians, suggests that historians are influenced in their work more by a sense of collective disciplinary 'craft' than by the pull of differing paradigms:

> History is a craft-like discipline governed by convention and custom, rather than by methodology and theory. (1995: p. 233)

A general sense of unanimity about the discipline's basic purposes and methods seems to allow historians to say with some confidence how history might be distinguished from other areas of inquiry that also concern themselves with the past. Thus, the eminent Australian historian Inga Clendinnen suggests there is a need always to show how the 'iron rules of the discipline' make the study of history different from such areas as historical fiction and cinema, or the new genres of 'ficto-criticism'. For Clendinnen, these 'rules', which relate to the fundamentally empirical and evidential basis of historical work ('a fidelity to what is found'), are what make history a 'critical discipline' at heart:

> History's social utility depends on it being cherished as a *critical* discipline and not as tempting source of gratifying tales. (2006: p. 69, emphasis added)

As we shall see later, this sense of a unity of purpose and general self-assuredness is not necessarily shared by all disciplines examined in the study.

3.4.2 Philosophy

For many, philosophy is the 'master discipline', but it is also one that defies any simple description of its purposes and methods. Robert Audi, in his preface to the *Cambridge Dictionary of Philosophy*, acknowledges these difficulties when pointing out to readers the impossibility of compiling an entry for the volume's most central term – 'philosophy'. Audi goes on to suggest that one would not want to hazard anything much beyond the following most tentative and qualified account – also notable, among other things, for the centrality afforded to the term 'critical'.

Perhaps a great many philosophers (though certainly not all of them) would agree that philosophy is roughly the *critical*, normally systematic study of an unlimited range of ideas. (1999: p. xxv, emphasis added)

The challenge in being more precise than this, Audi suggests, is to find a rubric that might adequately accommodate thinkers as diverse as Plato, Aristotle, Aquinas, Descartes, Hume, Kant, Hegel, Mill, Heidegger and Wittgenstein, and fields as varied as epistemology, ethics, logic, metaphysics, and aesthetics. (p. xxvi)

Although highly diverse in its traditions, there has been a tendency over the last half century for philosophy's many different strands to divide into two broad, distinct groups (Critchley 2001). On the one side is the analytical tradition, associated with the work of Bertrand Russell and G.E. Moore in Britain and the logical positivists in Vienna, and taking in such areas of inquiry as formal logic, philosophy of language and scientific method; on the other side is the continental tradition, associated with such schools of thought as phenomenology, hermeneutics, post-structuralism, feminism, critical theory of the Frankfurt school, and some branches of Marxism (Critchley 2001).

The points of difference between these traditions are many, but they are often encapsulated in terms of their divergent views towards the concept of the 'real'. The analytical view, for example, holds that reality (and the related quality of 'truth') is somehow directly accessible to us, whether this is by means of the senses, or through the agencies of thought and analysis. By contrast, the general position within the continental tradition is to reject the idea that things can ever be known in themselves, and to insist instead that our knowledge of them is always contingent in some way (Solomon 1988). Perhaps, the most extreme expression of the anti-realism of the continentals is to be found in Derrida's famous slogan – *il n'y a pas de hors-texte* ('there is no "outside-the-text"') – usually interpreted to mean that in human culture, at least, there is no reality that exists prior to descriptions of that reality (Milner and Browitt 2002). As already noted, it is in the growing embrace of continental schools of thought that the origins of the 'new humanities' are to be found.

The interactions between the two traditions have played out in different ways. In some instances, there have been efforts by some thinkers to find points of contact and convergence between the two streams (e.g. Wheeler 1986; Green 1999). More often, however, the relationship has been a less-than-felicitous one, expressed in its most extreme form in the campaign mounted in the early 1990s by a number of prominent analytical philosophers to prevent Derrida from receiving an honorary doctorate at Cambridge. The fraughtness of this affair is well illustrated in the following extract from a letter sent to *The Times* by the analytic group, among whose signatories was one of analytical philosophy's more eminent figures – W. V. Quine.

M. Derrida's voluminous writings in our view stretch the normal forms of academic scholarship beyond recognition. Above all – as every reader can very easily establish for himself (and for this purpose any page will do) – his works employ a written style that defies comprehension. ... When the effort is made to penetrate [this style], however, it becomes clear, to us at least, that where coherent assertions are being made at all, these are either false or trivial. (cited in Humphries 1999: p. 255)

The situation in Australian universities has seen patterns both of accommodation and discord between the two traditions. Whereas in some philosophy departments, co-existence has been relatively unproblematic (see, for example, the University of Melbourne; Harney 1992), this was not the case at the University of Sydney, where relations between the two groups became so strained in the late 1970s that each eventually broke off into separate departments – with the creation of the Department of Traditional and Modern Philosophy 'for the Analytics', and the Department of General Philosophy 'for the Continentals' (Franklin 2003). The episode, now infamously known as the 'Sydney disturbances', has been described by one observer as 'a two-part toxin that polluted the atmosphere for a generation' (Price 2004).

More recently, the generally leaner times for the humanities have allowed for far less indulgence within academic philosophy, and the main energies of the discipline appear to have been devoted to just ensuring its relevance and survival (Coady 1998). Franklin suggests that the greatest relevance over the last decade has been found in the area of applied ethics, where the many dilemmas (and also scandals) that characterize contemporary public life have created a demand for training in professional ethics, thus providing an unexpected source of employment for many philosophy graduates (2003: p. 408).

3.4.3 Literary/cultural studies

If the recent history of philosophy has been largely one of segregation and separate development, the situation for our final discipline has been marked by a form of ongoing insurgency, as suggested by the additional 'cultural' tag given to the discipline's name in the study – literary/cultural studies. The unsettling effects of the conflict between more traditional studies of literature and the recent expanded field of cultural studies are well summarized by John Frow:

> There is no longer a general agreement about what the [discipline's object of study is] – Is it the text, and if so which ones? Is it literariness or textuality or a historical literary system? (1992: p. 24)

Part of this lack of accord in the discipline is expressed through the conflicting views that are held about the relationship between studies of culture and of literature. For those more aligned to the cultural perspective, literary studies is viewed as just one branch of the discipline, albeit a very important one (see Hoggart 1970). For those of a more traditional literary bent, the cultural component is viewed mainly with disdain – as a kind of alien intrusion that has been only a bane for the discipline (see Bloom 1994).

One place to locate the origins of these controversies is in Raymond Williams' reflection on the idea of 'culture', discussed earlier in the introduction to this book. In *Keywords*, Williams notes two distinct, and seemingly oppositional, uses of the term: a more normative meaning, referring to 'processes of intellectual and aesthetic development' (hence 'being cultured', or 'cultivated'); and a more anthropological sense – the one preferred by Williams – denoting 'the way of life of a whole people' (1976: p. 80). It was an overall shift in the humanities towards this latter meaning from the 1960s onwards that saw a challenge to more traditional approaches to literature, ones that had previously been devoted to what Arnold called 'the best that has been thought and said' and which 'makes for the beauty and worth of human nature' (cited in Milner and Browitt 2002: p. 26).

The effect of this shift on many literature departments was quite momentous, with a turning away from the English canon (especially that particular version of it favoured by F. R Leavis and others in the 'New Criticism' movement), and an embracing of alternative and popular forms of literature, and later, of cultural texts of all forms. This change in what literature studied saw a change also in the underlying purpose for studying it – not to appreciate how great literature is created, but rather to understand how texts in all their forms are made and consumed, a development characterized by Zygmunt Baumann as a shift in the role of the critic from cultural 'legislator' to that of 'interpreter' (1992: p. 24).

As long and difficult works of literature progressively fell off university reading lists, another type of difficult reading was introduced to take its place – this was theory, mainly Continental Theory, which provided the tools of the trade for the interpreter critic. Terry Eagleton, one of the standard bearers of the new movement, while acknowledging the sometimes 'obscurantist' tendencies of the new theoretical approaches, is at pains to point out that the 'emphasis' on theory, in fact, had its origins as a counter to the 'obscurantist' methods of Leavisism. For Eagleton and others, the expansion of higher education in 1960s and 70s, and the arrival of new kinds of students in literature departments meant that the 'cultivated' and largely intuitive methods of New Criticism – ones that assumed a particular 'cultural breeding' in one's charges – were no longer tenable:

> Theory was a way of emancipating literary works from the stranglehold of 'civilized sensibility' and throwing them open to a kind of analysis in which, in principle at least, anyone could participate. (1996: p. vii)

The situation for more traditional literature academics amid these developments is often portrayed as a grim one, as personified, for example, in the troubled protagonist of J. M. Coetzee's best-known novel *Disgrace*. In the face of various departmental rationalizations and shifting student preferences, the main character, David Lurie, once a professor of Romantic poetry, is only able to keep his tenure by agreeing to teach something called 'communications', a subject which he finds 'preposterous'. This is not, however, to suggest that the more traditional approaches have been entirely overwhelmed by the contemporary tide. For example, Harold Bloom – over the course of his long career – has remained a steadfast adversary of the cultural studies approach, which, as he scornfully suggests, seeks to substitute 'Batman comics, Mormon theme parks, television movies and rock' for 'Chaucer, Shakespeare, Milton and Wordsworth' (1994: p.519). For Bloom, like those from the traditions of New Criticism, the chief purpose for studying literature must ultimately be the personally ennobling ones of aesthetic pleasure and self-insight.

There are signs nowadays that a version of the traditional approach to literature is undergoing some kind of revival in the academy. Indeed, Terry Eagleton has recently shown himself to be something of an apostate, with suggestions that the study of literature needs to return to earlier grand themes of truth and morality (Eagleton 2003: p.155). In Australia, such issues have come to the fore with educators of various persuasions beginning to assert the need to arouse in students a renewed enthusiasm for literature, and to do more 'contextualising of great literary works' (Haines 2006).

3.5 The Disciplines at University X

If some of the dynamics within the broad discipline areas are to be understood in terms of the varying degrees of influence of the 'new humanities', at the local institutional level, the other factor we have identified – neo-liberalism – has been arguably the more potent force. The experience of many arts faculties in Australia, as elsewhere, has been one of a general decline in commitment to the humanities (Nightingale 1998). Nowhere has this been more evident than in the continual processes of restructuring and rationalizing that have seen the traditional departmental base of faculties give way to larger cross-disciplinary schools (Pascoe 2002: p. 15).

The Faculty of Arts at University X has been no exception in these processes. Thus, going back to more bountiful times in the mid-1980s, the faculty was divided into 17 different departments – an arrangement which saw a high degree of overlap between disciplinary and administrative boundaries, with separate departments of literature, history, philosophy, sociology, politics and linguistics, among others. Twenty years later, at the time the investigation was conducted, the faculty's departmental structure had been largely dispensed with, with most disciplines restructured into six schools. These processes of amalgamation, which occurred over several years in the late 1990s, were guided to some extent by considerations of disciplinary 'affiliation', but also, as one informant from the study described it, by the 'inevitable byzantinism of faculty politics'. The disciplines studied in the present project experienced different outcomes in these processes. What follows is a very brief account of these recent administrative histories, along with some background information about the teaching offerings of each of the schools.

3.5.1 History at University X

History, as a department, managed to survive the faculty's restructuring virtually intact as a discipline, with staff in the former Department of History moving into a newly created School of Historical Studies. Included in the new structure was archaeology, which had previously been a part of the Classics Department. Classics, which was closed down in 1998, was a controversial casualty in the faculty's restructuring processes (*The Age* 1998). The sub-discipline of gender studies was also briefly a part of the new and larger school, but moved not long afterwards, after what one history informant euphemistically described as 'some disagreements about role'. It was relocated within the faculty's major social science grouping – the School of Social and Political Inquiry.

The School of Historical Studies, one of the larger schools in the faculty, teaches a broad range of histories, with research strengths given as: 'Australian social and cultural history (including indigenous history); South and South East Asian history; modern Europe; medieval and Renaissance history, and classical history'. The following is a representative sample of subjects offered at undergraduate level: *Australian History; Modern Asian History; Contemporary History; Renaissance Europe; Nations at War; The Vietnam War; American Civil War; Ancient Civilizations; The Golden Age of Athens.*

Describing the general dynamics and outlook of the school, one informant (formerly the head of the school) thought that it was the particular historical interests of the school's academic staff that contributed most to the school's overall character, as opposed to the subscribing to any specific research paradigms or theoretical positions. As she explained: 'I think here we're all of us particularists, and then only optionally look for a more general kind of frame'.

3.5.2 Philosophy at University X

The considerably smaller area of philosophy also emerged from the processes of amalgamation in the late 1990s as a standalone discipline. Initial cohabitation with linguistics was abandoned after a period of a year – mainly due to perceptions by staff from both areas of the very different intellectual orientations of the two departments[1] and the philosophers found their disciplinary independence restored in the renamed School of Philosophy and Bioethics. The inclusion of the sub-field of bioethics in the school's title, it was explained, was recognition of the department's research strength in this area, including the major international reputation of one of its staff members.

One informant described the general outlook of the school as 'one strongly in the Anglo-analytic tradition of philosophy', though the degree of affiliation to this tradition, it was suggested, varied among individual academics. The informant went on to explain that in the case of University X, the main teaching of continental philosophy took place not within the School of Philosophy and Bioethics, but more in one of the faculty's literature strands – in the Centre for Comparative Literature and Cultural Studies (CCLCS). For him, this situation reflected the particular history of the disciplines at University X; at other universities, he explained, the arrangements were different.

The school's 'research concentrations' are listed on its website as: logic and metaphysics; applied ethics and moral philosophy; and history of philosophy. The following are the main subjects taught on the undergraduate programme: *Contemporary Moral Issues; God, Freedom and Evil; Science, Religion and Witchcraft; Language, Truth and Power; Crime and Punishment; Metaphysics; Thinking, Biotechnology, Justice and the Law.*

3.5.3 Literary/cultural studies at University X

The circumstances of the teaching of literature at University X (and its companion field of cultural studies) have been more complex, and attest to the fragmentary nature of the discipline area, as discussed in the previous section. Unlike the other disciplines in the study, the broad area of literature had a history in the faculty of being taught within two different administrative units, with more traditional literature taught for many years within an English literature department, and the more 'contemporary' variety based in its own dedicated unit – the Centre for Comparative Literature and Cultural Studies (CCLCS). It is worth noting that the origins of the latter unit lay not so much in the types of theoretical disputes described earlier, but from a push from staff in parts of the faculty – notably those from modern language departments – to expand the faculty's offerings to include non-Anglo varieties of literature (Pascoe et al. 2003: p. 60).

In the restructuring process of the late 1990s, the two literature streams were briefly brought together within the one school (School of Literary, Visual and Performance Studies), an arrangement that saw a greater degree of cooperation between them than had previously been the case. The amalgamation however, was not to last, and staff in the Centre for Comparative Literature Cultural Studies decided to relocate again several years later – this time to take up in the School of Languages, Cultures and Linguistics. According to one informant from CCLCS, the principal reason for this reversal was the desire of the centre's staff to preserve their 'academic independence'.

The different orientations of the two literature strands are suggested in the website information that is provided to students, and also in the range of subjects offered by each. The more traditional English department gives an account of itself on the departmental website as follows:

> *The School of Literary, Visual and Performance studies offers a wide variety of courses in English studies at undergraduate level. Some subjects emphasise the study of English language, some the study of a particular author in depth, some the formal elements of literary genres, some the critical and scholarly methods of studying and writing about English literature.*

Some of the literature subjects offered by staff in the department at undergraduate level include: *Reading Literature; Modern English Literature; Short Fiction: Classic and Contemporary; Poetry: Text and Performance; Australian Urban Fictions; Romantic Literature; Shakespeare.*

The contrasting synopsis from the Centre for Comparative Literature and Cultural Studies (CCLCS) emphasizes both the broader range of literature and text-types that are studied on programmes, as well as the centre's interest in particular theoretical approaches:

> *Comparative literature at University X is the study of literature in ways that go beyond particular national or linguistic boundaries … Cultural studies at University X is the study of literature in its political and social contexts and in relation to other arts and media, especially newspapers and magazines, film and television. We study the inter-relationships between texts and codes, both 'artistic' and 'popular', verbal and visual. [The Centre draws on] a whole series of contemporary approaches to literary and cultural criticism, for example hermeneutics, semiotics, post-structuralism, psychoanalysis, and so on.*

Subjects offered at undergraduate level include the following titles: *Text and Context; Narrative Practices; Introduction to Cultural Studies; Postmodernism and the Novel; Science Fiction: From Monsters to Cyborgs.*

The disciplinary histories sketched in the preceding sections – unavoidably brief and partial as they are – are intended to give a sense of the dynamic and complex landscape in which notions of critical thinking have been developed and taught by the academics who participated in the study. This landscape includes both the broader horizons of the discipline as a whole, and also those in closer view – the vicissitudes of local faculty and departmental life. In offering these brief sketches, the intention is not in any way to presuppose or to predict the outlook of the study's participants. It is assumed that all academics, while no doubt influenced by the various contexts of their academic work, will engage with the developments and dynamics of their disciplines and also of broader educational discourses in quite individual – even idiosyncratic – ways.

Thus, in the conduct of the study, an effort has been made to heed Geertz's caution and not to rely too much on any 'Linnean classification of scholarly species', but rather to be open, as Geertz urges, to 'what is really going on out there where men and women are thinking about things and writing down what it is they think' (1983: p. 7). For the purposes of the present research, we might also add to these activities, what it is that these men and women say about this 'thinking', and indeed what the 'thinking' is that they wish to encourage in their students.

3.6 The Study's Participants

A total of 17 academics (ten men and seven women) were recruited to participate in the study – six from history, five from philosophy and six from literary/cultural studies. Table 1 provides details of these participants, including their disciplinary backgrounds and research interests. (Pseudonyms have been used in each case.) As was explained earlier, academics in the literary/cultural studies grouping were based in two different administrative units, with two (numbers 12–13) coming from the more traditional English literature department, and the remaining four (numbers 14–17) from the Centre for Comparative Literature and Cultural Studies. Where relevant, an effort has been made in the data to indicate these different administrative affiliations, with those from the traditional English literature department designated *literary/cultural studies – Eng.*, and those from the centre, *literary/cultural Studies – comp.*

Most of those participating in the study were colleagues with whom I had some acquaintance. In some cases, the relationship was a fairly close working one, involving previous teaching or research collaboration. Others were colleagues known only from around the faculty. In the first instance, recruitment was organized on the basis of informal encounters – chance meetings in corridors, conversations after faculty meetings and the like – where I briefly explained the project to them, and asked about their willingness to participate. There was a small additional group of informants whom I did not know previously, but who were recommended by initial informants on the basis of an interest they were known to have in the area (e.g. 'X would be a good one to talk to about this, because she actually teaches her students all this stuff').

All participants were tenured members of the faculty, and had worked at the university for relatively long periods – in most cases more than ten years. Some occupied, or had occupied, senior positions in the faculty. One, for example, was a former faculty dean; another three, at the time of interview, were heads of school or centre. All participants had had a strong involvement in teaching activities in the faculty, including extensive teaching experience on undergraduate programmes.

Table 1 Summary of informants (discipline, research interests).

DISCIPLINE AREA	ADMIN'TIVE UNIT	INFORMANT*		INFORMANT'S RESEARCH INTERESTS **
HISTORY	School of Historical Studies	#1	Edward (M)	European social history; Enlightenment; French Revolution
		#2	Hannah (F)	Ptolemaic and Roman Egypt; Greek and Roman history; early Christianity
		#3	Katherine (F)	South East Asian history; Vietnam war
		#4	Nell (F)	Australian social, political and religious history; women's history
		#5	Michael (M)	British nineteenth century urban and working class history; Australian regional political history
		#6	Nigel (M)	Australian history, American history
PHILOSOPHY	School of Philosophy and Bioethics	#7	Eric (M)	Ancient Greek and Roman philosophy; metaphysics; aesthetics; moral philosophy
		#8	Henry (M)	Philosophy of language, philosophy of science, philosophy of religion, aesthetics, logic, metaphysics
		#9	Jonathon (M)	Cognitive science, metaphysics, critical thinking
		#10	Kim (M)	Bioethics; ethical theory; moral psychology
		#11	Lauren (F)	History of women's ideas; philosophy of language; continental philosophy; Sartre and de Beauvoir
LITERARY/ CULTURAL STUDIES	Department of English Literature	#12	Bruce (M)	Nineteenth and twentieth century novel; Dickens
		#13	Quentin (M)	Literary stylistics; translation studies; poetry and prosody, Shakespeare

(continued)

Table 1 (Continued)

DISCIPLINE AREA	ADMIN'TIVE UNIT	INFORMANT*		INFORMANT'S RESEARCH INTERESTS **
LITERARY/ CULTURAL STUDIES	Centre for Comparative Literature and Cultural Studies	#14	Brian (M)	Literature, politics and society; cultural studies; utopia, dystopia and science fiction; Bourdieu, Jameson, Williams
		#15	Nora (F)	Modernism and postmodernism in European literature and film; realism in Russian, French and English literary canon; Dostoyevsky
		#16	Lois (F)	Romanticism; ecophilosophy; ecocriticism
		#17	Zoe (F)	Media and communication; modernity and postmodernity, the culture of the everyday

*   pseudonyms used; M= Male, F= Female
** as indicated on school websites

3.7 Brief Notes on Methods: Towards a Textography

As discussed in the previous chapter, it was Wittgenstein's notion of 'meaning as use' that formed the methodological basis of the study. In the following account, Wittgenstein suggests a method of investigation for how one might get access to 'meanings as use':

> The meaning of a word is what is explained by the explanation of the meaning, i.e. if you want to understand the use of the word 'meaning' look for what are called 'explanations of meaning'. (1958a: p. 149)

Wittgenstein seems to be suggesting here a method in two parts: the first is to seek 'explanations of a meaning', and the second is to interpret what is 'explained' by such explanations. In broad terms, the investigation sought to follow such a procedure; that is, it asked academic staff to talk about their understanding of critical thinking (the explanation of meaning), and then sought to draw on these explanations as texts to be interpreted (the explanation of the explanation).

3.7.1 Phenomenography

The procedure, as outlined by Wittgenstein, is in some ways an arcane one, and probably was never intended to be operationalized as a research method. His account, however, does have associations with at least one established, though not broadly known, social scientific method – phenomenography. In the name of this method, there is a clear lineage with the Husserlian 'phenomenological' tradition, whose central tenet is the idea that knowledge is rooted in an individual's immediate experience of the world. Ference Marton, the Swedish educational psychologist most associated with phenomenography as a method, describes it as 'a research specialization aimed at the methodical examination of the variable ways in which people experience, conceptualize, perceive, and understand … various phenomena in the world around us' (1988: p. 178). The phenomenographer's task therefore involves interpreting 'the descriptions of another's conception of something' – a project which seems congruent with Wittgenstein's idea of seeking meaning by examining the 'explanations of a meaning'.

Phenomenography, as Marton (1988) explains, has a strong basis in educational research and has been used particularly with students to investigate the outcomes of their learning. One common phenomenographic protocol, for example, is to ask students about their preconceived ideas of a phenomenon at the commencement of a programme of study, and then to see how these ideas might change as a result of their educational experiences. Marton gives the example of an investigation in which economics students were queried about their understanding of the notion of 'price'. The analytical aim of such research is to arrive at what Marton calls 'categories of description' or 'themes', which are the most crucial structural aspect of the individual's account of the phenomenon (1988: p.182). Thus, in the study of 'price', students at the beginning of their studies were found to have two distinct 'categories of description': one group saw price as a quality of a commodity (an intrinsic value), and the other saw it as a relation between the supply of and demand for the commodity. The principal method used in phenomenographic research is typically the open-ended interview, which has the aim of seeking out 'the qualitatively different ways in which any given phenomena … is seen or apprehended' (1988: p. 186).

Relating this to the present investigation, the phenomenon to be investigated is 'critical thinking'. The interest here is not in the students' perceptions of the phenomenon, but in those of their teachers. This is a different agenda from Marton's, but, within the phenomenographic tradition, seems one worth pursuing. In higher education, or indeed in any education setting, the way that individual teachers conceive of a concept (their 'category of description') becomes, in effect, its normative form – and such conceptions in their institutional collectivity then become the *habitus* with which students must contend.

3.7.2 Other methods – towards a textography

While phenomenography provides a broad methodological framework for the project, there are several problems with it; these are discussed below, along with some alternative methods that were drawn on for the study. One criticism, which comes from an alternative qualitative research tradition, ethnography, is that the key data gathering process – the interviewing of subjects about their understandings of a concept – is an artificial one (Mishler 1980). It is questioned whether, within an interview format, it is possible for an individual to authentically experience the phenomenon in question, as well as to reflect and reliably report on it. In this way, ethnography draws a clear distinction between a person's actual experience of a phenomenon, and their conceptual reflections on it (Mishler 1980). Such a criticism suggests the need for an observation-based approach – that is, to observe the workings of the phenomenon in question in the actual experience and practices of the 'life-world'.

In the present investigation, the use of observation was thought to be impracticable. This was because it seemed unlikely that such a method would allow for sufficient focus on the key term, 'critical thinking. While one might assume that any teaching processes observed would be underpinned to some degree by a critical approach, it seemed there would be no clear way of establishing in any resulting discourse exactly what such critical elements might be, or indeed how they might be distinguished from other 'non-critical' elements in the teaching.

As an alternative, the approach adopted for the study was to rely on the interview as a key research method, but to introduce into these interviews certain discursive elements from the life-world, in the form of various documents used by lecturers in their teaching. Thus, the method employed was a form of 'text-based interview', aimed at eliciting what the method's originators have called, that 'socially learned information, which has been silently transformed into functional [acts]' (Odell, Goswami and Herrington 1983). The document types drawn on in the study were:

i.   Statements in subject outlines that refer to the modes of thinking, approaches to study, and so on, that students are expected to adopt in the subject;
ii. Exercise tasks set for students and intended to develop particular skills and approaches to study in the subject; and
iii. The rubrics of essay questions set for students.

In the study, these documents were used as 'stimulus' material for the interviews, but were also appraised on their own as objects of independent textual analysis.

Another criticism that is made of phenomenography concerns not its methods of data collection, but the basis of its analysis. As mentioned above, Marton notes, in relation to the findings of phenomenographic studies, that the understandings of a phenomenon often fall into a limited number of qualitatively different 'categories' – as in the example of the commencing economics students who, it was suggested, saw the concept of 'price' in one of two distinct ways. This trend in phenomenography has been criticized for being excessively reductionist (Mishler 1980). The problem here would seem to arise from the fact that, in the process of interpreting a participant's account of the phenomenon, the researchers' own conception of that phenomenon will unavoidably come into play. There is a phenomenological paradox here; and one wonders whether the categories used in this type of research can ever be *a posteriori* ones, as is claimed – or whether they are, by their nature, necessarily *a priori*.

These problems, ones that recall Wittgenstein's critique of metaphysics discussed earlier, suggest the need for some additional form of analysis. For the present investigation, a more basic unit of analysis was also relied upon – simply words; or, that is to say, a text analysis approach. Wittgenstein's injunction, as we have seen, was not 'to think' (about concepts) but instead 'to look' (at words). The question, however, if one wishes to pursue such a text-based approach, is what specifically one should look at? How should such an analysis proceed?

The starting point for the framework developed for the study was the phenomenological maxim, first proposed by Franz Brentano, that 'consciousness is always consciousness of something' (cited in Gardner 1985). Such a notion, as noted previously, is affirmed by McPeck in his response to the generalist critical thinking position when he states that: 'thinking, by definition, is always thinking about something, and that something can never be "everything in general" but must always be something in particular' (1982: p. 4). In the context of university study, we need to ask what this 'something in particular' might be. Indeed what kind of epistemic entities are students called upon to consider?

Interestingly, Robert Ennis, the generalist, who is more interested in the skills of thinking than the actual content they are applied to, cannot help giving away some idea about what he thinks these epistemic entities should be. Thus, in the following examples from his 'taxonomy of critical thinking skills', a range of entities (shown in italics) are identified – *lines of reasoning, certain statements, conclusions* (1987: p. 11). In these elements, we can begin to grasp Ennis's particular notions about the types of knowledge with which a critical thinking programme should fundamentally be concerned.

i.   judging whether there is ambiguity in *a line of reasoning*
ii. judging whether *certain statements* contradict one another
iii. judging whether *a conclusion* necessarily follows

The preceding analysis is organized around a semantic category, which in the present study I have called the *object of inquiry*. We can see, if we 'look' in this particular direction, that a particular vocabulary begins to emerge, one which may help us to understand the type of thinking that is envisaged.

In the items that make up Ennis's skills taxonomy, there are two other linguistic categories that are of interest. The first is the verbal element contained in each descriptor – which in all cases above is given as *judging (whether)*. Thus, a picture is gained here of the desired mode of thinking that this particular theorist has in mind, but one can, of course, imagine many other types of thinking that students might be called upon to be engaged in. The second element is the types of judgement that Ennis suggests need to be made – in i) it is a judgement about the presence or not of *ambiguity*; in ii) it is about *contradiction*; and in iii) it is about whether something *necessarily follows* (a criterion, perhaps, of logic).

This kind of analysis can also be applied to the rubrics of assessment tasks commonly set for students in their courses of study. For example, in the following essay topic, taken from a politics subject, we can see that the epistemic entity that students must consider is a *theory* – specifically, Marx's theory of surplus value.

Evaluate the usefulness of Marx's theory of surplus value.

Further, the type of thinking required in this instance is *evaluating*, and the criterion by which students are expected to 'evaluate' the theory is with respect to its *usefulness*. The point of such an analysis is not to attempt any formal categorization of the type of critical thinking involved in such an essay task; rather, it is to see with which kinds of terms the practice seems to be associated.

Another essay topic example is the following, also from a politics subject:

Were the actions of the Parisian students in May 1968 legitimate in your view?

The object to be inquired into here is seemingly of a different type, not some kind of textual entity (such as a *statement* or a *theory*), but one that has a real-world quality about it – the actions of a group of people (*Parisian students*). The type of thinking evoked is one of *viewing*, and the criterion to be used as the basis for this viewing is one of *legitimacy*.

Table 2 summarizes the findings from the preceding analyses (both of the sample essay topic and of Ennis's sample accounts of critical thinking skills). An attempt is also made to show how the categories used in the analysis above have been derived. It will be noted that the terms opted for here – *process, object* and *content of inquiry* – can be roughly related to more general linguistic categories used in both traditional and Hallidayan (1994) grammar.

In summary, the approach used in the study was broadly similar to that employed by Swales in his university building study referred to earlier. The term that Swales coined to denote his approach is 'textography', described by him as 'something more than a disembodied textual or discoursal analysis, but something less than a full ethnographic account' (1998: p. 1). This is broadly true of

Table 2 Analytical categories used in textual analysis.

Ennis descriptor #1	*judging (whether)*	*certain statements*	*contradict one another (contradictory)*
Ennis descriptor #2	*judging (whether)*	*a conclusion*	*necessarily follows (logical?)*
Ennis descriptor #3	*judging (whether)*	*a line of reasoning*	*ambiguous*
Essay topic #1	*evaluating*	*Marx's theory of surplus value*	*useful*
Essay topic #2	*viewing*	*actions of Parisian students*	*legitimate*
Traditional grammar	**VERB**	**NOUN**	**ADJECTIVE**
Hallidayan terms	**PROCESS**	**PARTICIPANT**	**EPITHET**
MY TERMS	**PROCESS OF INQUIRY**	**OBJECT OF INQUIRY**	**CONTENT OF INQUIRY**
	What type of thinking processes is it envisaged that students will be engaged in, including the outcomes of these processes? (e.g. *judging, evaluating, viewing*)	Which epistemic entities specifically are to be analysed? (eg. *statements, conclusions, theories, actions*, etc.)	By which criteria or categories are these entities to be analysed? (e.g. for their *logic, usefulness, legitimacy* etc.)

Table 3 Summary of research methods.

Type of data	Method of analysis
Interviews with academics (including reference to teaching documents)	Phenomenography
Teaching documents	Textual analysis

the present study. The study used several types of data, and also relied on several different methods of analysis, which are summarized in Table 3.

The findings of the research are described in the following two chapters. Chapter 4 describes the findings from the interview section of the study; and Chapter 5 those from the textual analysis.

Chapter 4

The Ineffability of Critical Thinking

4.1 Introduction

This chapter reports on the findings from the first part of the investigation; that is, the conceptions of critical thinking as discussed in interviews by the study's informants. Before presenting these findings, I provide some background relating to the conduct of these interviews.

All interviews took place in the Faculty of Arts, located in a large, eleven-storey building at the central campus of the university. The physical and administrative layout of the building is a traditional one, with the different disciplines investigated here each occupying their own dedicated spaces in the building. Thus, my interviews with the historians took me to the School of Historical Studies on the sixth and seventh floors of the building, and meetings with the philosophers to the School of Philosophy and Bioethics on the ninth floor. My literature informants were to be found between the philosophers and the historians on the seventh and eighth floors. As explained previously, the two literature floors represented something of a sub-disciplinary divide, with the more traditional literature academics located on the lower floor in the larger School of Literary, Visual and Performance Studies, and the others – of a more theoretical bent – on the floor above in the Centre for Comparative Literature and Cultural Studies (CCLCS). It is interesting to note that some of my informants showed themselves to be aware of the faculty's various geographical orderings, drawing on a number of spatial references to explain perceived differences in outlook. An historian, for example, in her discussion of the nature of logic in her field, commented that 'those *on the ninth floor* [i.e. the philosophers] would probably see things quite differently'. (All italics indicate my emphasis). In characterizing that particular 'way of see[ing] things', one of the philosophers referred to the 'robust sense of reality that exists *up and down our corridor*'. In a more extreme contrast of views, another philosopher spoke of the perception held by some in his school that 'what happens *downstairs* [in the Centre for Comparative Literature] is a kind of philosophical netherworld'.

Most of the interviews ran from between one to two hours. The first question asked of informants was arguably the most important – this was whether the academic in question found the term 'critical thinking' relevant to their practice as a teacher, and to the types of qualities they wished to encourage in their students. They were then asked to elaborate on the particular 'qualities or capacities' they associated with being 'critical' in their subject areas. In the later stages of the interview, attention was given to specific academic activities – for example, what it might involve to be a 'critical reader or writer'. In the final part, informants were asked about specific assessment tasks they set for students, and to discuss the ways in which a 'critical approach' might be required to complete these tasks. These tasks were collected from informants and later analysed independently for the research (see Chapter 5). An interview schedule was used in the sessions, although the nature of the exchange was typically conversational and open-ended.

The following two interview extracts give a flavour of the nature of the talk in the interviews. The first is taken from the early stage of an interview (Figure 1). Here Lauren (philosophy) and I (Tim – interviewer) discuss the use of the term 'critical'. The second extract comes from the later stage of an interview, where Brian (literary/cultural studies informant) discusses the idea of what is involved in being critical in the writing of essays in his discipline area (Figure 2).

TIM: Now, do you use the term 'critical thinking' with students, or the term 'critical'?

LAUREN: Yeah, I think we do use the term 'critical', a bit. We often use the term 'criticize'.

TIM: Criticize?

LAUREN: In fact a very standard way of proposing an essay question, or a short task. Critically evaluate or …

TIM: What about 'critique'? That's a term I've noticed that's used around the faculty.

LAUREN: Well, probably expound and criticize. I think critique is not [the word] that we like quite so much, because it's a noun.

TIM: I guess in some usages it can be a verb.

LAUREN: I don't really like it as a verb. But critically evaluate we use all the time.

TIM: Alright, so when you use that in your essay rubric, what have you got in mind? So critically evaluate …?

LAUREN: Well it would usually be critically evaluate an argument, and we would have given fairly precise instructions as to what we want when we say critically evaluate …

FIGURE 1:   Transcript sample from interview, early stage (philosophy)

TIM: So what does it mean for a student to be critical in a literature essay?

BRIAN: Well, the most exciting thing is when in a sense students move sideways – where they make a connection between the text you've given and something else that you haven't given at all, either in another text from elsewhere or their own personal experience.

TIM: So making connections is …?

BRIAN: Yes connections, it's the lateral thinking. You can't be random though.

TIM: Right.

BRIAN: But having said that, you also sometimes get terrible essays which are a stream of consciousness rambling without engaging with the material. You have to engage the material. Part of the argument for text-based disciplines – be it philosophy, literature, art history – is that the text imposes a discipline on things.

TIM: Mmm. You've also mentioned theory as a way of disciplining one's approach?

BRIAN: Well, theory is vital. I think … you can't make sense of anything without theorizing. Everybody theorizes. People who say they don't believe in theory, it just means they're not aware of it.

FIGURE 2:   Transcript sample of interview, later stage (literary/cultural studies)

4.2 Use of the Terms 'Critical' and 'Critical Thinking'

The first general statement to be made about the interviews is that all the informants, without exception, thought the idea of being 'critical' was absolutely central to their teaching, and to their academic outlook generally. For example, Eric, one of the philosophers, said that the idea of 'critical thinking' was, for him, 'absolutely philosophy's bread and butter'. Another philosopher, Henry, mentioned how he had deliberately sought to teach one of his subjects – *God, Freedom and Evil* as 'a critical thinking subject'. Similarly, Zoe (literary/cultural studies – comp.) thought that critical thinking was 'crucial' in her subject and was key to being 'successful' in it. For Nigel (history), evidence of 'critical thinking' in students' essays – 'the ability to probe beneath the surface', as he described it – was the most important element of writing in history, and also what he believed distinguished the more able from the less able students. Another historian, Nell, who had been involved in the development of educational policies across the university, was strongly committed to the term and mentioned how she had 'worked quite hard' to ensure that the term 'critical' was used explicitly in key university documents.

Although all informants thought the idea of 'critical thinking' was crucially important in the teaching of their discipline area, it was interesting to learn that a number thought they did not use this exact formulation – 'critical thinking' – in their specific discussions with students. One exception was a philosopher who taught a subject with 'critical thinking' in the title. He described this as a thinking subject *per se*, where 'the critical thinking side of it is just right up front'. For others, the 'critical' part of the expression was indispensable, though they thought they were inclined to use terms other than 'thinking'. Several historians, for example, indicated a preference for the term 'critical analysis' over 'critical thinking':

> **EDWARD** (history): I think probably what historians mean by critical thinking is probably what would be better termed critical analysis.

> **HANNAH** (history): Critical thinking and critical analysis? Are they the same? When I thought of what we are asking our students, I think I ask them more to do analysis.

Another variant, one favoured by the philosophers, was 'critical evaluation'. Other related terms to emerge in discussion, and which informants believed they used with students were: 'critical examination', 'critical awareness', 'critical reflection', 'critical discussion', 'critique' and the general variant – a 'critical approach'.

An alternative perspective was for informants to accept the term 'critical', but to avoid using it explicitly in their communications with students. For example, one historian expressed a clear awareness of 'critical thinking' as some desirable educational objective, but thought it unhelpful to present the concept in these terms to students. A better strategy, she thought, was to try to be specific about what exactly she wanted her students to do:

> **KATHERINE** (history): I mean, I recognize that critical thinking is the way this kind of thing is framed in objectives and outcomes, but it's not a term that I would use much with students. … I would not say that that's what I want them to do. I would try and move them to doing it by asking them to develop an independent argument and support it with evidence … I think [to say I want them to be critical thinkers] might confuse and intimidate the students.

The same caution in the use of terms was expressed by another historian, Michael, who also felt it preferable to characterize the desired intellectual activity in more concrete terms – in this case 'the challenging of assumptions':

> **MICHAEL**: Critical thinking, I have to say, is not a term that I usually use [with students]. I tend to use more specific terms like … 'challenging assumptions' rather than me saying I'm encouraging critical thinking.

In passing, we note here that in their efforts to be more precise, the two historians present slightly different accounts of what critical thinking fundamentally involves – for one, it is the 'developing of an independent argument', and for the other, it is the 'challenging of assumptions'. It is variations like this in informants' understandings that will be discussed in detail in later sections of this chapter.

4.3 What is Critical Thinking? – Multiple Definitions

All informants affirmed that some version of critical thinking was indeed an indispensable part of study in their subject area. The task then in the interview was for them to provide some account of the notion – that is, to say what they thought was involved in 'being critical' in the context of study in their discipline area. For some informants, this was initially a daunting task. Several, for example, felt the need to lead off with certain qualifications ('Well, I'm just talking off the top off my head here but …'; 'I don't have a particularly good sense of what critical thinking is, however …'). For others, any tentativeness came from a recognition that there was probably no adequate single definition of the concept:

> **JONATHON** (philosophy): Critical thinking is probably going to turn out to be a very, very broad diverse set of things and some of them will have nothing in common except some very basic connection.

> **NELL** (history): It's a wonderful word isn't it? You can probably make it mean anything.

The impression given in the literature is that academics typically find it difficult to articulate their understandings of the idea of 'being critical'. For example, Resnick (1987), who was quoted earlier, argues that it is a good deal easier for academics to recognize higher order thinking skills than it is to actually describe them. Fox makes a similar claim, suggesting that 'critical thinking is hard for faculty members to talk about' – mainly because, as she suggests, 'it is learned so intuitively' (1994: p. 125). My experience of interviewing academics in these three disciplines in an Arts Faculty does not bear these impressions out. All my informants ultimately had much to say on the subject, and while in some cases the understandings they had may have been 'intuitive' ones, their talk suggested that this was an issue about which most had done a good deal of thinking and reflecting on. Their talk – whether it was about the specific matter of critical thinking, or more generally about learning and teaching in the academy – was also highly interesting; in some cases, quite inspiring.

In what follows, I present the main themes that emerged from the interviews. The definitional accounts of my informants fell into eight broad groupings, which can be summarized thus:

i.   critical thinking as judgement
ii. critical thinking as a sceptical and provisional view of knowledge

iii. critical thinking as a simple originality
iv. critical thinking as a careful and sensitive reading
v. critical thinking as the adopting of an ethical and activist stance
vi. critical thinking as a form of rationality
vii. critical thinking as a facility and awareness of language
viii. critical thinking as a form of self-reflexiveness

The ordering of this list roughly equates to the prominence given to the particular theme in discussion. Thus, those categories towards the top of the list were ideas given some airing by most informants; and those towards the bottom were ones which were described by only some. Each of these themes is discussed in some detail in the following sections.

4.3.1 Critical thinking as judgement

In the earlier discussion of definitions of the term 'critical' (Chapter 2), it was suggested that critical as 'the exercise of careful judgement or observation' is the notion that has the most resonance within the university, and also within the critical thinking movement. In fact, in the interviews this was the main definitional strand to emerge. For many informants, the idea of critical thinking as judgement and evaluation was salient. This was true across the three discipline areas. Thus, Nell (history), for example, was sure that critical thinking 'always means judgement and the making of distinctions of some kind'. Eric (philosophy) saw the activity in similar terms – as the 'rendering of verdicts' on the ideas students need to engage with. As he pithily put it:

> **ERIC** (philosophy): I like to say to students – would it profit you to read the entirety of Aristotle's work, and form no view whether it's bullshit or not?

Nora (literary/cultural studies – comp.) also identified judgement ('the taking of a stand') as a key element to be critical in her discipline area:

> **NORA** (literary/cultural studies – comp.): ... Being critical, it's about taking a stand. You have to commit as a critic.

In elaborating on this idea of judgement, informants also gave a sense of the types of judgements they would expect students to be making. As suggested in Eric's colourful account, perhaps the most basic type of judgement is one between 'good' and 'bad'. A number of informants discussed the judgements they require students to make in these very broad terms. Kim (philosophy), for example, said he typically told students that his bioethics course was mainly concerned with 'analysing arguments and deciding whether they're *good* arguments or not' (emphasis added). Henry (philosophy) talked about one of his subject areas, *Philosophy of Religion*, in very similar terms, with students mainly engaged with the 'primary question of whether there are *good* arguments for or against the existence of God'. Similarly, Hannah (history) discussed the importance in her field of students being able to make judgements about the types of sources they might rely on in their work – to decide between '*good* historical and archaeological sources' and ones that 'they should really keep well away from'.

A number of other – perhaps more precise – evaluative terms came up in discussion. A prominent one was the notion of 'validity', which was mentioned by informants from all discipline areas. For Edward (history), the term was central to his general account of critical thinking:

> **EDWARD** (history): ... critical thinking would be thinking about something in an evaluative sort of way and thinking particularly about the ways in which it might be *valid* or *invalid* (emphasis added).

In literary/cultural studies, Nora likewise spoke of the need for students to understand what a '*valid* ... interpretation of a text' might entail. For the philosophers, the concept was particularly salient. Eric (philosophy), for example, discussed *validity* as one of a number of key evaluative concepts that students need to learn as part of the procedures in that discipline for assessing the worth of arguments. ('We explain validity as structural goodness – that is, if the premises lead to the conclusion'). Jonathon (philosophy), one of whose subjects had a dedicated critical thinking component to it, elaborated on this point, relating validity to the notion of argumentative support:

> **JONATHON** (philosophy): Giving students the idea that the question of whether a view is true or not is quite separate from the question of whether it supports another view. So the notion of justification or support is different from the notion of truth. I think that idea is still terribly important. It derives, of course, from the notion of formal validity. Formal validity is all about the structure of an argument independent of whether the premises are true.

Judgements of 'truthfulness'

In the quotation above, Jonathon makes a distinction between notions of validity and truthfulness. 'Truthfulness', as a criterion for judgement, was also mentioned in the interviews – though usually accompanied by a fair amount of explanation and qualification along the way. In a few rare instances, the term was mentioned unproblematically, typically as part of a more general point that was being made about critical thinking. For example, Hannah (history, archaeology), when discussing the general principle of subjecting any archaeological interpretation to critical scrutiny, talked about students having to decide whether an interpretation 'rings true'. The same kind of incidental usage was noted in the discussion by a philosopher concerning the timeless nature of ideas in his field, and his practice of setting comparative essay questions to bring this point out:

> **ERIC** (philosophy): I will frequently give students a mix of possible essay topics, some of which invite them to assess the *truth* of what Aristotle is saying against examples and problems drawn from modern sources

In most references to 'truthfulness', however, the notion was treated with a good deal of circumspection and qualification. Not surprisingly, given the discipline's anti-positivist leanings, it was the literary/cultural studies informants who reacted most strongly to the concept, as seen in the following exchange with Brian:

> TIM: You probably find the word 'true' quite difficult?

> **BRIAN** (literary/cultural studies – comp.): Abhorrent in fact. Yeah well I do. I start by saying in first year that nothing's true, and we try to deconstruct that.

Later in the interview, however, Brian thought he should qualify this view, suggesting that it is not helpful to allow students to come away from their studies believing that an extreme relativist position is actually a tenable one:

> **BRIAN**: I tell them that in the real world you can't wander around saying it's all relative. You won't get on the bus if you think that. You really do have to make decisions.

Brian went on to relate this to commentaries on texts, insisting that while it is certainly not possible to speak of a 'true' interpretation of a text or of any single correct reading of it, it is nevertheless important to hold to a view that some readings and interpretations are better than others, and that yet others are simply wrong:

> **BRIAN**: I mean there are many things that can be said about any particular text. On one level I suppose you could go on indefinitely saying things. But nonetheless, some of the things you say are wrong, and some may be just foolish.

The strongest advocate for the notion of 'truth' as an evaluative criterion was an historian, Nigel. His increasing commitment to this position, he explained, came from a belief that a 'deconstructive' outlook, as he termed it, had become rather too dominant in the education system – not just at universities, but also in the secondary system. Nigel went on to explain – somewhat disdainfully – that some of his 'brighter' history students coming out of the secondary system were, in his view, 'very good at deconstructing evidence ... but not so good at putting something in its place'. This situation, he explained, had prompted him to take on a gadfly role in his teaching:

> **NIGEL** (history): I like to use the term 'truth' [with students], but it discomforts them. ... They clearly don't expect me to be talking about [these things]. But I tell them as an historian I think that my job is to tell the truth.

Like Brian, however, Nigel was quick to temper this position, rejecting any absolutist view of truth as readily as Brian did any extreme version of relativism. It is interesting to note that the final positions of the historian and literary/cultural studies academic would seem to be not that far apart:

> **NIGEL** (History): Well there may not be such a thing as big 'T' truth ... nonetheless, we have to maintain the capacity and judgements about what is more likely to be true, right, correct and so on.

The idea of judgements of 'truthfulness' was most often invoked by the philosophers. In a number of instances, it was mentioned as a part of the established protocols used in that discipline for the evaluating of arguments. Eric (philosophy) talked about the need for students to assess the truthfulness of statements when making some overall judgement about the adequacy of ideas. He mentioned here the general framework operating in the discipline that sees an 'argument [as] sound just in case it is both valid and in fact has *true* premises'. Jonathon (philosophy) referred to similar criteria that students need to consider 'when they come to write about an argument'. The first of these, he suggested, was deciding 'whether the views presented are *true* or not'.

But, while the concept of truthfulness was seen as a necessary part of philosophy's evaluative framework, my informants were wary of the role it might play in critical processes. Jonathon, for example, was keen to stress the discipline's greater interest in what he termed 'the structural characteristics of arguments' (such as validity) over notions of truthfulness. Establishing the latter ultimately relied on empirical procedures, which, for Jonathon, lay outside the ambit of the discipline:

> **JONATHON** (philosophy): I do present truth as a separate category and actually I don't spend much time on it. This is partly because, as I say to [students], that authenticating some truth is difficult and may involve going to a laboratory or doing a survey or something. From the armchair there is only so much you can say about it.

Henry (philosophy) also recognized the problematical nature of 'truthfulness' as a criterion, suggesting that even though the term is often used in a standard way in the discipline, he was more comfortable using less stringent criteria with his students, such as 'acceptability' and 'reasonableness':

> **HENRY** (philosophy): The word that I would use [with students] is *acceptability*. Are the premises acceptable which is not necessarily asking them to judge whether they are *true*. But whether in your judgement someone else who believed them or failed to believe them would thereby show themselves to be irrational. Could a *reasonable* person accept them – something more like that.

For Kim (philosophy), the preferred criterion was 'plausibility':

> **KIM** (philosophy): I suppose plausible and implausible are the two terms that I would use most commonly as ways of evaluating arguments [so that] students don't think that I'm asking them to determine whether or not ... something is completely justified, or *true*.

Judgements by other criteria

The preceding discussion has emphasized the notion of judgement as a key theme in informants' understandings of critical thinking, and has also identified a range of judgement types that had some commonality across the disciplines (notions of goodness, validity, truth, etc.). It needs to be noted, however, that some of the criteria mentioned appeared to have quite specific disciplinary applications. A term, for example, that emerged strongly in the data from the history informants, but less so elsewhere, was 'reliability'. This was mainly discussed with reference to the historical sources that students needed to engage with in their work. For example, in discussing the ways that students could be 'uncritical' in their studies, Nigel (history) talked about 'an absence of judgement about the *reliability* of different kinds of sources'. Edward (history) also mentioned how assessing the reliability of sources has always been a key judgement type for students in history, but even more so now with the access that students have to non-traditional sources via information technologies:

> **EDWARD** (history): [the use of a critical approach] is very marked, of course, when we're trying to deal with websites. ... we actually have discussions in tutorials. How can we tell whether this is a *reliable* site or not? So its evaluation of who is producing this, in what context, and for what purpose – that's what we're pushing (emphasis added).

For the literary/cultural studies informants, notions of 'usefulness' and 'helpfulness' had a prominence which was not evident in the other disciplines.

Lois, for example, mentioned that a key element in her first-year course was to introduce students to certain theoretical concepts, and to help them recognize how these can then be applied to the analysis of texts and other cultural phenomena:

> **LOIS** (literary/cultural studies – comp.): so we just really introduce concepts, critical concepts, and students need to recognize how these are *helpful* tools which enable them to see things rather differently.

For Zoe (literary/cultural studies – comp.), a key judgement to be encouraged in students was decisions about the relative utility of different perspectives and theories, and for them to also realize that such judgements are dependent on what it is that the particular perspective (or theory) is being applied to:

> **ZOE** (literary/cultural studies – comp.): What I try to teach my students is that in certain contexts, certain perspectives become more *useful* than others … So I try to give them a sense that the use of theory is that it's context specific, and the idea of a theory being more useful than another theory.

For Bruce, coming from the more traditional literature stream, a key evaluative quality was 'beauty':

> **BRUCE** (literary/cultural studies – Eng.): I might say that one of the things that we do, that I do anyway, is to reveal the *beauties* of literature or what makes them truly beautiful.

Bruce went on to explain that on his course, where the literary works studied tended to be more 'canon-like', the key critical issue was not so much one of whether a work was 'beautiful' or not, but rather how this beauty is manifested in the work:

> **BRUCE**: We tend not to ask – Is this a successful piece of literature or is it flawed? In a sense we have already given the work the benefit of the doubt. We almost say they are beyond criticism. So we become, in fact, people who reveal the beauties of past texts. We demonstrate why they are beautiful or how they are beautiful

Finally in this initial survey of judgement types, it is important to note that the particular terms used by informants should not be seen as any rigorous epistemological account of the methods of a particular discipline area. We have already noted, for example, the non-systematic usage of certain categories, such as 'truth'. A certain kind of desultoriness in the use of evaluative categories was, in fact, a feature of the talk of a number of informants. We can see this, for example, in the following exchange with Hannah (history), where a number of different criteria for judgement are invoked – 'validity', 'rightness', 'truth', 'evidentiality', 'sense':

TIM: You've mentioned the term 'valid' a bit, as in when you want students to ...

HANNAH (history): Yes, is it a *valid* argument?

TIM: So what do you have in mind for the students to be deciding yes it is valid? On what basis do they say that something is valid?

HANNAH: Looking at the argument that a scholar has put up ... In other words does it seem *right* to you, does this argument ring *true* to you, if it's something he or she has sort of *given the evidence* for and shown their methodology, if you like, as they've gone through it. Yes, does this argument make *sense*? (emphasis added)

4.3.2 Critical thinking as a sceptical and provisional view of knowledge

In the earlier discussion of critical thinking traditions in Chapter 2, a key theme that was identified in the literature was the idea of critical thinking as the adopting of a sceptical frame. A belief in scepticism, as noted, was a foundational idea of the Enlightenment, and has also been a key strand in recent theorizing about critical thinking. Dewey, for example, contrasted a 'thoughtful' approach with 'a disposition to pass judgement on the basis of mere custom, tradition and prejudice' which he suggested 'shuns the task of thinking' (1933, p. 34.). Scepticism is also invoked in some of the kernel definitions of critical thinking discussed earlier, as in McPeck's account, namely, 'the appropriate use of reflective skepticism' (1981: p. 7).

In the interviews, the notion of students bringing a sceptical attitude to the knowledge and ideas presented to them was a key theme, and was seen by some informants as a quality equally important as any capacity for judgement. While the idea itself was considered most important, it needs to be noted that the specific term 'scepticism' was not used frequently in the interviews. It was more common for informants to discuss the notion in terms of not *accepting* or *acquiescing to* certain ideas and beliefs, or *taking issue* with them:

LAUREN (philosophy): Well, I suppose that ... critical thinking is not just *accepting* what somebody tells you.

KATHERINE (history): In general terms, I would say [critical thinking is] the capacity to cut through *accepted* ideas ... to recognize and examine them.

ERIC (philosophy): And there is, I think, this important emphasis in philosophy in not *acquiescing* and believing things for inadequate reasons.

QUENTIN (literary/cultural studies – Eng.): I think the best essays begin by *taking issue* either with the question or, at the same time, with certain critics, and then kind of arguing against them and producing some kind of interesting response.

The philosophers, perhaps not surprisingly, had a good deal to say on this issue, seeing a sceptical outlook as fundamental to the spirit of inquiry in their discipline. Eric (philosophy), for example, chose to invoke one of philosophy's more iconic images to convey the centrality of this notion – that of Socrates famously challenging the assumptions of his hapless interlocutors. In the following statement, it is also apparent that, for Eric, the act of challenging accepted wisdoms needs to have primacy over any act of judgement:

ERIC (philosophy): What's Socrates' characteristic activity? It's to buttonhole somebody who has pretensions about knowing something and shows that his beliefs are inconsistent. And there is, I think, this important emphasis in philosophy in not acquiescing and believing things for inadequate reasons. It is better to be in a state of suspension of judgement than not to be critically aware.

Jonathon (philosophy) also stressed this type of critical thinking – though sought to characterize the disposition more as a form of contemplation than one of an active challenge. Thus, for Jonathon, encouraging students to 'wonder about' or 'to stop and give some thought' to the various notions to which they are exposed was integral not only to a philosophy education, but also, he thought, to higher education generally:

JONATHON (philosophy): These [students] are still very young, and they have just left high school, so one wants to say to them, 'Look, you know there are lots of things in life that we all acquire when we are young, all sorts of beliefs and views and so on. And you can wonder about them.' And I think that is something that everybody, not just in philosophy, everybody around the university does it. And for me university education in general is an opportunity to stop and give some thoughts to things.

Similar ideas were expressed by informants from other disciplines. Among the historians, Michael was perhaps the one who most associated critical thinking with the notion of challenging ideas, seeing this as a key part of the first-year modern history course he taught. An important caveat for Michael, however, was to distinguish between practices that 'challenged' students' assumptions and those that might 'undermine' them:

TIM: So in the context of your teaching, which qualities or capacities do you most associate with critical thinking?

MICHAEL (history): Well challenging attitudes. I want to challenge their assumptions, and challenge the ideas that perhaps you put to them in what they read, or what we put to them as well hopefully. So that's reasonably high and that's what I see as a large part of [my subject] *Contemporary Worlds*. A large part of what I do is actually not undermine their assumptions but to challenge their assumptions and that's what I see critical thinking as.

The targets of sceptical thinking

In Michael's account – and also in those of Eric and Jonathon above – we can identify perhaps two types of targets of this form of critical inquiry. The first of these is the acquired ideas, attitudes, beliefs and so on that students bring with them to the academy – what Jonathon referred to as 'the sorts of beliefs and views we all acquire when we are young', and what Michael called 'the assumptions [that students] are brought up with'. The other target is the ideas that students are then presented with and need to engage with within the academy. Michael, for example, thought it important that students not be overawed by the ostensible authority of academic texts. As he succinctly put it: 'it's about getting [students] to think "well just because this guy writes it in a book it's not something you have to *accept*"'.

The same distinction between the critiquing of notions students bring to the university and those they are exposed to once they are there was made by Lois (literary/cultural studies – comp.). She mentioned that in her first-year subject – *Text and Context* – which introduced students to new 'quite theoretical' approaches to the study of literary texts, it was important in the first weeks of the course for students 'to critique their commonsense' understandings of what literature is – or 'to challenge their taken-for-granteds', as she described it. Lois sought to do this, she explained, by getting students to investigate a variety of historical definitions of 'literature', so that they could recognize 'the relativity of the term' and see that '[the idea of literature] is not some kind of universal given, in all times and all places'.

The same critique, Lois thought, also needed to be made of ideas presented in the course, a process she described as the 'undoing of dogma'. For Lois, this was particularly called for in the type of literature she taught because of the tendencies of both scholars and students to 'accept certain theories as dogma' – attributable, she thought, to the sense of 'charisma attaching to some of the originators [of these theories]'. Lois cited the example here of Freud and how his ideas have assumed a quasi-religious status in some areas of the discipline:

LOIS (literary/cultural studies – comp.): I mean, for example, Freudian psychoanalysis. There is a certain amount of evidential basis for it. However, there is also a high degree of imagination and sort of creative modelling involved in Freud's theory. Yet, students, indeed not only students, will often be tempted to … adopt it as the new Bible and it then becomes the truth. … [and] you then get this phenomenon of the theory being accepted without question.

For Quentin, coming from the more traditional literature strand in the faculty, the main source of problems lay in an uncritical embrace of theory in general:

QUENTIN (literary/cultural studies – Eng.): To be honest I think that one problem with the spread of critical theory … in the lesser minds it turns into a kind of orthodoxy, almost a sort of theology, which is accepted totally uncritically.

He went on to explain what he saw as the worst possible outcome of this kind of exposure – students seeking to adapt their work to suit the theoretical preferences of their teachers:

QUENTIN: I mean some places like University Y, for example, are very much out in the open. Other places like here, they're less overt, you know. I had a student coming from University Y who had been exposed to a fair dose of critical theory. … She wanted to know what my theoretical position was so she could tailor her essay to it.

This line of critique within the literary/cultural studies fields – of certain theories being accepted without question – was also made by informants from other disciplines, an issue that will be taken up later when cross-disciplinary comparisons are considered.

The theme of critical thinking as the adopting of a sceptical frame was particularly prominent in informants' accounts of what it is that students do when they are being 'uncritical' in their studies. Most of the discussion here was of observations made about the way that certain students engage with reading materials. Edward (history), for example, talked about how students will often read a secondary account of an historical event or phenomenon and accept it as in some sense 'factual' – as opposed to seeing it as an interpretation being advanced by an individual historian. To illustrate this, he gave the example of students' uses of secondary material in a writing task he had set requiring an account of nineteenth century attitudes to crime:

EDWARD (history): Now if you're talking about nineteenth century attitudes [to crime], the secondary source … at best it will give you the historian's analysis of a range of those sources, in which case it might be evidence of a kind – second-hand evidence. At worst, it is simply an assertion about what people in the nineteenth century thought and in that sense it's not evidence at all. So that, I would say, is a marked absence of the kind of awareness of sources and a critical use of sources.

Nora (literary/cultural studies – comp.) also recognized a lack of 'critique' in students' uses of sources. She linked the problem to a difficulty she saw students having in being able to distinguish their own authorial identity from that of the author of the text they were reading. For her, part of the problem was 'a lack of self-confidence':

> **NORA** (literary/cultural studies – comp.): What they [the uncritical students] do, is assimilate a secondary source, they assimilate somebody else's ideas. Then they operate with these ideas as if they were gospel truths. That is what you're talking about, this unselfconscious inability to distance oneself from the text you have just appropriated. It boils down to a little bit of a lack of self-confidence

Underlying notions of scepticism

For many informants, the key to students adopting a suitably critical and sceptical stance – and indeed developing the confidence to create a distance between themselves and their sources – lay in their capacity to take on board certain epistemological notions about the nature of knowledge in the academy, or at least in the humanities. Two recurring themes on this issue were the idea that knowledge is always 'provisional', and that it is fundamentally a type of 'cultural construct'. On the first of these themes, Lauren (philosophy) mentioned how in her discipline the view that was always impressed upon students was that any position one might wish to advance 'is only provisionally defensible'. Eric (philosophy) also mentioned the importance of students understanding the 'provisional character' of any 'positions' or 'theories' they might draw on in their work:

> **ERIC** (philosophy): I frequently say [to students] that you're applying what the best philosophical position is, and not the one for which there are overwhelmingly positive arguments. It will often be the one that seems to … land us with the fewest puzzles and problems. The best theory is often the least worst theory … I mean it is always provisional.

On a related issue, Michael (history) thought that the more capable students in his first-year subject were those who were able to see the study of history in fundamentally 'historiographical' terms, and to recognize that there can be no final and definitive accounts of an historical episode. These students, he said, could 'get the idea' that there will always be different interpretations of events and periods put forward by historians, and there would inevitably be major disagreements between them:

> **MICHAEL** (history): Something that's really good is just that recognition where there are [different points of view]. Some [students] get that there are disagreements between historians and they're actually able to display that quite strongly.

The other epistemological precept that informants felt students needed to take on board – and which underlay the necessary sceptical stance – was the idea of seeing knowledge in fundamentally 'constructivist' terms – that is, unavoidably as the product of modes of thought from a particular time and place. Several of the historians saw this as crucial for students to come to grips with the way they need to approach the reading of historical materials. Nell (history), for example, in a discussion about the role of primary and secondary sources in history, explained how eventually students have to recognize that secondary accounts have no particular privileged status as forms of knowledge – and in the end they need to see them as cultural artifacts like any other type of documentary evidence they might engage with:

> **NELL** (history): I never used to be able to persuade the first years to [see the secondary sources as a type of primary source] until really quite late on, maybe not until second year. And that's one of the [ways] I want them to be critical ... to understand that ... everything is socially produced and culturally produced.

Michael (history) related the notion of the 'constructed' nature of knowledge to a broader realm – to certain reified ideas and concepts that go to construct our understandings of the world and of worlds in the past. Examples he gave from his modern history subject were the associated ideas of 'the nation-state', 'nationality', 'national identity' and so forth – pointing out that there is a tendency for students to simply see these notions as 'givens', and as somehow naturally occurring:

> **MICHAEL** (history): I try to get [students] to the idea ... that the nation-state is not the only way of organizing the world, which is so central to [our understandings of] twentieth century history ... so I try and get them to think of the idea that the nation-state is a construction .... I get them to think – are there other ways that the world could operate? But [some] students can't get past the idea that things are just natural, that they're permanent and that's how things will continue.

The literary/cultural studies informants – perhaps not surprisingly – saw these types of understandings as especially salient in their field. In fact, a number mentioned that it was virtually impossible to proceed in the discipline without assimilating them to some degree. Nora, for example, drew heavily on the terminology of 'construction' to characterize the necessary theoretical perspective. She described this under the broad rubric of 'phenomenology', which she contrasted with certain 'realist' approaches to knowledge:

> **NORA** (literary/cultural studies – comp.): Phenomenology is about representation of reality. Reality can only be represented. It cannot exist for us in the raw ... it's not directly accessible to us. Everything between us and nature has to be representation and a construction of reality [through] language.

Lois (literary/cultural studies – comp.), coming from a similar theoretical tradition to Nora, drew on similar ideas to explain how students, in whichever area they are studying in the humanities, often need to undergo a shift from a naive realist to a more sophisticated constructivist understanding of knowledge. Lois related this to her own experiences of studying history as an undergraduate:

> **LOIS** (literary/cultural studies – comp.): I became so despondent then, because I was after truth, I thought I was going to find the truth about the past ... But one has to sort of rediscover [historical writing] as a work of interpretation ... You have to be able to substantiate the interpretations that you're making. ... There is an ethics of paying attention to all of the facts that one can ... but in the end one is telling a story.

Finally, Brian (literary/cultural studies – comp.) recognized the difficulty that these processes and understandings present to students. Interestingly though, he thought that one of the surest signs of a lack of a critical approach was a type of engagement that somehow did not acknowledge these difficulties:

> **BRIAN** (literary/cultural studies – comp.): The worst writing from students is that which does not give a sense that ... this [grappling with knowledge] is problematic.

The benefits of scepticism

As the preceding discussion has shown, informants provided a range of views about what a sceptical approach might entail – as well as how it might be enacted in their specific disciplinary contexts. Despite the differing forms it was thought to take, there was, however, a good deal of agreement that the encouraging of a sceptical outlook in students was of paramount importance. For Edward (history), it needed to be seen as one of the principal goals of a humanities education:

> **EDWARD** (history): I think that not just historians, but most people in social sciences ... say well one of the functions of the arts faculty is to teach people to critique assumptions, to think things through rather than simply accepting at face value what they're reading ... that willingness to question is absolutely essential.

Others were certain of the benefits that such attributes would have for students in their lives beyond the academy. For Katherine (history), the development of a sceptical and critical frame was crucial in providing students with the 'strength' to deal, in an analytical way, with whatever situations they might encounter:

> **KATHERINE** (history): I want [my students] to be as critical ... as sceptical in their analysis as they possibly can be. I want them to have those skills that will make them feel strong to go out and analyse anything.

Eric (philosophy) also saw the nurturing of this outlook as a type of bolstering. His image was one of being armed – as he termed it, to become 'the sharpest knife in the drawer'.

> **ERIC** (philosophy): I say to students ... even if you think you don't care about the issues much, you want to ... [learn to be critical] because it will in fact make you sharp. Stick with us and we will make you the most dangerous person in the corporate boardroom. You will be the person past whom people cannot push bullshit ... You'll be the sharpest knife in the drawer.

4.3.3 Critical thinking as a simple originality

In the preceding section, we saw how critical thinking was characterized largely in terms of a 'challenge' to knowledge – whether it is directed at the extant knowledge that students bring to the academy, or at that which they are exposed to once they arrive. Other terms used by informants were 'questioning', 'rejecting' (or not 'accepting') and 'deconstructing' – and with Eric's knife image above, a suggestion of 'being incisive' or 'cutting through'. While most informants saw this outlook as fundamental to critical thinking, and one to be wholly encouraged in students, there was an interesting dissenting view that emerged in the interviews, one that took issue – or indeed was 'critical' of – a routinely sceptical outlook. According to this view, the essence of a critical approach is for students to be less engaged in the challenging of ideas, and concerned more with producing them. The position is well summarized by Nigel (history):

> **NIGEL** (history): A critical thinker has to argue on the basis of the critical thought. [But] it is not enough just to have critically negative thoughts. You actually have to … put them into something, to produce something.

In the various critiques made of an overly sceptical approach, it is interesting to note some of the images drawn on by informants. Many of these pick up on the notion of critical thinking as a form of assault on knowledge. Thus, Henry (philosophy) was bothered in the first instance that philosophy as a discipline was inclined towards an excessive negativity – the overvalued practice of 'poking holes in arguments', as he described it – though he thought this was also a tendency across the whole faculty:

> **HENRY** (philosophy): Because of the nature of philosophy, it's much easier to publish a paper in which you take an argument and *poke some holes in it*. So I think we can systematically overvalue critique. But I don't think it's just … philosophers who do that, I think it's true of large parts of the faculty that we place too high a value on critique.

Lois (literary/cultural studies) drew on a similar assailant metaphor, expressing concern that students can feel they have a licence to 'do hatchet jobs' on certain unfavoured thinkers in her field. It is a nice irony that one of the thinkers that Lois felt needed some defending against the attacks of her charges was indeed one of scepticism's greatest champions, Descartes, now, according to Lois, an all-too-easy target in the discipline:

> **LOIS** (literary/cultural studies – comp.): recently I've found myself calling upon students to be less damningly critical because you also get [a] distortion that can come into play, whereby they assume that they are the enlightened ones … and that they are now going *to do a hatchet job* on all these bad guys in the past … like Descartes, who led us all up the garden path.

An alternative motif to emerge in this type of critique was that of the dismantling – even demolition – of knowledge. Nigel (history), for example, spoke of students' 'readiness to *dash the foundations out from everywhere*, and end up with ruins'; and Lauren (philosophy) noted that some students were inclined to think 'they can *knock almost anything down*'.

As the comments above suggest, a concern on the part of informants was the tendency for this type of sceptical thinking to breed in students a basic disrespect for the ideas they are introduced to. Another undesirable consequence that was identified – in some respects the obverse of this latter tendency – was for students to become excessively equivocal about ideas, and to find it impossible to draw any firm conclusions in their work. On this point, a number of informants expressed some frustration at receiving a type of essay in which the views of various thinkers are typically laid out, but where the student strenuously avoids committing to an identifiable position:

> **HENRY** (philosophy): The kind of essay that you really hate getting is the one that says there are two points of view here ... and it's hard to say either way – and that's it. There are lots of students who do that and [they] wonder why they get a bare pass.

> **EDWARD** (history): As a kind of knee-jerk response, some students tend to say in their work: 'There is no correct answer to this question, because all historians are biased.' But this is really a bit of a *cliché* - it doesn't get us anywhere. The job for students is to go out on a bit of a limb.

An alternative to scepticism

A number of informants were thus somewhat 'sceptical' about the value of a 'sceptical' frame – at least in its more excessive guises. The alternative account proposed was one that saw critical thinking more in terms of students drawing their own conclusions about issues, and making their own modest contributions to knowledge. Lauren (philosophy), for example, while acknowledging the need to be cautious in one's approach to knowledge, recognized that eventually one must make decisions. For Lauren – who was notable for being virtually the only philosopher in the department teaching within continental traditions of philosophy – the existentialism of Sartre and de Beauvoir provided some guidance on these matters; that is, how one might reconcile the problem of the provisionality of knowledge on the one hand, and the need to commit to a position on the other:

> **LAUREN** (philosophy): [I say to students] I mean I don't think scepticism is such a bad thing, but there's a sense in which you know scepticism is a kind of dead end. [In the end] you have to kind of choose to believe. I guess I'm rather influenced by Sartre and de Beauvoir ... that the more you exercise critical thinking, the more you see that no set of beliefs is absolutely justified and justifiable. But that you then finally ... you have to make decisions.

Nora (literary/cultural studies) was aware of the same tension – and also of the need to help students find a clear epistemological voice amid all this provisionality. For her, the best encouragement was to indicate to students how rhetorically they might lay out a position they wished to argue for – not, as she suggested, in some detached objective way ('This might [be] the case'), but in a way that

confidently affirmed their subjectivity ('This is the case, according to my interpretation').

> **NORA** (literary/cultural studies – comp.): what I say to students is you can't
> beat around the bush. You can't say 'this might have been the case'. You have
> to say, 'this is the case, according to my interpretation'.... Being critical, it's
> about taking a stand. You have to commit as a critic, put your head on the
> line. It is always reducible to a person, to a personal point of view.

Some informants recognized the considerable challenge that students face in
projecting themselves in this way. Indeed a number of the statements above
attest to the inherent risk of such practices – with Michael (history) wanting
students to 'go out on a limb', and Nora insisting – perhaps more dramatically
– that they had to 'put [their] heads on the line'. A number of informants were
well aware of these risks, and thought it important to be realistic about what
type of contribution an undergraduate was capable of making at that stage in
their studies. Several, in fact, suggested that it did not really matter if what was
proposed in a piece of writing was flawed (with 'holes in it', or simply 'wrong');
what was important was that there was evidence of the student having made an
'honest' attempt to present some kind of conclusion:

> **HENRY** (philosophy): What you want is someone who's got a conclusion and
> they make a case for it. But even if the case has got some holes in it, that
> doesn't matter. It doesn't have to be anything big, just as long as they've got
> something to argue for.

> **KATHERINE** (history): I want [students] to come to their own conclusions
> about problems which have been framed for them and other people have
> already explored … I don't care whether they're right or wrong, as long as
> their position is reasonably well defended and there's an honest journey
> there.

This making of a contribution was characterized in interviews in a variety of
ways. Perhaps the images most relied upon were ones that suggested various
kinds of manufacturing processes – 'putting together', 'building', 'constructing' and so on – in contrast to the metaphors of dismantlement and deconstruc-
tion, discussed earlier. Henry (philosophy), for example, talked about students
needing 'to *make* a case', and 'to take some reasonably interesting proposition
or theory and *do something with it*'. Similarly, Edward (history), in discussing the
importance of students developing their own arguments, spoke of how they
needed to '*build* on the sources, or *organize* them in a particular way to *construct*
a particular … picture of the past'.

Another type of characterization was one that evoked less a sense of 'the building up' of knowledge, and more a kind of lateral engagement with it. For a number of informants, this type of engagement was suggestive of some originality of thought. Michael (history), for example, spoke about a group of students he had taught that year (from third year) who had impressed him by offering their own particular interpretations of an historical period: 'They were quite creative', he said, '[for] taking things *outside* the accepted ... historical interpretations'. For Lois (literary/cultural studies – comp.), the type of thinking to be encouraged was one where students 'headed in a different direction'. In elaborating on her concerns about students being too readily dismissive of certain ideas – the 'doing of hatchet jobs', discussed earlier – Lois thought that a genuinely 'critical' approach was one where students did not see a text primarily as an object to be evaluated, but rather as something that might stimulate them to pursue a different course:

> **LOIS** (literary/cultural studies – comp.): so you actually develop something positive out of your critical engagement with a text rather than just damning it. That's what I've been trying to impress upon students – don't just go in and do a hatchet job, have a look and see if there is ... a redeeming element here that you could pick up and run with, *to head in a different direction* (emphasis added).

Brian (literary/cultural studies), from the same discipline, saw the contribution that students can make in the same lateral terms – as a 'sideways' movement, involving the drawing of 'connections' between different sources.

> **BRIAN** (literary/cultural Studies – comp.): Well, the most exciting thing is when, in a sense, students *move sideways* – where they make a connection between the text that you've given and something else that you haven't given at all, either in another text from elsewhere or their own personal experience. It's the *lateral thinking* that counts (emphasis added).

Kim (philosophy) also mentioned the importance in his area of ethics and bioethics of the 'making of connections', suggesting that this was one of the ways that students can somehow be 'original' in their work:

> **KIM** (philosophy): And so I try to explain to them how they can actually be original ... it's more just about them thinking how to *bring together* two different sorts of arguments and perhaps *connecting* them in ways that no one else has (emphasis added).

Like others, Kim felt it was important that students have a realistic perspective on what it might mean to be original, especially in study at undergraduate level.

He explained that students needed to think of any potential contribution they could make at this level in modest terms:

> **KIM** (philosophy): But students sometimes think … they've got to come up with an original ethical theory, a full-blown theory that's original. But I'm not asking for something ambitious … I quickly disabuse them of that assumption.

4.3.4 Critical thinking as careful and sensitive readings

One of the other more prominent themes to emerge from the interviews was critical thinking as the careful and sensitive reading of texts. For many informants, the notion of being able to grasp the basic meaning of reading material was seen as fundamental to the activity of critical thinking. The point was particularly emphasized by the philosophers, perhaps as a consequence of the typically difficult reading requirements of that discipline. Jonathon, for example, emphasized the point several times, suggesting that the ability to make basic sense of texts lay at the heart of all critical practices:

> **JONATHON** (philosophy): Put rather bluntly, just trying to figure out what somebody is on about is what underlies everything that we are looking at. I think the connection [of critical thinking between all disciplines] would be a connection of careful reading.

> Over the last couple of semesters, I've devoted a lecture to sort of saying, what's fundamentally involved in [being critical] is figuring out what a person is saying.

For Eric (philosophy), this 'figuring out' needed to be most directed at the 'identifying of arguments' in a text, seen mainly in terms of a relationship between a series of premises and a conclusion. For him, the ability to 'read' texts in this way was what much of the initial training in the discipline involved:

> **ERIC** (philosophy): So we think of, particularly first-year philosophy, as being geared towards building skills in identifying arguments. That is, being able to tease out from a block of normal English prose something where you can identify the premises and show how they are supposed to support a conclusion.

Eric also emphasized the need for students to develop these skills within a comparative framework:

> **ERIC**: [what I mainly want in] an essay at first year is one that gives you a clear exposition of a couple of different authors with divergent views and … puts

them against one another and shows how they line up and where the points of disagreement are. So it's maybe 70% exegesis in terms of just getting the ideas down.

While the philosophers perhaps had the most to say about this aspect of critical thinking, similar views were expressed by informants from the other disciplines. Bruce (literary/cultural studies – Eng.) also stressed the need for students to have a sound understanding of the texts with which they were engaged, suggesting that no meaningful critique in literature was possible without this:

BRUCE (literary/cultural studies – Eng.): First of all [being critical] is something that's really dependent on students having demonstrated a working understanding of the text that is being used.

Hannah (history) also saw this ability as paramount, to the extent that she initially discouraged students from expressing a 'point of view' of their own in the subject. Like Eric, Hannah thought the main 'critical capacity' to be developed in the early training in her discipline was just an ability to identify and make sense of a range of interpretations advanced by scholars in the field:

HANNAH (history): And so really [I want the students] to pick up on what these [writers in archaeology] have said and pick up relevant points ... I don't necessarily want them to put their point of view, which will often go off on a tangent. That's not really asked of them until they get to second year. Initially it's just let's have a look at what others say.

This need for the staged development of students' critical abilities was emphasized by a number of informants, with several outlining specific techniques they typically used on their courses to facilitate this development. Nell (history), for example, saw value in setting simple 'summary tasks' for her first-year *Australian History* students. Among other things, these exercises, she explained, were aimed at getting students to appreciate the difference between acts of representing ideas and acts of evaluating them:

NELL (history): The [first task we set] in first year is actually just a summary. And a summary which is really meant to be only a summary ... I mean they're not meant to criticize the argument, and when they do you tell them no, no that's later, don't do that yet.

Eric (philosophy) saw the same value in drawing on this kind of 'exegetical' approach early on in the philosophy degree. Much of the assessment in the first year of the philosophy degree, he explained, was organized around a series of 'expository exercises', aimed principally at getting students to grapple with the meanings of key philosophical texts in the subject. As he explained in his particular idiomatic style:

> **ERIC** (philosophy): so the expository exercises are really geared at getting [students] to get down and dirty with a fairly short piece of reading and try and demonstrate their actual grasp of the important concepts.

For Eric, the 'critical' element in this type of exercise was for students to manage to establish some distance from the text and its specific wording, and to be able to express their 'grasp of concepts' in their own terms:

> **ERIC** (philosophy): So I say to students: 'Don't just tell me, don't just use Marx's jargon, for example. Try and tell me what you think it's all about.'

Although these informants were sure of the importance of these skills of careful reading, there was uncertainty expressed in a few quarters about whether this type of careful, analytical reading should be thought of as part of some broader critical thinking activity, or whether it related to a separate and distinct cognitive domain. Such uncertainty, for example, was expressed by Lauren (philosophy) in an initial discussion about the role of reading in her subject area:

> **LAUREN** (philosophy): It's not clear whether you think of [reading] as part of critical reasoning or something like a *prelude* to it.

As this particular discussion with Lauren continued, however, it became apparent to her that the two areas could not really be separated, and that one 'intimately implied' the other. She discussed this notion in relation to the processes of critiquing philosophical arguments, suggesting that how one reads and interprets a text will invariably affect the way that it is subsequently evaluated:

> **LAUREN**: If you've got a fairly complex piece of writing … how you evaluate the argument will depend very much on … [your] expository account of what the argument actually is.

These ideas about the importance of understanding ideas are very much in line with conceptions of critical thinking presented in the literature. Indeed, in a number of the accounts of critical thinking we saw earlier, the ability to represent one's comprehension of a text figures prominently in the various lists of putative skills that have been produced. For example, Facione and his colleagues include in their list of 'core CT skills' the 'clarifying of meaning' – which is characterized as the ability 'to restate what a person said using different words or expressions, while preserving that person's intended meaning' (1990: p. 7). There is a similar emphasis in Robert Ennis's 'Taxonomy of critical thinking dispositions and abilities' (1987) with the basic comprehension of texts (what Ennis refers to as 'grasping the meaning of statements') being the first ability that is identified on his list. According to Ennis, this comprehension is a pre-condition for all other cognitive activities included in his taxonomy – for example, 'judging whether a text is ambiguous', or 'whether a conclusion necessarily follows', or 'whether a definition is adequate' and so on.

Other readings

While many informants in the study recognized the imperative for students to have some basic and literal understanding of the texts they need to read on their courses, a number of additional aspects of critical reading were also identified as important. It is notable that some of these additional aspects are quite absent in the various skills outlined by proponents of the critical thinking movement. The first of these was the ability to read beyond a text's literal meanings and to be able to engage with its broader rhetorical purposes. For those informants who spoke about this aspect of reading, it was important for students to develop a sensitivity to the circumstances in which a text might be written, and to be able to give some account of its underlying 'motives', 'intentions' and 'agendas'. This dimension of reading was emphasized particularly by the historians, who saw it as a crucial part of a student's training in the discipline, particularly in a student's engagement with primary source material. Nell (history), for example, spoke of the need for students to 'go further into a [historical] document', and to have 'a shot at working out its intentions'. Hannah (history) and Michael (history) – in separate discussions of specific document exercises set in their respective first-year subjects – also emphasized the importance of going beyond a simple literal understanding of a text, to a more nuanced, interpretative reading:

> **HANNAH** (history): I set a document analysis task on Thucydides. He certainly has an agenda there … And so we get students to look at the document, and we get them to try and analyse that … not only what he is saying, but why he might go to the trouble to say these things.

> **MICHAEL** (history): We want [students] to understand the assumptions within … these documents … why are they being produced, the agendas, that sort of thing.

For Michael, the development of such an approach to reading involved showing students how they need to move continually between the text itself and the context in which it was produced:

> **MICHAEL:** [students need to think about] what's surrounding the [document], why it was created in those different circumstances and then also what

the author of the document is trying to achieve through it … not just superficially what they're saying in the document but also getting behind and seeing the other agendas which may have been there within that historical context.

It is perhaps not surprising that this focus on more contextual readings of texts should be a specific concern of those working in the area of history. This is to be explained by the interest of that discipline in the temporal dimension of texts and in the role that such texts often play in processes of historical change.

This type of contextual reading however seemed not to be the sole province of the historians, and was discussed by informants from the other areas. Lauren (philosophy), for example, mentioned that, although the more conventional approach in philosophy was to lay out the content of arguments 'as they appeared on the page', there were occasions when students needed to see these ideas in some broader domain. An example she gave was a subject she taught that focused on the writings of Jean-Paul Sartre and Simone de Beauvoir. Lauren mentioned that while the principal aim of the course was to understand the arguments contained in the seminal works of each of these writers (*Being and Nothingness* and *The Second Sex*, respectively), she also wanted students to have some understanding of these works in the context of the personal relationship that existed between the two thinkers, as well as other aspects of the social and intellectual milieu they were writing in:

> **LAUREN** (philosophy): The course on Sartre and de Beauvoir takes a somewhat different form, not entirely different, but in some ways it's more expository because [the students are] filling in the historical background … and there are quite directed kinds of questions which are along the lines of what do they say, what are their arguments, and why are they saying these things.

Similarly, Eric (philosophy) indicated that in a subject on Greek philosophy he was inclined, from time to time, to set essay topics that required students not only to summarize and evaluate the arguments of certain philosophers, but also to consider the purposes they might have had for advancing a particular argument.

Another type of contextual reading mentioned was one focused not so much on identifying the underlying intentions and purposes of individual authors and texts, but on understanding a text in relation to broader paradigms of writing and thinking at the time. Such a view perhaps reflects a more postmodernist notion of text, where meaning is thought to derive less from the subjectivity of individual authors, and more from larger discursive structures of which the text is a part. Thus, Nell (history) thought that a 'really critical reading' was one that showed awareness of 'the kind of code that an author writes in because of the particular form that they were using … and the particular discourse they had to write in'. This type of discursive approach – one that seeks to understand a text in relation to its own conventions – was elaborated on by a number of the literary/cultural studies informants:

> **LOIS** (literary/cultural studies – comp.): [Another] aspect of critical thinking I bring to bear is an appreciation of the historical context in which these people [theorists] are writing and thinking, … that you can't necessarily expect people to have the same kinds of assumptions that you're making.

For Lois, this type of reading involves an 'empathic' kind of engagement with a text – and, for her, needs to be understood as fundamentally non-judgemental:

> **LOIS**: The point [in such an approach to reading] is not to try to condemn, but rather to understand the legacy of a certain way of thinking, which became predominant under a particular circumstance, and at a certain time.

Bruce (literary/cultural studies) also spoke of the need for students to bring an empathic and non-judgemental attitude to their reading of texts. Interestingly, the critical faculty that Bruce thought needed encouraging was a kind of intellectual and moral humility – and to disavow students of the notion that they necessarily operate at the end point in some inexorable march of progress.

> **BRUCE** (literary/cultural studies – Eng.): Some students do come in with the assumption that we are more enlightened than our parents' generation, and certainly our grandparents' generation. And one of the uses of reading literature from the past is that it can make them critical of … that easy assumption that we know more than our predecessors.

Underlying conceptions of reading

The preceding discussion has highlighted some divergence between more 'literalist' approaches to reading (where the aim is to grasp the essential message of the author contained within the text) and more 'relativist' approaches (where a text is open to broader and variable interpretations, especially through reference to material beyond the text – context, biography, discourses, etc.). These differing accounts undermine the notion of any single critical orientation to reading, and suggest that the approach a student needs to adopt will depend to some degree on the nature of the particular reading task, and also on the subject matter with which they are engaged. But we can, also detect in these variable accounts some broad epistemological differences about the nature of reading processes, and the kinds of meanings that are thought to be available to the reader.

One informant to take up these kinds of differences was Brian (literary/cultural studies – comp.). In a fairly spirited commentary, Brian elaborated on the distinction alluded to above – that is, between a postmodernist view of reading on the one hand, and what he described as the 'traditional humanist view' on the other. For Brian, this latter view, which he thought continues to be the predominant one in the academy, is founded on a number of assumptions about reading processes that cannot really be sustained. The first is the idea that a text unproblematically expresses an author's intended meaning, and that the sound reading of a text will be principally directed at identifying this basic meaning:

> **BRIAN** (literary/cultural studies – comp.): I don't accept that there is an original authorial truth that is transmitted through the text and that our only problem is to read it and find it.

For Brian, it was folly not only to imagine that there is some objective and unitary meaning residing in a text, but also to believe that one can use the text to establish with any certainty what an author's intention was in writing it:

> **BRIAN**: Even if you could find out what an author intended, and that is by no means obvious, the argument that it's obvious what Shakespeare meant – well it's not because all we have is the text.

Also problematic for Brian was any reliance on the notion of 'context' as a way of getting at a text's meaning. He explained that it was important for students to appreciate that any putative 'context' (whether it be the author's life and times, their social milieu, the larger historical period and so on) does not have any objective status independent of texts, but rather needs to be seen as something which is ultimately constructed from the reading and interpreting of a range of other texts:

> **BRIAN**: We're a text-based discipline, and what students do is they read texts … literary texts, philosophical texts and they criticize them … In the course, we think of texts as artefacts that exist now – and yes [students] would like to rely on some sense of the contexts when they, say, read Milton, but the seventeenth century has gone. It's just not available as an immediate object of empirical study. We tell [students] all we can do is study text – historical texts, historiographical texts – but they're still just texts … they're archives. The seventeenth century is simply not available as an object for study in the way that materials are available in physics and chemistry. It's mediated by text, and this is why we say all we can do is study text.

Drawing on these broad ideas, Brian thought that the most useful way of thinking about reading is not as a fundamentally receptive activity, but rather as a productive, even creative one – as 'a form of re-writing', as he described it. He was mindful, however, of the criticism typically made of this strongly subjectivist position – namely, that any interpretation of a text can ultimately be held to be valid – and was at pains to point out that the position he favoured did not in any way preclude one from distinguishing between good and bad readings:

> **BRIAN** (literary/cultural studies): Reading is a form of re-writing, but there are bad readings … there are worse and better readings. But it's not that there is a right reading … You can't rely on the naive humanist notion that there is a truth there, but you do know that some readings just don't work.

For Brian, the distinguishing quality of a 'good' reading is the extent to which it is 'informed' by the reading of other texts – a notion which he felt was most important to impress upon students:

> **BRIAN** (literary/cultural studies): So… we try to give a sense of what a good reading is – which would be one that's aware of previous readings, that would be critical of previous readings, [and] that would bring in theoretical resources from outside the text to bear.

The main critics of such a view were to be found among the philosophers. Eric was the one to elaborate most on the rival position. In his discussion, Eric showed a keen understanding of the alternative, receptionist view favoured in the 'continental tradition':

> **ERIC** (philosophy): My impression is that the continental tradition much more invites students to get inside a paradigm. Here is how you read a text like a Marxist. Here is how you read a text like a phenomenologist. And these are tools for sort of re-imagining the world. This is because [those working in the continental tradition] take very seriously the idea that our access to reality is always sort of conceptually mediated by a kind of theoretical framework of which we're seldom aware.

Eric was not actively dismissive of such a position, but was keen to point out that he and his colleagues in the School of Philosophy mainly felt themselves to be a part of a very different epistemological tradition, one committed to the notion that meaning (and indeed reality) exists independently of how one perceives it:

> **ERIC**: This is a department strongly in the Anglo-analytic tradition of philosophy, which is relatively untouched by post-structuralist theory, and postmodernism. … I think the tradition in the Anglo-analytic school tends to be a much more Aristotelian methodology. The starting assumption … much of what we believe is that there can be a sort of accurate representation of the world that is independent of how we perceive it.

The strong emphasis that the philosophers placed on the idea of students being able to produce clear and unadorned exegetical readings of texts can be seen as an expression of this particular view.

Reading and knowledge

While the preceding discussion points to divergence, and even tensions, regarding specific theoretical understandings of reading, the comments of a number of other informants suggest that in practice the differences may not be so acute. In particular, there appeared to be a good deal of agreement about the need for students to read widely and to be able 'to bring other resources to bear' on whatever they were considering. Lauren (philosophy), for example, was sure that the reading of a philosophical text was always more 'critical' if informed by other relevant readings, and suggested that it was this ability that often distinguished the more able and critical students in her classes:

> **LAUREN** (philosophy): Well … one thing [that distinguishes these students] is being able to bring in material from elsewhere that is relevant.
>
> TIM: Like another philosopher or another type of argument or…?
>
> **LAUREN**: Yeah. Well seeing similarities or … objecting to things that I say.
>
> TIM: OK.
>
> **LAUREN**: You know, when a student says, 'but what about such and such who wrote on this'.

Edward (history) was also sure that extensive reading of this kind was crucial to adopting a critical approach in his area. Thus, any legitimate form of critical evaluation, he thought, was dependent on one being aware of the debates surrounding a particular historical question, and also being aware of alternative answers and views that might have been proposed:

> **EDWARD** (history): So it [being critical] is very much dependent on a certain level of knowledge in the subject which … is why we say to students you must do adequate reading otherwise you cannot respond to the questions [that we pose]. You might find a perfectly reasonable answer in a single book on this topic, but you're in no position to evaluate that unless you've read alternatives.

Edward's broad view – perhaps an intuitive understanding that many academics have of their students – was that, more than anything else, it was good reading practices that lay at the heart of all successful academic engagement:

EDWARD (history): What is very clear is that those students who do a lot of reading will be better at whatever they are called to do than students who don't do very much, including the adopting of a critical approach.

The accounts of the various informants mentioned above suggest that 'careful and sensitive reading' needs to be seen as an integral part of being a critical thinker, perhaps to a greater extent than has traditionally been suggested by those within the critical thinking movement. It is also fair to say that the views expressed by many of the academics interviewed go a good way further than the somewhat rudimentary conceptions of reading that have emerged from within the movement. Thus, the typical characterizations of reading in the critical thinking literature – as 'the clarifying of meaning' (Facione 1990), or 'the grasping of the meaning of statements' (Ennis 1987) – would seem to capture only a single dimension of reading processes, and also to obscure the fact that any act of 'grasping meaning' would appear to mean rather different things in different contexts of study.

The emphasis that a number of informants placed on the importance of extensive reading raises questions about the connection between the ability to think critically and possessing relevant disciplinary knowledge. As we saw in the earlier review of the critical thinking literature, debates about this issue revolve around the question of whether critical thinking is best viewed as a general skill that can be developed irrespective of content, or whether the accumulation of relevant content knowledge is in fact crucial to this development (Glaser 1984). The comments of some informants in the later part of the discussion above – especially Edward's conclusion about the keener critical capacities of the more informed and better-read students – would appear to lend some support to the latter position. But, these are only preliminary observations. Issues of the role of content and disciplinarity are considered in more detail in the next chapter.

So far we have considered a variety of definitions of critical thinking – namely, as judgement; as a sceptical view of knowledge; as a simple originality; and as a careful and sensitive reading of texts. These were the more prominent themes in informants' talks about critical thinking. The remaining definitions – characterized here as: i) the adopting of an ethical and activist stance; ii) a form of rationality; iii) a facility and awareness of language; iv) a form of self-reflexiveness – figured less prominently in the interviews. In line with the more limited attention given to these themes, the discussion of each in the following sections is commensurately briefer. As with the more prominent themes, it will be seen in the following discussion that while these aspects of critical thinking were thought to be an important part of being critical, informants did not necessarily agree about the precise nature of the aspect in question, nor about the extent of its significance.

4.3.5 Critical thinking as the adopting of an ethical and activist stance

Those informants who saw an ethical and activist dimension to critical thinking tended to be those who emphasized the broad social mission of universities – that is, to see a university education being concerned as much with 'life in the world' (as one informant described it) as with training in a specific discipline area. Thus, for these informants, the definitions of critical thinking needed to be extended beyond acts of cognition, and to incorporate some notion of critical action. One informant to elaborate on this dimension was Kim (philosophy), who worked in the area of practical ethics:

> **KIM** (philosophy): It's important for students to confront issues in a fairly personal way and to try and figure out for themselves where they stand on [these issues] and to be able to defend them.

The issues Kim referred to were a range of moral issues covered on his course, ones typically related to the health and medical domains – euthanasia, abortion, therapeutic cloning and so on. It is perhaps unsurprising that on a course devoted to medical ethics that critical thinking should be conceived of in this way. Kim, however, wanted to make it clear that the consideration of the moral issues on the course was designed to be personally relevant to students, and not – as he described it – 'just an intellectual exercise'.

A similar view was expressed by Eric (philosophy), whose particular area of philosophy was not specifically concerned with ethics. Eric explained that a key principle he tried to impress upon students was that philosophy is not a 'value-free inquiry', and that it was important for students to think that they can be bold and speak up for the things that matter to them:

> **ERIC** (philosophy): I say that this is not a value-free inquiry. You think of the important value as the love of the truth. If you think that [something] is just bullshit, and you've got some reasons for thinking this, then you need to bring this out.

Eric and Kim were both sure that a part of being 'critical' involved taking a stand on issues of a broadly social nature; other informants were more specific about the type of stand they thought the term necessarily implied. For Nell (history) and Bruce (literary/cultural studies), being 'critical' meant being broadly critical of the political and academic 'establishments'. In their respective discussions of this notion, we see expression of a type of criticality referred to earlier in the literature – that is, 'the university as institutionalized critique', where a key purpose of study is to be engaged in a permanent 'problematizing' and 'critiquing' of cultural structures and practices (Delanty 2001: p.10). Bruce, for example, spoke of a commonly held view – at least in the circles he inhabited

– that saw the 'duty of the university as in some sense [being] opposed to the establishment in society'. He likened the role to a 'corrupting of youth':

> **BRUCE** (literary/cultural studies – Eng.): We like to say to students: 'That's the monolith over there and the university's job [and your job] is to be, in a sense, subversive of it.'

Nell also affirmed the importance of this type of socially-engaged critique. For her, it was this type of thinking and engaging with knowledge that gave studies in the humanities their distinctive quality. She went on to explain how in her former role as dean of the faculty, she and some of her colleagues had worked hard to have this 'activist' view of critical thinking included within the faculty's educational policies:

> **NELL** (history): So [in the documents we produced] 'critical' was a value-laden term … it meant critical in the sense of being critical of the established order, and setting up values that you then compared politics against, or history or teaching at the university, whatever. So it was critical in the sense of having – not exactly a radical – but at least a reformist kind of agenda; in other words, not being satisfied with the status quo.

For Nell, the values of which she spoke needed to serve as a 'kind of prism' through which disciplinary knowledge could be viewed. Thus, in the study of history, for example, she thought that students always needed to have some moral perspective on the events they studied – that is, not only to consider the 'what', 'how' and 'why' of history, but also to make some assessment of the ethical quality of these events:

> **NELL** (history): It does mean not just accepting what you have, what you've come to, but asking questions about it. And usually not just questions about how did it happen, but how did it happen and is it a good thing.

Other informants were more specific about the kinds of values and ideals they thought should inform this socially critical view. A number of broad political ideals were mentioned here, including 'emancipation', 'liberation', 'freedom from oppression' and 'a general egalitarianism'. In values such as these, there is a connection with that particular form of criticality associated with the critical theory tradition – specifically of the Frankfurt school, referred to earlier. In fact, Brian (literary/cultural studies – comp.), one of the keener advocates for such values, mentioned how the critical approach which he sought to develop in students was strongly rooted in this tradition:

> **BRIAN** (literary/cultural studies – comp.): For the Frankfurt school this … knowledge is not neutral. They argue, and I would too, that it's often

implicated in man's oppression ... And the point of this kind of critique is to liberate human beings ... It's the idea of emancipation, which is to do with the idea of enlightenment critique.

Another informant to elaborate on this 'transformational' form of critique was Nigel. While less explicit than Brian about the theoretical basis for such an outlook, Nigel was sure of the need to have this activist ethic included as one of the goals of higher education. For him, the underlying approach in his teaching was to make students aware of the privileged position they occupy as students of a university, and to appreciate the sense of social responsibility that goes with such a position:

> **NIGEL** (history): So there is [a sense of] being critically responsible ... one of the burdens of being [a] capable [person] is the burden of feeling responsible for the state of the world ... the job of talented, fortunate people is to be able make decisions in the world ... that don't [necessarily] favour them.

A dissenting view

All this is not to suggest that this activist version of critical thinking was embraced by all. One notably dissident voice here was Nora's (literary/cultural studies – comp.). Far from encouraging students in this type of thinking, Nora was generally disapproving of the tendency for some students to push – and be encouraged to push – a particular moral position in their work; for example, to take a view that 'all violence is bad'. At best, Nora thought, such intrusions were irrelevant; at worst they demonstrated an unthinking form of 'political correctness':

> **NORA** (literary/cultural studies – comp.): There are no value judgements [in critique] as in this is a good way to be, this is a bad way to be. So, for example, if you're talking about violence, you don't have a contentious judgement which proclaims 'all violence is bad' because that's sort of not relevant.

Nora believed there were additional problems with an activist approach beyond this clumsy kind of moralizing, which she felt was evident in some students' work. For her, allowing one's 'subjective' values to impinge on the appraisal of a work of literature (or whatever is being considered) can only serve to undermine the 'objectivity' of the critique, and pushes one necessarily into the realm of 'ideology'. Thus, in contrast to other informants who thought that taking an ideological stance is always implicit in the idea of being critical, Nora believed the two notions to be wholly 'incompatible':

> **NORA**: if [in one's thinking] there is a kind of element of good or bad, that is not being critical, that is not critique. That is value judgement of a

subjective and emotional kind, and it always reduces to ideology. You don't have ideology in critique.

Nora went on to explain how her views on these matters did not necessarily accord with those of her colleagues in the Centre for Comparative Literature and Cultural Studies:

> **NORA**: Somebody quite well placed here said that we are using the ideology of critique in this centre. Well, that's a contradiction in terms. It's a misunderstanding of what critique is. Critique and ideology in fact are incompatible terms.

The particular controversy described by Nora here is a familiar one. Such debates surrounding 'activist' versus 'neutralist' modes of scholarship are played out typically in many fields of inquiry, and often involve, in some guise, those oriented towards more Marxist traditions of critique on the one hand, and those working in non-Marxist (or even anti-Marxist) paradigms on the other (see Fairclough 1996; and Widdowson 1995, 1996 for examples in the field of applied linguistics). Such debates are of intrinsic interest; however, for the purpose of our investigation, the particular disagreement noted here among the literary/cultural studies academics is perhaps most interesting for the way it provides an additional perspective on the source of variation in informants' ideas of critical thinking. Thus, whereas some of the previous disagreements we have seen would appear to stem from certain interfield differences (e.g. the disparate accounts of critical reading offered by the philosophers and the literary/cultural studies academics), in this particular instance, a clear difference of view was evident among those from the same sub-discipline area – indeed within the same administrative unit. To see such divergences at this local level adds to the impression gained of the complex network of understandings that surround our term, and of the different types of 'conversations' of which it is a part.

4.3.6 Critical thinking as a form of rationality

Another of the less prominent themes was critical thinking as a form of rationality. As noted earlier (Chapter 2), this conception figures substantially among the views of many from within the critical thinking movement. It is of interest that as a theme it had arguably less prominence in the discussion with the informants in the study. Significantly, it was the philosophers who most emphasized this dimension of critical thinking. For Jonathon (philosophy), it is the spirit of rationality that lies at the heart of all critical activities. Jonathon was also keen to stress that it was this rational aspect of critical thinking that gave it its universality:

> **JONATHON** (philosophy): There is a sense that to some extent all intellectual work is engagement with a rational project, it is not surprising that it is

a commonality ... but of course I am coming from a view according to which what we mostly think of as critical thinking is similar and universal.

Henry (philosophy) also held to a universalist position, and spoke specifically about the efforts made on his course – *God, Freedom and Evil* – to develop rational habits of mind in his students. Henry indicated that – particularly on this subject, which involved questions of a religious nature – students needed to understand the unacceptability of claiming certain truths without providing some kind of substantive reasons for them. Interestingly, he thought that this could be as much a problem for those who held to an atheistic position as for those who came to the course with certain religious convictions:

> **HENRY** (philosophy): Even after they've been doing the course for a while, they'll be a lot of students who will have this response. You give them an argument and say: 'What do you think?' You want them to criticize it. And initially all you get is: 'I disagree with the conclusion'.

> TIM: What, because they just do?

> **HENRY**: Yes, for no particular reason. So they might say: 'I'm an atheist, so I disagree with the conclusion that God exists.' After a while in *God, Freedom and Evil* that's not an acceptable response.

While it was mostly the philosophers who emphasized the importance of students having a reason-based approach to their thinking, several informants from other disciplines also touched upon this notion. Bruce (literary/cultural studies – Eng.), for example, spoke of the common problem of students arguing by assertion without providing adequate support for whatever particular assessments they made of a work of literature. For Bruce, it was this mode of thinking that needed to be particularly emphasized to students in the assessment of their work:

> **BRUCE** (literary/cultural studies – Eng.): For me, it's one of the main things that I assess an essay on ... whether it supports [an] argument not just by assertion, but is backed up in some logical way through reference to the text that's being discussed.

For Hannah (history), the lack of a rational approach was seen as a particular 'occupational hazard' on one of the subjects she taught – Ancient Civilizations. She explained that, of the various courses she taught, this course was attractive to quite a range of students, including some of 'a more exotic bent' (as she described them) who were inclined to 'all manner of theories' about certain archaeological controversies considered on the course:

HANNAH (history): [From some students], it will be hypothesis on top of hypothesis, and eventually [they] get so far away from the actual evidence that we've got. It's not unusual to have students assert, for example, that the pyramids were actually built by extraterrestrials.

As an antidote to this highly speculative approach, Hannah talked about the importance of impressing upon students the basic 'rational' and 'critical' framework that the discipline operated in:

HANNAH: So when they come up with these way-out theories, [we say to them]: 'Let's follow it through … let's think rationally about it, let's think critically about it.'

Critiques of reason

While those informants who referred to these matters generally agreed on the need to instill principles of reason and logic, uneasiness was expressed in some quarters about the extent to which these principles should be emphasized. Scepticism about the potentiality of reason was a strand of thought touched on in the earlier discussion. It was noted, for example, that criticisms of western notions of rationality have been particularly strong within post-structuralism, and especially among certain feminist thinkers from within this larger circle (eg. Le Doeuff 1980). In the present investigation, it is of interest that concerns about the 'rationality' of critical thinking were expressed most keenly by some of the female informants.

Lauren (philosophy) elaborated at length on these issues. In explaining her concerns, she was keen, in the first instance, to distance herself from what she saw as an extreme 'anti-rationalism' of the type advocated within some strands of feminist thought:

LAUREN (philosophy): There was a movement, about which you may be aware, which more or less said that rationality or reason is a male kind of construct, and then there was an attempt at some kind of anti-rational female way. I personally think that that is an insane position.

While holding firmly to a view that some general notion of rationality is essential, Lauren nevertheless felt concern about what she called that 'overblown conception' of rationality that has tended to predominate within analytical traditions of philosophy. For her, such a position, which typically seeks to draw a rigid distinction drawn between ideas of reason and emotion, has limited resonance for many people, especially women.

LAUREN (philosophy): I don't think that reason and emotion really are opposed. I mean, I think that you can't get anywhere without a certain amount of emotion.

LAUREN: Women have historically conceptualized reason in ... much more emotional terms. They haven't really fallen into ... the trap of thinking of a kind of totally disembodied, disengaged and ... non-passionate reason. They have always thought of reason in a way which almost went in line with a kind of reasonable, caring emotion.

A similar view was expressed by another female informant – Nell (history). She also did not wish to dismiss out of hand the importance of a logical and rational approach, though felt it was necessary for students to understand not only the potential of a certain logical habit of mind, but also the limitations it could impose upon one's thinking:

NELL (history): I do believe there are processes of logic that are appropriate and inappropriate. But where I have problems with logic is that it's just a tool ... and it's a tool that within its own rules can actually stop you doing things, as well as allow you to do things.

Like Lauren, Nell favoured a less 'purist' kind of logic – one that does not need to be established in one's writing in explicit and 'transparent' terms. For her, what was to be encouraged was a more inner logic of 'connections' and 'layers', rather than one that followed any specified logical procedures:

NELL: I don't require students to be sort of transparently logical by any means, providing [their writing] has a kind of inner logic, or a set of connections, or an opening up, a continual opening up that doesn't have to be strictly logical.

In the preceding discussion, it can be seen that while many held to the view that critical thinking necessarily entailed being rational and logical in some way, there was a range of opinion about the forms that such a logic should take, particularly how strictly prescribed it should be. Elaborating on this notion, Edward (history), who at the time occupied an educational leadership role in the faculty, thought that it was important in one's teaching to recognize the different 'logical' modes that students typically bring to their studies.

EDWARD (history): ... there are [students] who it would seem are born with particular kinds of approaches to the world, and some ... have a very questioning approach to everything, and others ... don't. And some are interested in logical progressions in what we might call linear logic. Other [students] are interested in more natural kinds of connections and associations.

And those who make these associations between things make accomplished art critics for instance, but may or may not be as good at some of the other types of critical activities we have been talking about.

4.3.7 Critical thinking as a facility with language

Another of the less prominent themes to emerge from the interviews was one that saw a close connection between being able to think critically and having a facility with language. As will be evident in the following discussion, there were two distinct strands in the various comments made by informants on this matter. In the first of these, the facility identified was described in more generic terms, and thought to involve the ability to be generally clear, precise and fluent in one's use of language. The second strand was one focused not on some generic competence, but rather on a student's ability to understand – and also to use appropriately – certain key terms and concepts related to their particular areas of study.

Generic accounts of language

In the more generic account, the following commentary by Bruce is fairly representative of the views expressed. For him, being critical involves not only being critical of whatever it is that one is considering (a text, for example), but also of the way that one chooses linguistically to frame the particular critique:

> **BRUCE** (literary/cultural studies – Eng.): When I advise my students that they should write a critical account of something, what I am saying is that not only should they look at [and think about] the text critically, but they should use their own language with discrimination. Therefore [they need to] be self-critical of their use of language.

Edward (history) also affirmed the importance of a discerning use of language, suggesting that this was another of the qualities that distinguished the more capable and critical students.

> **EDWARD** (history): Well one of the crucial things [that the more critical students] do is [demonstrate] linguistic precision, whether it be verbal or written, because one of the things that critical thinking certainly requires is the ability to express sometimes very fine nuances of meaning and to do so clearly. And clarity is very much a part of it. I think that's a generic ability.

These notions of clarity and precision in language were taken up by several other informants. Lauren (philosophy), for example, saw this precision arising from someone having a healthy preoccupation with the meanings of words – a propensity 'to worry about words' as she described it:

> **LAUREN** (philosophy): [critical thinking] also, I suppose, involves being aware of … well worrying about the meanings of words and attempting to be clear in what one is saying.

Brian (literary/cultural studies – comp.) thought another sign of a critical attitude was a concern for a kind of grammatical 'fluency':

> **BRIAN** (literary/cultural studies – comp.): On one level … [being critical] is about being fluent and articulate in writing and speech. Those are interesting skills. The fact that you are able to write suggests that you are actually able to think. And in a sense one enables the other.

For both Lauren and Brian, a lack of sensitivity to these aspects of language – as demonstrated in the misuse of certain key words, or the construction of ill-formed sentences – was a clear indication of the lack of a critical approach:

> **LAUREN** (philosophy): One aspect in which I find people rather uncritical in some areas is that they use words without really thinking about what those words mean. Of course if you don't really know what the words mean, then you don't really know what you're saying and then you can't really be critical.

> **BRIAN** (literary/cultural studies – comp.): So people who write sentences that don't have verbs, there is a problem when you come to reading it. What did he want to say – it's just not propositional.

Language for specific purposes

The other strand in discussions about language was focused not on some general facility, but rather on students having an understanding of the language and terminology related to a specific area of study – or what we might call the 'discourse' of a particular discipline. Zoe (literary/cultural studies – comp.), for example, explained that in her subject *Media and Communications*, a major challenge for students was coming to terms with the 'particular language we speak' (as she described it), and especially to have a grasp of the particular inflection that a term can assume within particular disciplinary contexts.

> **ZOE** (literary/cultural studies – comp.): It is a really big problem that we face in first year. [In cultural studies] we speak a very particular language, and students have a lot of trouble getting their heads around that.

Zoe went on to explain that, for her, as good a method as any for determining a student's grasp of material in the subject was evidence in their work of a 'critical and informed' use of terms:

> **ZOE**: I've read countless essays where [students] use a basic term like 'political' or 'ideology' in a slightly weird way and you think they haven't quite got it. When you're marking, I use those sorts of things to gauge their level of understanding in the subject.

Lauren (philosophy) also emphasized the importance of understanding key terms. While in the earlier discussion above, Lauren mentioned the need for students to be concerned in a general sense with the meaning of words ('to worry about them', as she described it), there were some specific terms in her field of philosophy that she felt required particular attention. Examples that she singled out were 'imply' and 'infer' – which, for Lauren, were indispensable terms in the discipline, but ones often confused by students:

> **LAUREN** (philosophy): I mean there are words that we [in philosophy] use in a precise way that a lot of students don't really use in quite the right way. … Well words like 'imply', where we can think that one sentence implies another, and 'infer' where we think of infer as something that people do, and that is a distinction that a lot of students don't get,

Nora (literary/cultural studies – comp.) also elaborated on this semantic dimension, explaining that ideas about the 'meanings of terms' were very much a part of the theoretical underpinnings of her subject. Drawing on this theory, Nora thought that what students needed was an appreciation of a term's history of usage (or 'biography', as she called it), and to understand that the particular meanings a word might have derive very much from the particular discourses of which it is a part. As the following quote suggests, a critical usage of a term would, for Nora, involve not only an understanding of its 'layers of meaning', but also the ability to justify one's usage of it if called upon to do so:

> **NORA** (literary/cultural studies – comp.): You've got to anchor your terms in specific discourses … Students have to know a word's biography. It's consistent with Bakhtin's theory of discourse. He said a word is not alone; a word looks over its shoulder to other words. And words are loaded in everyday language, in discourses of all sorts, and you just have to unpack the layers and tell me what you are using it as, and in what context.

Reflecting on this need for students to be sensitive to field-specific language, several of the informants above (Nora and Zoe) thought that critical thinking could be understood ultimately as a form of linguistic (or discursive) competence. Thus, for Zoe, students really had a critical grasp of the subject when they could 'fluently speak' (and one assumes also 'write') in the particular idiom of the field:

> **ZOE** (literary/cultural studies – comp.): ... if they can speak the language fluently, in a way that relates to how I speak it for example, then that's a student who's got it. So it's that idea of critical thinking being about being able to speak the language.

Nora (literary/cultural studies – comp.) also spoke about the development of students' critical abilities in the same linguistic terms – becoming 'a critic' [in this field], she suggested, was 'like learning a foreign language'. Nora was keen to emphasize the productive and creative potential that the acquisition of this language can provide. For her, when a student has developed a genuine 'fluency', they are then able to use the language in an 'original' way, and significantly, according to Nora, it becomes a 'tool' for their thinking:

> **NORA** (literary/cultural studies – comp.): What [the really good students] do, they don't just mimic a secondary theoretical text ... they actually somehow appropriate it. They use the terminology very fluently and in their own original combinations, to such an extent that they can turn it into their own tool ... When [they] can use the paradigm with such fluency, then you can see that they are there as a critic.

Language and thinking

Among other things, the foregoing discussion in this section raises the complex issue of the relationship between thought and language; that is, whether acts of thinking and of speaking need to be seen as somehow separate and distinct activities, or as ones inextricably related to each other. In the relevant literature on this issue, those favouring the former view tend to be of a mentalist disposition, and mainly see language as the medium through which thoughts – often pre-existing thoughts – are expressed (see, for example, Piaget 1967). The corollary of such a view is that processes of language and literacy learning are thought to inhabit a separate realm of development from those associated with the acquisition of thinking skills. This is broadly the view held by various proponents in the critical thinking movement, who see no particular role for language, beyond the need for students to learn to express themselves clearly. We have heard, in the comments of various informants, some echo of this position – especially from those who emphasized the generic nature of language use.

The alternative view, one advanced by a number of thinkers (e.g. Whorf and Vygostky), insists on an inextricable relationship between the two realms. Rather than being the medium through which thoughts are expressed, language is thought to be the stuff that enables thinking to occur. Thus, according to Vygostky: 'Thought is not merely expressed in words, [but] comes into existence through them' (1962: p.125). The corollary of this position is that the thinking of which one is capable is thought to be dependent in some way on the repertoire of language that one has come to acquire. A version of this position was seen in Brian's earlier observation that there is something about linguistic fluency that enables thinking. Perhaps even closer to this view was Nora's suggestion above, that the real significance of learning the terminology in a field is that it provides one with a critical vocabulary (or set of 'tools'), which in turn gives substance and shape to one's thinking. Much as this is a most interesting issue, it is beyond the scope of this chapter to explore it in any direct way. However, issues of language use – including the discipline-specific nature of this use, will be considered in detail in the next chapter.

4.3.8 Critical thinking as a form of self-reflexiveness

A final notion was an understanding of critical thinking as a form of self-reflexiveness. In many of the previous themes considered so far, 'critical thinking' has typically been thought of as a type of thinking that students need to direct at the knowledge (or whatever it is they are engaged with) in their studies. In this final theme, the particular type of thinking identified is not one directed at a form of knowledge as such, but rather turned back at the originator of these thoughts – the thinking self. This particular understanding of critical thinking was articulated most succinctly by Zoe (literary/cultural studies – comp.):

> **ZOE** (literary/cultural studies – comp.): ... when students are given [material to consider], then for me critical thinking is ... about not only being able to critique the material in front of you, but also to critique your own assumptions about what's in front of you. ... So [it's a] sort of self-consciousness, or self-reflexiveness.

The first of the definitional strands discussed in this paper was the idea of critical thinking as the making of judgements. For those informants who discussed the idea of reflexivity, critical thinking needed to be understood as much as a developing 'awareness' or a 'self-consciousness' about how judgements are made, as the actual judgements (or 'interpretations) themselves:

> **LOIS** (literary/cultural studies – comp.): What we try to assist the students in doing is to become much more self-conscious about the way that they are

making sense of texts. So critical thinking in that context is very much to do with [students] being aware of how they have arrived at the interpretations that they're making.

These ideas would seem to accord, to some extent, with accounts of critical thinking from within the critical thinking movement. In the earlier discussion of kernel definitions, it was noted that an 'awareness' of one's thinking processes was considered an essential quality by a number of writers. Thus, Robert Ennis referred to critical thinking as 'reasonable, *reflective* thinking' (1987: p. 10), and Richard Paul as 'disciplined, *self-directed* thinking' (1987: p. 214). This aspect of critical thinking is also picked up in the list of skill and sub-skills compiled by the Delphi 'panel of critical thinking experts' (Facione 1990), referred to earlier. The cognate skill they identify here is 'self-examination', which involves, among other things, 'the ability to reflect on one's reasoning' for the purpose of 'verifying both the results produced and the correct application of the cognitive skills involved' (1990: p. 10).

Rival metacognitions

While there would appear to be some broad agreement about the particular capacity in question here (i.e. as a form of metacognition or 'thinking about one's thinking'), one notes the very different ways in which it is described. For those in the critical thinking movement, the capacity appears to be thought of mainly in procedural terms – as a form of monitoring, especially to ascertain whether certain pre-existing 'cognitive skills' (or criteria) have been 'correctly' and 'objectively' applied (Facione 1990). In contrast, the informants in the study – or at least those who discussed this aspect of critical thinking – saw both critical thinking, and the way in which it might be reflected upon, in much looser and more organic terms. Zoe, for example, felt that critical thinking was best understood not as an objective set of skills (upon whose application one could then reflect), but as a less circumscribed, and more personal capacity – as an 'attitude' or an 'approach':

> **ZOE** (literary/cultural studies – comp.): I think [of] critical thinking as an attitude, rather than as a specific set of skills. I think of it as an approach to material.

Lois also thought of critical thinking as a more 'contingent' activity, one in which the thinker's own subjectivity invariably plays a role. For Lois, such a view – which she believed was held in many parts of the academy – has its basis in a Kantian epistemological outlook which precludes the possibility of any entirely objective knowledge (or indeed objective critique) of things:

LOIS (literary/cultural studies – comp.): In the back of my mind is Kant's first critique – the critique of pure reason. That's something that I think a lot of people basically now just assume – that one can't know things in themselves; that one's knowledge is always contingent, and is always shaped by one's own perceptual and conceptual apparatus.

Brian, from the same discipline area, also emphasized this contingent quality and thought that to have an appreciation of the 'problem of knowledge' – as well as one's permanently 'fraught' relationship with it – lay at the heart of a genuinely critical outlook. For him, it was those students whose engagement with the subject gave no indication of this type of 'reflexivity' who really struggled:

BRIAN (literary/cultural studies – comp.): Knowledge of whatever is a much more fraught process than we might initially think .... The worst writing from students is that which does not give a sense that all this is problematic.

Thus, we can recognize in these statements a rather different view of the desired form of metacognition. Whereas those in the critical thinking movement tend to see reflection as a means to improving the quality of one's thinking, the informants in the present study who commented on these matters saw the basis for this thinking in more ontological terms – that is, to ultimately have a better understanding of one's self:

LOIS (literary/cultural studies – comp.): So [critical in this sense is] being aware about how you come to make certain kinds of judgements and argument.

NELL (history): [critical thinking] also has an element of reflectivity ... of self-criticism in it, the idea being that when we teach students well, they will understand themselves better.

4.4 Conclusions

The preceding discussion has outlined the ways in which academics from a range of disciplinary backgrounds understand the notion of critical thinking. There are several conclusions that can be drawn from their various commentaries. The first is that, far from being a largely 'buried' and 'ineffable' concept within university education, as is suggested in some of the literature, it would appear that academics – or those who took part in the study at least – have quite developed understandings of the notion, ones that they are able to articulate in cogent and often very engaging ways.

Another conclusion is that the idea of critical thinking would seem to defy reduction to some narrow and readily-identifiable cognitive mode. Instead,

much variety emerged from the interviews in the way that academics understood the term. This was evident not only in the differing accounts of various
informants, but also, on occasions, in the variety of conceptions articulated by
a single informant. Along with seeing critical thinking as a fundamentally polysemous term, the evidence from the interviews suggests that it is also a contested one. This was evident in a number of quite divergent, even incompatible,
accounts by informants – for example, in the different views expressed about
whether critical thinking is at heart an 'evaluative' mode, or a more 'constructive' one; or whether the term necessarily entails the adopting of an ethical and
activist stance towards the world.

While the semantic field surrounding our notion is clearly a most rich and
complex one, one can nevertheless recognize in this complexity the potential
for a fair amount of confusion. One thing that seems clear from the findings
described so far is that any simple, minimally-worded directive to students 'to
adopt the right critical approach' in a subject is unlikely to be very helpful or
enlightening. Indeed, such a suggestion, on its own, would seem to imply quite
an array of possible modes and outlooks. The interview material clearly shows a
diversity of understandings; what is not so clear at this point in the investigation
is what the main source of this variation might be. In the next chapter, the
intention is to explore these variations in a systematic way by looking at the ways
in which the concept finds expression in a range of teaching materials from
within the specific disciplinary groupings.

Chapter 5

Critical Thinking: The Disciplinary Dimension

5.1 Introduction to the Textual Analysis

The previous chapter considered some of the different conceptions of critical thinking held by academics, as reported by them in interviews. While data of this kind – the reported accounts of individuals – can provide useful insights into the phenomenon in question, there are some clear limitations to such an approach. As mentioned in Chapter 3, doubt is expressed in the literature about whether, within an interview format, it is possible for an individual to experience authentically the phenomenon they are considering; that is to say, in this case, whether an academic who is asked about the nature of critical thinking on their particular programme can fully describe what this actually involves in practice (Mishler 1980). Reservations such as these have led some to question the nature of results obtained from survey investigations into the teaching and assessment practices of academics. It has been queried, for example, whether the results reflect what an informant actually does, or whether it is more what they think they do; or even, as one critic has suggested, what they in fact aspire to do (Horowitz 1986). Thus, as was suggested in Chapter 3, there is a need to supplement the findings described in the previous chapter with data more directly related to the teaching practices themselves.

In this chapter, these conceptions of critical thinking are investigated further by drawing on data of a textual nature. These data, consisting of various documents and assignment tasks set for students on their courses, constitute an important part of the actual teaching practices within a discipline. Three different types of texts were collected and analysed for the investigation:

i.   advice protocol documents
ii. exercise tasks
iii. essay tasks

The 'advice protocols' were documents produced within the disciplines investigated, and which were designed to advise students about appropriate modes of study and thinking in the discipline area, with an emphasis – in most instances – on how students should go about preparing and writing assignments.

The 'exercise task' documents were tasks typically set for undergraduate students in the early phases of courses with the objective of developing the basic skills and approaches necessary for effective engagement in the discipline area. In the rubric of some, but not all, of these tasks, the nature of these skills and the rationale for their development are explicitly outlined. The final type of data, the 'essay tasks', were the main assessment tasks set for students by the various informants who took part in the study. The corpus collected for this final type of data was larger than for the other two, with the subsequent analysis of the 'essay task' texts constituting the major part of this section of the research. The justification for this particular emphasis is to be found in the central place that the essay task occupies in undergraduate programmes (Dudley-Evans 2002). It is arguably in these tasks – which prescribe explicitly the type of materials students need to engage with, as well as the nature of that engagement – that ideas about critical thinking as an educational ideal are most clearly inscribed.

All documents considered in this part of the research were provided by the study's informants. It is important to stress that the analysis conducted here was not intended to be evaluative in any way – that is, to provide commentary on such matters as the adequacy of these materials, or their likely effectiveness as instances of pedagogical discourse. As has been stressed, the investigation was conceived within a broadly ethnographic framework, with a focus more on describing conceptions of critical thinking – along with the educational practices through which these conceptions are expressed – rather than subjecting them to any explicit critical scrutiny.

The analysis of the documents collected for this part of the study was conducted in two stages. The first stage involved a 'macro reading' of the documents, with the purpose of identifying their main contents, especially in relation to the nature of the thinking prescribed, or suggested, in them. In the second part, a discourse analysis of the documents was conducted using the linguistic framework outlined in detail in Chapter 3. To recap briefly, this framework, designed to enable a systematic exploration of 'critical' elements in the documents, takes in three semantic categories:

i.   object of inquiry
ii. process of inquiry
iii. content of inquiry

as summarized below in Table 4. As explained earlier, in the analytical procedure, the first of these categories – the *object of inquiry* – was considered the primary category, and was used as an anchor for the analysis of the other two categories.

Whereas the previous chapter was organized along thematic lines without explicit attention given to disciplinary-based variation in responses, this chapter seeks to explore the issue of interfield variation in a direct way. The findings in the chapter are thus presented in order of the three disciplinary groupings

Table 4 Summary of categories used in analysis

OBJECT OF INQUIRY	PROCESSES OF INQUIRY	CONTENT OF INQUIRY
Which epistemic entities specifically are to be analysed? (e.g. *statements, conclusions, theories, actions, events* etc.)	What type of thinking processes is it envisaged that students will be engaged in, including the outcomes of these processes? (e.g. *judging, evaluating, viewing* etc.)	By which criteria or categories are these entities to be analysed? (e.g. for their *logic, usefulness, legitimacy* etc.)

being considered – namely, history, philosophy, literary/cultural studies. The interest in the analysis is both in what appears similar and what appears different in the ways that the idea of critical thinking is constructed in the documents analysed from these disciplines.

5.2 Advice Protocol Documents in the Three Disciplines

A feature of undergraduate study in the contemporary university is the growing provision of pedagogical materials aimed at facilitating students' studies on their courses. This trend can be seen in part as a consequence of the considerable expansion in recent decades in the number and diversity of students undertaking tertiary study – and a recognition on the part of faculties and departments that students nowadays do not necessarily commence their courses with the familiarity and preparedness for university study that could once be assumed (Baldauf 1996). Indeed, the problems described earlier regarding students' often incomplete understandings of the notion of critical thinking might be seen as part of this perceived need. One type of material now often available to students to assist in their 'transition' to university study is what is referred to here as 'advice protocol' documents. Whereas in the past, the purpose of such documents was mainly confined to providing students with information about specific citation and referencing conventions in the field, nowadays the coverage is often quite comprehensive. In many of these documents, there is a focus on the types of assessment tasks that students will encounter in their study, along with advice about how they need to go about researching, writing – and indeed thinking – about these tasks in order to be successful in their academic work.

The particular advice protocol documents selected for analysis were those identified in the study as the principal information sources provided, or recommended, to students at the beginning of their studies in each of the three discipline areas. Some of these were made available in hard copy and typically contained in subject outline documents, or else were included on school websites and recommended to students for them to access. While most of these documents were not designed to directly address the issue of critical thinking *per se*, it will be seen that the term 'critical' is used frequently in them, and emerges as a key theme in many of the ideas and suggestions they present.

5.2.1 History document

The main material provided to history students to guide their academic work in the School of Historical Studies at University X was a document entitled *History Essay Writing Guide*. This document, running to about 9,000 words, was recommended to all students studying in the school and was available on the school website. It was also printed in various subject outline booklets that were provided to students. It was explained by several informants that the document had 'official status' within the school, having been produced under the auspices of the school's Education Committee, and involving input from a number of the school's staff. Although the bulk of the guide's content was put together by one particular staff member, it was explained that an initial draft was circulated in the school, and was revised subsequently drawing on input from a range of others. In this way, the document might be said to reflect a collective disciplinary view – as opposed to a particular individual view – regarding the way in which students are expected to engage with knowledge in the subject area. The perspective provided in the *History Essay Writing Guide* is also a generic one in the sense that it outlines a general approach for students to adopt, without seeking to make account of any possible variations related to such factors as type of essay task, area of historical study, level of study and the like.

Description of contents:

As the title of the document suggests, the *History Essay Guide* was mainly concerned with explaining to students the approaches and methods they need to adopt in order to produce effective written work in the school. Although focused on the particular skills of essay writing *per se* – described as 'one of the most important aspects of study in an arts degree' – the guide does seek to give a general account of how students should approach their studies in history. Brief coverage is also provided, for example, about other types of assessable work set for students in the school – 'tutorial exercises and examinations'. In the introductory section, entitled *the purpose of essay writing*, an attempt is made to outline both the skills underlying successful writing and study in the faculty in general, and those relating to history in particular. The former list includes the following putative skills:

5.01   *the ability to summarize and paraphrase the work of other writers, the development of arguments and conclusions, and the effective use of evidence to support a case*

Those skills relating particularly to history are given as:

5.02   *research, analyzing different forms of source material, using different kinds of evidence, and writing strong, critical and clear arguments*

While one detects in these two different lists some overlap of categories (e.g. 'the development/writing of arguments'), among the history-specific items there would seem to be some additional emphasis on skills related to the analysis and use of different forms of 'source material' and 'evidence'.

The remainder of the opening section of the document elaborates on what might be involved for students in presenting an 'argument' in their work (also referred to in the document variously as 'contention', 'thesis', 'position', 'case' and 'point of view'). It is pointed out, for example, that the best essays have 'a clear line of argument', one which is 'supported and defended', which is 'developed point-by-point' and which 'arrives at strong, clear conclusions'. An additional point made in an accompanying section (called *who is an essay written for?*) is the idea that students should always argue on the basis of what they genuinely believe to be the case (based on 'information they gather and also their review of different historical interpretations'), rather than seek to 'target [their] arguments for particular lecturers'. It is suggested further that some of the more successful arguments produced by students are in fact those with which lecturers 'do not necessarily agree', or which 'challenge their [particular] interpretations'.

Much of the remainder of the document is concerned with outlining for students the various processes and steps they need to undertake in order to produce an effective essay. There are sections, for example, on *comprehending the question or topic; coming up with an argument; planning the draft; writing the draft; introducing the argument* and *using different kinds of evidence*. As these section titles suggest, there is a fair amount of additional elaboration on the idea of students presenting an argument in their work. To make this clear to students, the document presents the following imaginary history essay topic:

5.03   *Would you agree with the argument that respect for the natural environment is a recent discovery for residents of Mars?*

It then outlines several possible 'arguments' that could be advanced by students in response, namely:

5.04   *Yes, because prior to the environmental movements of the 1960s, the majority of Martians were more interested in exploiting than respecting the natural environment.*

Or:

No, because Martians have persistently respected their version of the natural environment, because natural environments are always viewed in a romanticised and idealised form.

It is explained that a successful essay will then be concerned with the 'development' and 'defence' of the argument that has been proposed.

This use of textual samples is a notable feature of the document. Thus, students are given examples of how they might go about 'developing and defending' one of the possible arguments above. It is suggested, for example, that a mounting of the 'no case' above would typically involve the presenting of 'appropriate evidence' (e.g. [*by*] *listing and giving examples of different idealizations of the natural environment in the nineteenth century*) along with some 'assessment of the interpretations of other historians' (e.g. [*by*] *reviewing the different interpretations of historian* [*who have written on the subject*], *and showing why* [*a particular interpretation*] *fits better with the evidence*). The remainder of the document is largely taken up with practical advice about the drafting and editing of work, along with information about methods for citing and referencing sources.

Analysis of 'critical' elements in history document

As explained previously, the purpose of analysing these 'advice protocol' documents was to see what light they might shed on broad discipline-based conceptions of critical thinking. In the preceding discussion, an account has been given of some of the general academic skills thought to be necessary for students to engage effectively in the discipline area, especially in relation to matters of researching and writing. To investigate specifically how critical thinking is conceptualized in the guide, a second stage of analysis was conducted with a systematic focus on those sections of the document that actually draw explicitly on the terminology of 'critique'. In this part of the analysis, the three 'critical' elements – *object, processes* and *content* – were relied upon.

The analysis of the *History Essay Guide* found a total of 10 mentions of the term 'critical' or the variants 'criticism', 'critically' and so on (1 token per 900 words). The first point to note is that the idea of 'critical thinking' (or 'being critical' etc.) was not specifically described or defined for students in the document, but rather was referred to in passing as some desirable quality that students need to adopt in their studies. The following extract (with two mentions of the term 'critical') is an example of this 'incidental' reference in the document.

> 5.05   *Don't take anything on trust: be a* **critical** *reader of all kinds of sources and texts, and use your* **critical** *analysis of both primary and secondary sources in your essay*

Employing the linguistic framework above, we can see, in this particular example, that what is specifically to be critiqued (*object of inquiry*) is 'all kinds of sources and texts' present in the first clause, and 'both primary and secondary sources' in the second. (It is not exactly clear whether the two particular denotations used for 'sources' here are intended to be synonymous.) The *processes* of critique that can be identified are 'reading' in the first instance, and 'analysing' ('use of your critical analysis') in the second. In this case, the evaluative criterion to be employed (*content of inquiry*) is one of 'trusting sources'.

Focusing on the *object of inquiry* category throughout the document, it was noted that students were enjoined to direct their thinking towards a range of epistemic entities (see Table 5 for summary).

Object of inquiry #1: Students' own arguments

The first, and perhaps most overarching, of these entities was students' own 'arguments', as noted in the list of requisite skills in history outlined at the beginning of the document:

5.06   *Essay writing in History is particularly aimed at helping you progressively develop your skills in research, analyzing different forms of source material, using different kinds of evidence, and writing strong,* **critical** *and clear arguments*

It is worth noting that this type of critique (i.e. one aimed at developing an argument or point of view in relation to a particular issue) fits very much with that particular version of critical thinking observed in the interviews that emphasized the more creative and constructive dimensions of critique (*critical thinking as simple originality*).

Object of inquiry #2: Texts – secondary

Other epistemic entities given prominence in the document were 'the primary and secondary sources', noted in the first example cited above (#5.05). Of these, the most commonly mentioned were the secondary sources (referred to as 'secondary interpretations of other historians' or 'work of other historians'), as in the following extracts:

5.07   [*a function of the history essay is*] *to develop and defend an argument or contention by discussing and analyzing a range of appropriate evidence, and by* **critically** *assessing the interpretations of other historians*

5.08   [*the desired outcome of essays*] *include developing skills ... in the* **critical** *analysis of secondary interpretations by other historians*

5.09   *You should argue the case which you think emerges most clearly from the evidence, and from your **critical** review of other historians' work*

5.10   *Basically, each stage of your argument should be developed and defended in turn, by showing your interpretation of the appropriate evidence, by **critically** reviewing the work of other historians, and by using example, case study and explanation*

The *processes* of critique referred to here include: 'analysing', 'assessing', and 'reviewing'. As can be seen in most of the statements above (#5.07, #5.09, #5.10), these *processes* of 'reviewing' and 'assessing' the secondary interpretations of historians are seen as, in a sense, subsidiary to the principal *process* of students 'developing and defending their own argument'.

Object of inquiry #3: Texts – primary

Reference was also made to primary texts ('documents', 'primary documentary sources'), although these were less numerous than references to the secondary works, and the information provided about the nature and purpose of the critique was less explicit. Students are informed, for example, that a skill to be developed in the process of essay writing is:

5.11   *a greater understanding of documentary **criticism** and interpretation*

In the extract below (#5.12), there is some indication of what this form of 'criticism and interpretation' might involve, including the identifying of points of view, assumptions, rhetorical strategies and the like:

5.12   *these types of sources [primary documentary sources] should ... be read **critically**: analysed for their point of view, for the assumptions, ideas and understandings which inform them, and for the strategies writers use to advance their arguments*

Object of inquiry #4: Students' own writing

One final entity mentioned that students needed to direct their thinking towards was 'their own writing', including the particular ways that they use language. Thus, in a final section entitled *writing clearly and effectively*, students are encouraged to adopt a critical approach to their writing, and especially to try to avoid any of the failings that may have been identified in previously submitted work.

5.13   *Take responsibility for **critically** ... assessing your own writing. Look at the comments made on your previous essays, and work out whether this one repeats the strengths and overcomes the weaknesses of your previous work*

Another reference to being critical in this section relates to the use of language – in particular, the need for students to avoid using 'discriminatory' language.

> 5.14   *It is also important to use language **critically**, which is one good reason for using non-discriminatory language. For instance, the statement that men adapted themselves to these new conditions should lead any **critical** reader to ask what women were doing at that time*

Summary

Table 5 summarizes the specific language used in the document around the notion of critique, according to the three categories of analysis. As mentioned, the analysis was organized around an initial identification of the different *objects of inquiry* which generate the different critique types indicated in Column 1. The main pattern to be identified in the data would appear to be the systematic distinction drawn in the document between the critiquing of primary sources on the one hand, and of secondary sources on the other (Type 2 & 3).

The limited linguistic data generated from the analysis (including the lack of any comprehensive language around the third category (*content of inquiry*) precludes too many additional conclusions being drawn at this point; there are,

Table 5   Critical elements in history advice protocol document – by *object of inquiry type*

T Y P E	OBJECT OF INQUIRY What type of entity is to be analysed?		PROCESS OF INQUIRY By which type of mental/ verbal process?	CONTENT OF INQUIRY By which analytical criteria/categories?
1	students' own arguments	(1)*	writing	clarity/strength
2	secondary interpretations/ works of other historians	(5)	analysing/assessing/ reviewing	ND**
3	documents/primary sources	(3)	analysing/discussing/ reading/interpreting	identification of point of view/assumptions/ ideas/argumentative strategies
2/3	all kinds of sources and texts	(1)	reading	trustworthiness
4	students' own writing (*including students' use of language*)	(2)	assessing	strengths and weaknesses/ non-discriminatory language

*   Number in brackets refers to number of mentions of term 'critical' collocated with particular *object of inquiry*

**   ND indicates no data in text for this category

nevertheless, several provisionally observed patterns that warrant some comment. The first was the tendency for the term 'critical' to be used more emphatically in relation to the secondary source material that students need to consider. Furthermore, one also detects some small variation in the types of *processes* collocated with each of these source-types. Thus, for the secondary sources, we see the use of verbs with a more 'evaluative' tenor ('assessing', 'reviewing'), compared to those used with the primary sources ('discussing', 'reading', 'interpreting') which are suggestive of a more 'interpretative' activity. These patterns of word usage are most clearly demonstrated in the following extract from the document where an attempt is made to lay out the principal intellectual tasks for students working in the discipline:

5.15   [*students need*] *to develop and defend an argument or contention by discussing and analyzing a range of appropriate evidence, and by* **critically** *assessing the interpretations of other historians*

5.2.2 Philosophy document

The main guide material recommended to students in the School of Philosophy and Bioethics was a document that was not in fact produced within the school, but one originating from a philosophy department at another university. The document, entitled *A Guide to Researching and Writing Philosophy Essays*, was posted on the school's website and was recommended to students as a 'useful resource'. Information provided in the document suggests that it was produced in a manner similar to the history guide – that is, authored principally by an individual staff member, but with input from a range of other philosophy staff, including staff from other institutions. It is not known how it came about that this particular material was selected for dissemination within the School of Philosophy and Bioethics. Despite its origins being from outside the school, the document would appear, nevertheless, to represent a collectively agreed-upon view regarding the necessary skills and approaches in this discipline area, and, like the history guide, also constitutes a generic approach to the field.

Description of contents

The general contents of the *Guide to Researching and Writing Philosophy Essays* were found to be similar in many respects to the history guide considered above. The document had the same practical focus, with the aim of giving those who were new to the discipline some 'preliminary advice' about how to approach their work. Issues covered included: *interpreting essay topics; researching and reading for an essay; writing and drafting; the documenting of written work* (footnotes etc.). Interestingly, the rationale given in the document for making such a guide available to students is the suggestion that studying and writing in philosophy is somehow distinct from certain secondary school subjects likely to be more familiar to students, such as literature and history – coincidentally the other disciplines considered in the present investigation.

5.16   *Most of you will have written essays in school for English, History, etc. A Philosophy essay is something a little different [from these]*

In explaining what is distinctive about studying and writing in philosophy, the document makes an initial distinction between 'having a philosophy' and 'doing philosophy'. The former is described as something everyone engages in – that is, taking on various 'basic beliefs and concepts', often in an unconscious way, 'about the world and ourselves'. In contrast, 'doing philosophy', the version of philosophy relevant to university study, is described as an activity involving the 'self-conscious unearthing and rigorous examination of these basic beliefs and concepts'. Such an examination, the document suggests, involves a continual process of asking questions, responding to these questions, and then asking further questions. This method is described as 'dialectic' and 'conversational' in nature, and suggested in the document as the basis of much thinking in the Western tradition:

5.17   *This dialectic of question and response is part of a tradition of thinking – a great conversation – that dates back to the Ancient Greeks and has been a fundamental influence in the development of the science, art, literature and politics of Western civilization*

The document goes on to give an account of the types of questions that students need typically to consider in their work in the discipline. Here a rough distinction is made between what are termed 'text-focused' topics and 'issue-' or 'problem-focused' topics. 'Text-focused' topics, it is explained, require students to focus on a particular writer's argument on an issue, as shown in the following examples:

5.18   *Discuss critically David Hume's account of causation in Part III of Book I of his A Treatise of Human Nature.*

Was Wittgenstein right to say that the meaning of a word is its use in the language?

In contrast, 'issue-focused' topics, as the document explains, are more concerned with 'a particular philosophical issue without reference to a particular text' as in the following:

5.19   *Is voluntary euthanasia morally permissible?*

What is scientific method?

The document goes on to suggest that, even though these topics are structured differently, in practice the types of responses they tend to elicit are often of a similar order. This is because, in responding to 'problem-focused' topics, students will typically draw on the particular texts of philosophers as a basis for exploring the problem being considered. Similarly, for 'text-focused' topics, the text(s) that one is called on to consider will typically be the attempts by a philosopher (or philosophers) to deal with a particular philosophical problem or issue.

Continuing in the same 'analytical' vein, the *Guide* goes on to suggest that irrespective of the type of essay that is being dealt with, students need to be concerned in their work with two essential 'functions' – 'exposition' and 'critical discussion':

> 5.20   *your essay [needs to] perform two basic functions (your understanding and your skills apply to both):*
>
> - **an exposition** *of the problem or issue in question (often as it is posed in some particular text); and*
> - **critical** *discussion of the problem or text.*
>
> (original emphasis)

The bulk of the document is then concerned with explaining the nature of these two functions. Under a subheading of *exposition*, it is explained that the main task for students is to outline 'in their own words' what they think an issue is, or what a text means. This exposition is described as an 'analytical' process, involving the 'breaking down' of a text or issue into its 'constitutive elements' and distinguishing the different parts that go to make up its meaning or argument. It is stressed to students that this expository aspect of their work should be aimed strictly at 'elucidating the meanings of a text or issue', without allowing one's own views to impinge on the account:

> 5.21   *Your interpretation ought … not serve merely as a 'coat-hanger' for putting forth your own favoured views on the matter in question.*

The opportunity for the expression of one's own ideas, the document explains, lies in the function of 'critical discussion'.

In the *critical discussion* section of the document, the idea of being 'critical' is given some explicit glossing. Thus, it is explained to students that the term derives from the classical Greek for 'to decide or judge', and that the goal for them in this aspect of their work is to come to some 'conclusion' or 'judgement' about what they have dealt with in their exposition. The document here has most to say about how students should go about judging specific philosophical texts or extracts of text (e.g. *Hume's account of causation in A Treatise of Human Nature*). These judgements, it is suggested, will be mainly positive or negative.

A negative judgement, it is explained, is arrived at by challenging the 'validity of an argument's reasoning', or querying any 'questionable assumptions' identified in it. Where one seeks to offer support, the best means to do this is by defending the argument against any criticisms (real or imagined) that could be mounted against it. The document stresses that being 'critical' therefore does not necessarily mean being 'destructive' or 'negative' as is often assumed by students, but can be equally 'constructive' about whatever it is that one is appraising. One notes in passing, however, that the suggested method here for being positive about an argument is, in fact, to be 'negatively critical' about any of the objections that may be made about it.

Analysis of 'critical' elements in philosophy document

As with the history text, investigation was made of the specific 'critical' elements in the philosophy guide (see Table 6 for a summary of these elements). A total of 17 mentions of the term 'critical' (or variants) were noted in the document (1 token per 1,000 words), a number proportionally similar to that found in the history document. As suggested above, the use of the term 'critical' was a little more explicit in the philosophy document, with the term actually defined for students, and also used in the title of a major section of the guide – *critical discussion*. Most references to the term were found in this particular section.

The specific epistemic entities (*object of inquiry*) to which students need to direct their critical thinking are in fact spelt out quite explicitly in the description of what is required in a 'critical discussion':

> 5.22 *Here* [*In the* **critical** *discussion section*] *you should attempt to develop a response to the issues which your exposition has made clear, and/or, in the case of a discussion of some particular text, attempt to give a* **critical** *evaluation of the author's treatment of the issue.*

Thus, it is made clear to students that the focus of their thinking will typically be on either an 'issue' or 'a particular text(s)' – a distinction that is in keeping with the analysis of essay types noted above.

Object of inquiry #1: Philosophical texts

The term 'critical' was invoked most frequently for the philosophical texts, referred to variously as a 'particular author's text', 'author's argument and/or views', or 'philosopher in question', as in the following additional examples:

> 5.23 *You ought to be patient and sympathetic in your exposition, even if you intend later to* **criticise** *heavily the philosopher in question. (Indeed, the better the exposition in this regard, usually the more effective the* **critique***.)*

>   5.24   *In the case of a **critical** analysis of a particular author's text, you can nega-*
>   *tively **criticise** the author's arguments by pointing out questionable assump-*
>   *tions, invalid reasoning, etc.*

>   5.25   *If you think that the text is good, then your **critical** discussion can be positive.*
>   *This can be done by revealing its 'hidden virtues'.*

The *processes* of critique referred to here include: 'appraising', 'discussing', 'crit-icizing (heavily)', and 'being negative or positive', with a greater overall empha-sis on the notion of negative evaluation. A number of additional processes mentioned relate to the specific ways in which one might be positive or negative in the appraisal of these texts, and indicate certain evaluative criteria to be applied (*content of inquiry*). Thus, in support of a negative judgement, students are advised that they should focus on any 'questionable assumptions' or 'invalid reasoning' they might identify in a text. What might be involved in the framing of a positive appraisal is a little less clear. It is suggested that students should seek to 'reveal [a text's] hidden virtues', either by showing that there may be 'more to an author's argument' than is otherwise apparent, or, as indicated above, by defending the text against the criticisms that may be made of it by others.

Object of inquiry #2: Philosophical issues

The other main *object of inquiry* contained in the document is a philosophical 'issue'; that is, some general philosophical question unattributed to any particu-lar philosopher or text (also denoted as 'belief', 'concept', 'view' or 'problem'). Examples of such 'issues' indicated in the document are the following essay topics:

>   5.26   *Is voluntary euthanasia morally permissible?*
>
>   *What is scientific method?*

As mentioned already, the term 'critical' was applied less often in the accounts of how students should engage with such 'issues'. In the limited references made, the *processes of inquiry* suggest less emphasis on the idea of 'negative appraisal', and more on the development of a 'constructive response', as in the following example:

>   5.27   *Where you are not primarily concerned with evaluating or responding to a par-*
>   *ticular text, your **critical** discussion can be more focused on your own construc-*
>   *tive response to the issue.*

Limited information is also provided about the type of criteria (*content of inquiry*) that should be applied in making this 'constructive response'. This is confined to the statement below, where it is suggested that students need to consider the 'rational grounds or justification' for the particular view they are considering (e.g. 'the moral permissibility of voluntary euthanasia'):

> 5.28 *In doing [Philosophy], we try to clarify the meanings of [certain] beliefs and concepts and to evaluate* **critically** *their rational grounds or justification.*

Object of inquiry #3: Objections and criticisms

In most instances, the *objects of inquiry* around the use of the term 'critical' were found to be either the attributed texts or unattributed issues. For each of these, however, a related epistemic entity is invoked, one that it is suggested students also need to devote themselves to in managing the function of 'critical discussion'. These are the 'criticisms' or 'objections' that might typically be made about an argument or position that students are considering. Thus, in relation to a particular issue, students are advised that as a matter of course they should deal 'critically' with any anticipated 'objections' or 'criticisms' that could be mounted against them as a way of 'defending' their position, as in the following:

> 5.29 *[you should] consider some of the various objections to and questions about your views that others might or have put forward, and try to respond* **critically** *to them in defence of your own line of thinking.*

Similarly, in dealing with a particular philosopher's text, it is suggested that a useful move is to defend the text against any possible or actual criticisms made by others. This is thought to be especially appropriate in those cases where students wish to argue for a text's virtues:

> 5.30 *[Being positive about a text] can be done by ... defending an author against possible and/or actual* **criticisms***.*

Summary

These additional *objects of inquiry* ('criticisms' and 'objections') are shown in Table 6. Their designations as 1A and 2A in the table are intended to indicate the dependent relationship they have with the two main *objects of inquiry* that we have considered ('texts' and 'issues'). This particular configuration of elements, one that suggests an argumentative sequence of *exposition of argument > criticism of argument > criticism of criticism (of argument)*, is very much in keeping with the 'dialectic', 'conversational' model of thinking outlined at the beginning of the guide. The extract below from the document (#5.31) – which outlines an objection to Descartes – is designed to show students how the two

Table 6 Critical elements in philosophy advice protocol document – by type of *object of inquiry*

T Y P E	OBJECT OF INQUIRY What type of entity is to be analysed?		PROCESS OF INQUIRY By which type of mental/ verbal process?	CONTENT OF INQUIRY By which analytical criteria/categories?
1	philosopher in question/ particular author's text/ author's treatment of an issue/David Hume's account of causation (*as example*)	(5)	critically analysing/ discussing critically/ evaluating/criticizing heavily/negatively criticizing/being negative or positive	questionable assumptions/invalid reasoning/hidden virtues
1A	criticisms of philosopher	(1)	defending philosopher	ND
2	issues/beliefs/ concepts/ views	(3)	evaluating critically/ responding/responding constructively	rational grounds justification
2A	objections to/questions- about view	(1)	responding critically in defence	ND

latter moves in the sequence (*criticism of argument* > *criticism of criticism*) might typically be realized in extended prose.

5.31   *'Norman Malcolm argues that Descartes is mistaken in assuming that dreams and waking episodes have the same content. However, Malcolm fails to appreciate the subtlety of Descartes' argument in the First Meditation, which allows Descartes to claim …'*

5.2.3 Literary/cultural studies documents

The use of advice protocol documents for analysis in the third discipline area – literary/cultural studies – was not as straightforward as it was for history and philosophy. Whereas for each of these two disciplines, a single document was available for students to refer to, on the literary/cultural studies programmes no such generic account was found to exist. In the earlier introductory discussion about the nature of the broad discipline areas covered in the study, it was noted that the field of literary/cultural studies has been marked by particularly high levels of difference and disputation, arguably to a greater degree than the other disciplines considered. These differences have been expressed, as we have seen, not only over the issue of how one should approach the analysis of literary texts, but also about the even more fundamental question of what constitutes a literary text in the first place (Eagleton 1996: p. 183). At University X, such differences, as described earlier, have played out in the partitioning of literary/cultural stud-ies into two separate administrative entities. The lack of a single protocol docu-ment for students studying in the area of literary/cultural studies can be seen as additional evidence of this divergence in the ranks.

Thus, in the absence of a single sustained account of recommended practices in the field, it was necessary in this part of the study to draw on two sets of materials – ones developed for the two different programmes: English literature and comparative literature/cultural studies. As well as having a different disci-plinary focus, the documents analysed were found to vary a good deal in their length, format and the extent of their distribution in the faculty. Details about the two documents used in the analysis are outlined below:

i.   Document 1: *Frequently asked questions: Literature* – web-based materials developed within department for first-year English literature students – 3,500 words.
ii. Document 2: *Introduction to the analysis of a literary text* – paper-based handout material developed by individual lecturer in the Centre for Comparative Literature and Cultural Studies and distributed to her first-year students – 2,000 words.

Because of the specialist nature of the data compiled for this part of the research, the presentation of findings below follows a slightly different format from that used in the preceding sections. The two documents above are discussed sepa-rately in turn, with an attempt later on to identify elements both common and different in each.

Document 1: 'Frequently asked questions' (English literature)

This web-based document, as explained by the informant who provided it, was developed as a cooperative activity within the Department of English Litera-ture, and was intended to guide new students in the preparation of their written work. The subject it was especially targeted at was a first-year unit entitled *Read-ing Literature*, referred to as 'your standard introductory literature subject'.

Description of contents

Using an FAQ format, the document is perhaps a little less systematic in its cov-erage of issues than in those from the other discipline areas. Some of the ques-tions considered include:

- How do I relate to the world of the text?
- How can I avoid 'just describing' in an essay?

- What analytical framework should I use when reading texts?
- How much should I read for an essay?

A number of broad themes emerge from the responses to these questions, many of which touch on the various conceptions of critical thinking that have been considered so far.

The first concerns the nature of literature, and the way students need to engage with it. This theme is mainly discussed in terms of the kinds of misconceptions that students bring to literary studies. Chief among these is a tendency for some to judge the 'world of the text' not on its own terms, but according to the values and standards of the world that the student-reader inhabits. Thus, the document advises students against falling too easily into simple judgements, especially moral judgements concerning the types of situations and people depicted in literary works. Any recourse to the making of such judgements, the document suggests, needs to involve reflecting on one's own assumptions and those of the culture that one inhabits.

> 5.32   *A student might want to say 'That's wrong, that's an inadequacy in the world view of the text'. They can say that, but it requires a lot of confidence on the part of the student. They would also need to have faced their own value system to make that kind of judgement.*

The document goes on to suggest that what students fundamentally need to do is make some 'imaginative leap', and try to enter sensitively into the historical and psychological world of a literary work. The purpose of such a reading, it is suggested, is to 'broaden horizons' and to be able to imagine other worlds. Such a view fits very much with the type of 'empathic' view of reading expressed by a number of informants in interview – for example, by Lois (literary/cultural studies – comp.), who thought that any engagement with literature should never be concerned in the first instance with judgement or condemnation of a work, but rather with trying to understand and appreciate 'the legacy of certain ways of thinking'.

Another theme to emerge in this document is the need for students not to just 'describe' what happens in a text (or 'to tell the story in one's own words'), but to provide some 'analysis' of it. As we have seen, the distinguishing between modes of this kind is a recurring theme in much of the protocol material considered, evident, for example, in the systematic distinction drawn in the philosophy document between 'exposition' and 'critical discussion'. In the case of the literature document, it is explained that the providing of an 'analysis' involves both identifying the 'crucial ideas (or 'themes') that lie at the centre of a story', and also showing in one's 'interpretation' how these ideas emerge through the various elements of which the work is comprised (for example, 'metaphors that are used, symbolic moments, actions or objects in the story'):

5.33   *An example of 'just description' is when you tell the story in your own words, or you provide a summary of the nature of the characters, but you neglect to indicate what the theme of the story is and how the various elements in the story contribute to making the theme more evident.*

In the document, the idea of advancing an argument is seen to consist mainly in the identification and demonstration of 'theme'.

A final area of focus is the need for students to distinguish between their own interpretation of a literary work (the primary text), and those found in secondary works. This distinction, it will be recalled, was a major theme in the history protocol. However, whereas in the history document engagement with secondary accounts was thought to be an indispensable part of developing a 'critical argument', the role of such sources is somewhat downplayed here. The best use to be made of the critics, the document suggests, is as a 'starting point' or 'stimulation' for the developing of one's own critical view, and to understand in advance of reading a text what the 'important critical issues' might be. However, the use of such sources, the document suggests, is optional; students are advised that very good essays can in fact be written 'without consulting a secondary source at all'. Thus, it is suggested that the focus of one's attention in the study of literature should always be squarely on the work itself. This involves, among other things, always seeking to develop an intimate understanding of the text:

5.34   *It is ... important to know the primary text in detail, so you must read it, and then you must read it again, and perhaps you might read it once more after that.*

Analysis of 'critical' elements in literature document

As in the history and philosophy documents, the term 'critical' (and its variants) was found to be used frequently in the literature protocol document, with a total of 18 references noted (1 token per 200 words). This proportion is in fact higher than for the other two documents, although it needs to be noted that a number of these instances – 6 out of 18 – are for the term 'critic' (as in 'literary critic'), a discipline-specific variant of the key word of our study. Many of the 'critical' elements in the document pick up on the key themes discussed in the preceding section (see summary in Table 7).

Object of inquiry #1: Literary texts

The main *object of inquiry* noted is, unsurprisingly, the literary text itself, as seen in the extracts below (#5.35 and #5.36). In Extract #5.35, we note the distinction drawn between students just simply 'describing' a text, and the need to

Table 7 Critical elements in literary/cultural studies advice protocol document #1 – by type of *object of inquiry*

T Y P E	OBJECT OF INQUIRY What type of entity is to be analysed?		PROCESS OF INQUIRY By which type of mental/verbal process?	CONTENT OF INQUIRY By which analytical criteria/categories?
1	literary texts/primary text	(5)	developing critical view/understanding/ interpreting/(*not to describe only*)	identification of themes/ metaphors/symbolic moment/action
2	critical readings/ criticisms/articles by the critics/secondary sources	(1)	using (*as starting point/ as stimulation*)reading discriminately/chal- lenging argument	strengths/weaknesses
3	student' own world/ assumptions about world/own culture	(3)	evaluating critically/ questioning/broaden- ing (*mental horizons*)	identifying complexity of issues

provide some 'analysis' of it; in Extract #5.36, we see the beginnings of an account of what this 'analysis' (or 'interpretation') might involve:

> 5.35 *Perhaps the most frequent problem students have is a tendency to just describe what happens in a text, when they should arrive at a* **critical** *understanding of why it happens.*

> 5.36 *The theme of the story is not usually encapsulated in some direct statement. The theme of a story emerges through your* **critical** *interpretation of the various ele- ments in the story. These elements can include, for example, metaphors that are used, and particularly symbolic moments, actions, or objects in the text.*

Object of inquiry #2: Secondary texts

A far less significant entity in the document were the secondary texts – com- mentaries on a work by 'critics', denoted as 'critical readings', 'criticisms' and 'articles by the critics'. In Extracts #5.37 and #5.38 below, we can see the subsid- iary role that is envisaged for these sources. As was noted earlier, it is suggested that students will often draw on such sources in only an incidental way in their work; for example, to 'use as a starting point' for the development of 'their own critical view' (#5.37); or as texts that 'show' the type of 'approaches' students should apply in their own interpretation of a work (#5.38).

> 5.37 *So, use secondary sources as a starting point or as stimulation for developing your own* **critical** *view of a text ....*

> 5.38 *The subject booklet alerts students to the various ways a text might be inter- preted. We supply some passages of* **critical** *readings. The bits of* **criticism** *that*

we print there come from various times in the 20th century, but they do show different sorts of approaches.

Object of inquiry #3: Students' own world and assumptions

A final *object of inquiry* evident in the document is one that can be said to exist beyond the text, as it were; this is the moral and cultural realm of students' own lives (#5.39 and #5.40). Thus, it is suggested that students see the reading of literature as a basis on which they might 'question' and 'evaluate' the assumptions they have about their own lives and the world in which they live (#5.39). According to the document, the best literature to be studied is that of a fundamentally moral nature – one that shows the complexity of issues, and which 'overlaps' with the 'world we live in' (#5.40).

> 5.39   *One of the reasons for studying Literature is to broaden mental horizons, and that involves questioning the assumptions of your own time and place, your own culture. You need to be aware too that there are possibilities for* **criticism** *of the world in which you live.*

> 5.40   *[A] text gives you an opportunity to evaluate* **critically** *your own assumptions. The really worthwhile literature very rarely simplifies its moral positions; it usually shows awareness of the complexity of the issues being talked about and this will overlap with the world we live in.*

Such a view, which sees processes of critique happening in a mainly affective and empathic way, relates to a number of the conceptions of critical thinking we saw expressed in the interviews, especially those that emphasized the sensitive readings of texts. It is also in keeping with more traditional, humanist paradigms of critique, such as those embodied in the Leavisite tradition, where a critical engagement with literature is thought to be tied intimately to the development of personal qualities and sensibilities, or an 'awareness of the possibilities of life', as Leavis (1948) described it.

Document 2: Introduction to the analysis of a literary text (text and context)

The other document analysed was created from within the other literature strand in the faculty – from the Centre for Comparative Literature and Cultural Studies. A feature noted about the protocol documents considered so far is that all were produced, to varying degrees, through some process of collective authorship within the discipline area. All were also widely available to students, being distributed both in hard copy and in digital formats within the respective department. The circumstances of this present document, entitled *Introduction to the analysis of a literary text*, were found to be a little different. Rather than being jointly authored, this was created by an individual academic (one of the study's informants – Nora). When asked about the lack of a collectively authored document emanating from the centre, it was suggested that this was due to the variety of approaches and orientations adopted by the centre's staff. Brian summarized some of the various affiliations and interests thus:

> 5.41 **BRIAN** (literary/cultural studies – comp.): Although we are in the centre together, there's no simple uniformity of view. I mean, B's a Deleuzian. It's fine, we disagree among ourselves and we have different interests as well. N is interested in Russian formalism. ... People have different disciplinary foundations. And L's interested in German Romanticism and eco-criticism. It's important to be up front about where one is coming from.

This lack of a 'uniformity of view', Brian thought, made the possibility of producing any single 'guide to criticism' for students unlikely.

Description of contents

The *Introduction to the analysis of a literary text* document differs quite markedly in both style and content from the one provided to students enrolled in *Reading Literature*. It is written in a more didactic and impersonal style, and also provides a more technical account of the way that students need to engage with the subject. The following extracts from the opening section of the document give a flavour of the style and approach adopted:

> 5.42 *A literary text, such as a novel or a play or a poem, is a structure. This structure is held together by its own – intrinsic – laws of composition. The most obvious component parts of this structure are: the plot or fabula (story-line); the characters; themes and motifs; the narrator; the dialogue or monologue*

> 5.43 *The most important question to ask in any structural analysis is: What is the function of this or that component part? In other words, all the component parts, such as characters, plot, narrator etc. are taken not at face value, but in their relation to each other as ideas or concepts*

Notable in this opening account is the document's advocacy for a quite specific type of literary analysis, namely a 'structuralist approach'. This is evident not only in the name given to the approach students need to adopt: 'the most important question to ask in a structural analysis is ...' (#5.43), but also in the way that literary texts are characterized: 'A literary text, such as a novel or a play or a poem, is a structure' (#5.42).

Although this initial material suggests important paradigmatic differences between the two literature documents, they do have a number of common elements. Both, for example, see the essential task for students to involve giving some account of a work's major 'themes' and 'motifs' – along with an appreciation of how certain literary elements (or components) in a work combine to realize this thematic content. In the earlier document, for example, it was suggested that many undergraduate essays suffer for not engaging fully with the thematic concerns of a story and 'indicat[ing] how the various elements in the story contribute to making the theme more evident' (#5.37). In the second document, this notion, although expressed in distinctly different terms, nevertheless suggests a similar emphasis on the identification of theme, and the need for students to arrive at some overall interpretation of the 'meaning' of a work:

> 5.44   *Themes and motifs are 'building blocks' in the structure of a literary work. Taken together, the themes and motifs may give the 'total' meaning of the work.*

The two documents also provide a similar list of literary elements that need to inform the interpretative activity of students. In the first document, these are laid out in somewhat desultory fashion, but include such elements as 'the arrangement of the plot'; 'the psychology and traits of the characters'; 'metaphors that are used' and 'symbolic moments, actions, or objects in the text'. In the second document, such 'components', as they are denoted, are presented more systematically, but nevertheless include a similar array of categories, including 'the plot or fabula (story-line)'; 'the characters'; 'the narrator' and 'the dialogue or monologue'.

The most telling difference between the two accounts, however, relates to the connections each sees between the world of the text and the material world inhabited by the reader. In the first document, this sense of correspondence was presented as crucial; it was suggested, for example, that recognition of the 'overlap' between these worlds enables students 'to reflect on their own assumptions' and generally 'to broaden their mental horizons' (#5.40). The second document, by contrast, sees any putative connections between 'word and world' as not relevant ultimately to the activity of literary analysis – or at least to the kind of 'structural' analysis being suggested:

> 5.45   *[In a structural analysis] one does not ask the question: how does this character or this plot or this narrator correspond to life or reality? Such a question, in a general context, does not make sense in a structural analysis. For the structure, which is the literary work, does not relate to a reality outside itself. What that structure does is to incorporate a reality of its own, which is autonomous and separate from nature, life, the writer's biography, even history.*

Such an approach, which insists on the 'autonomy of texts', fits very much with strongly formalist approaches to literary criticism. In this particular tradition, as

Eagleton explains, the literary work is viewed adamantly as an entity to be analysed, rather than as a source of insight into the world, and the mind of its author. As he describes it:

> the literary work in [formalist traditions] is seen not as a vehicle for ideas, nor a reflection of reality, nor the incarnation of some transcendental truth: it is material fact, whose functioning can be analysed rather as one can examine a machine. It is made up of words, not of objects or feelings and it is a mistake to see it as the expression of an author's mind. (1996: pp. 2–3)

The document is in fact quite conscious of the particular view of literary analysis it presents. In its explication of the approach to be adopted, there is a fair amount of juxtaposing with other approaches to literary criticism that students may be familiar with, usually referred to in the document as 'older approaches'.

Analysis of 'critical' elements in literary/cultural studies document

The term 'critical' (and its variants) was used in the second literature document. A total of 9 instances were noted (1 token per 200), with most appearing in a final summary section at the end of the document. The uses of the term are summarized in Table 8.

Object of inquiry #1: Literary text

As might be expected in a 'structural' account, the main *object of inquiry* indicated in the document – in fact almost the only one invoked – is the 'text' itself, as seen in Extracts #5.46 and #5.47.

Table 8 Critical elements in literary/cultural studies advice protocol document #2 – by type of *object of inquiry*

T Y P E	OBJECT OF INQUIRY What type of entity is to be analysed?		PROCESS OF INQUIRY By which type of mental/ verbal process?	CONTENT OF INQUIRY By which analytical criteria/ categories?
1	literary texts (*novel*, *play* *poem*)	(5)	analysing/writing down (*one's thoughts*)/interpreting/ segmenting the text	identification of salient features
2	critical approaches (*to literature/theoretical notion*)	(2)	adopting a structural approach	–

5.46   *to write down one's thoughts about the text in any form ... necessitates a **critical** approach.*

5.47   *... you [need to] recall salient features of structure when you ... go over the text for the purposes of writing a **critical** analysis.*

In these 'critical' clauses, only limited information is provided about the *processes* with which students need to engage in their appraisal of these texts. In Extracts #5.46 and #5.47, it is suggested they 'write down their thoughts' as they read a text, and also that they need to 'recall the salient features of structure' when writing up their analysis. These 'salient features', as indicated previously, take in such elements as plot, characters, themes and motifs, narration, dialogue and so on. In Extract #5.48 below, there is an attempt to characterize, in general terms, the modes of thinking that inhere the type of criticism expected of students – described as 'segmentation'.

5.48   *There is no other path into **criticism** of a text than via segmentation ... All literary texts must be segmented in this way prior to analysis.*

For the writer of this document, the process of 'segmentation' is seen as particularly crucial; it is suggested, in fact, that it is this process that underlies all critical thought:

5.49   *Literary **criticism** is ...a model of all **critical** thought. No **critical** or analytic thought can take place without this segmentation of the whole.*

While some claims are made here for the universality of the method described, one notes that the types of processes found in this document are suggestive of a rather particular approach (i.e. the formalism referred to earlier). A clear contrast is to be made here with the previous literature document. Whereas in the first document, these processes are of a looser, more empathic nature ('interpreting', 'understanding'); in the second they have a much more technical, even clinical, character to them ('analysing', 'segmenting').

Object of inquiry #2: Approaches to literary criticism, theoretical notions

The only other *object of inquiry* referred to in the 'critical' elements in the document is particular 'approaches' to literary criticism, referred to earlier and evident in the extracts below:

5.50   *What in older **critical** approaches is called the 'author' has been replaced in structural **criticism** by the theoretical notion of the fictional narrator.*

5.51   *There can only be an interpretation of an historical event. The same is true of*
        real-life prototypes of the fictional characters. In older literary **criticism***, it was*
        de rigueur to trace the real-life prototypes of the fictional characters.

It is notable that while the idea of being critical is associated here with adopting a particular 'approach' (or 'theoretical position') to literary criticism, the document does not indicate how students should engage with these approaches; that is to say, there is no specification here of relevant mental or verbal *processes* (e.g. 'analyse', 'evaluate', etc.). This absence seems significant, and suggests that the intention in this case is not to have students engage critically, as it were, with the different approaches on offer, but rather for them to be instructed in the methods of *a* particular approach.

5.2.4 Summary of protocol analysis – all disciplines

In the preceding sections of this chapter, protocol documents from the three discipline areas have been analysed. A total of four documents were considered, one each from history and philosophy, and two from the area of literary/cultural studies. The analysis therefore, had to it both an inter-field and intra-field dimension.

In the analysis, both commonalities and differences were seen across the four documents. Perhaps the most important common element was the centrality in all documents afforded to the key term of our study – 'critical'. Also common was the tendency in all discipline areas to see acts of being critical as something directed principally at texts – whether these were works of literature, philosophical tracts, historical documents and so on. A final commonality was the idea that being 'critical' needed to be distinguished in some way from a different type of 'non-critical' activity – variously referred to in the documents as being 'expository' or 'descriptive', or relating to such skills as 'summarizing and paraphrasing'. These latter modes, while seen as an important part of study in each discipline, were generally held to be a necessary, but not sufficient, mode of engagement with material.

Some of the main differences noted between disciplines concerned the key category of the analysis, *object of inquiry*, and in particular the varying emphasis placed in each document on the notion of primary and secondary texts (see summary in Table 9). In the history document, for example, this distinction was held to be paramount, with students advised to see both as being essential to their studies, and each needing to be appraised in a critical way. By contrast, in the literary/cultural studies documents, much greater emphasis was placed on the primary literary work, with minimal reference made to secondary works. Where there was mention of secondary texts, some difference was noted between the two literary/cultural studies documents: in the first document, from the more traditional literature stream, these were 'articles by the critics';

Table 9 Summary of critical elements: advice protocol documents (by discipline)

DISCIPLINE	PRINCIPAL OBJECT OF INQUIRY	PRINCIPAL PROCESSES OF INQUIRY	PRINCIPAL CONTENT OF INQUIRY
HISTORY	primary text(e.g. *historical documents*)	interpretative	thematic (e.g. *motive, agenda, argumentative strategies*)
	secondary text(e.g. *works of historians*)	evaluative	epithetic (e.g. *trust-worthiness*)
PHILOSOPHY	primary text(e.g. *arguments/ objections of philosophers*)	evaluative	epithetic (e.g. *ratio-nality, validity*)
LITERARY/ CULTURAL STUDIES	primary text(e.g. *literary work*)	interpretative/ana-lytical	thematic (e.g. *theme, character, metaphor*)
	secondary texts		
English Literature	(e.g. *articles by the critics*)	evaluative	epithetic (e.g. *strengths, weaknesses*)
Comparative Literature	(e.g. *theoretical notions*)	ND	ND

in the second literature document they were characterized as 'theoretical notions'. The philosophy document was notable for making no distinction at all between source types, tending to view all relevant material as 'primary' in some sense – whether these be the arguments of a philosopher, or the counter-arguments or objections of a respondent.

Table 9 also shows variation in the patterns for the other categories – *processes* and *content*. A distinction can be seen between *processes* that are largely 'interpretative' (and which require a more 'thematic' engagement with the text), and those having a more 'evaluative' quality (requiring the application of certain evaluative criteria). The term 'epithetic', defined by Halliday as 'a subjective attitude towards an entity' (1994) has been used for these latter judgements. The data show a range of different judgement types, both within and across the discipline areas.

One final point of difference worth noting relates to the non-uniform nature of the data used in this part of the analysis; that is to say, a difference between discipline areas that have been able to work towards the production of a single consensual account of approaches in the field (as seen in the history and philosophy documents), and another discipline which would appear to eschew the laying out of any unitary method (literary/cultural studies). In this way, the two literature documents stand in clear contrast to those from history and philosophy. This is not to suggest that these latter two disciplines do not also rely on a range of methodological paradigms, nor is it to suggest that they are not prone to their own particular theoretical arguments and disputes. However, we can say – at least on the evidence of these documents – that the critical approach impressed upon the history and philosophy students would appear to be a generally agreed upon one. In the next section, the investigation shifts to looking at how these broad disciplinary configurations might translate into actual academic tasks set for students.

5.3 Exercise Tasks in the Three Disciplines

The focus in this part of the analysis was on a range of 'exercise tasks' set for students at undergraduate level in the three discipline areas. Within assessment regimes in Australian universities, such tasks are normally set as first pieces of academic work for students, and are usually required to be submitted in the earlier part of a semester of study. Along with allowing students to receive early feedback on their performance in a particular subject, such tasks also have the function of developing certain academic skills thought to be necessary for the effective participation in the particular discipline area (Ramsden 1992). The pedagogical basis of such tasks can be seen in the following extracts from history and philosophy course information material:

5.52   *In units in History, you will be given written exercise tasks to complete. These tasks are designed to help you work on specific skills in the critical evaluation of different kinds of evidence, and writing evidenced arguments*

History Handbook

5.53   *The exercises set in Philosophy will help you in coming to terms with the requirements of study and thinking in Philosophy*

Philosophy Green Guide

It is thought, therefore, that such tasks have the potential to shed additional light on the way that thinking is conceived in these particular disciplinary contexts. The corpus of exercise tasks analysed in this part of the research was collected from a range of first-year subjects offered under the three different discipline areas. The analysis was focused on a number of exercise samples from each discipline corpus identified by the researcher as distinctive in some way. As with the analysis of the protocol data, the approach employed here was a discoursal one, with a focus on the exercise samples as linguistic data. The organization of this section is also similar to the one used for the advice protocol documents above, with an extended description provided for the exercise samples in the three discipline area, along with an effort to summarize their main 'critical' elements at the end of each section.

5.3.1 History exercise tasks

In the analysis of the *History Essay Writing Guide* document, it was noted that a distinction was drawn between a student's engagement with sources of a primary and those of a secondary nature. The analysis noted very provisionally that the type of critical engagement for each appeared to be a little different – with a stronger sense of students needing to be more explicitly 'evaluative' of the secondary sources. In the corpus of history 'exercise tasks', this distinction between source types is also maintained, with some exercises aimed at developing skills related to the use of secondary sources, and others focused on those related to primary material. As will be seen, the nature of these tasks suggests the development of a different form of critical engagement for each of these source types.

Sample 1: 'Secondary source summary'

The first type of exercise identified in the history corpus was one related very closely to a key skill mentioned in the introduction to the *History Essay Writing Guide* document – namely, 'the ability to summarise and paraphrase the work of other writers'. In the following sample exercise (Figure 3), entitled 'secondary source summary', this information is in fact given in the first lines of the task rubric, and is the rationale provided for the task:

5.54   *One of the most important skills in conducting research in history is the ability to comprehend a particular text and then summarise its major arguments and conclusions in your own words.*

Exercise 1: Secondary source summary

5   One of the most important skills in conducting research in history is the ability to comprehend a particular text and then summarize its major arguments and conclusions in your own words. A good summary is not simply a blow-by-blow recapitulation of the text; instead you should show the main arguments and conclusions, describe the most important evidence provided by the author, and restate what you regard as the author's *main* contention or thesis.

10   For this exercise, you need to read Henry Reynold's chapter in *In the Age of Mabo: Native title and historical tradition: past and present* and then write a 500 word summary. This exercise should be handed in at the tutorial.

Australian History HSY 1040

FIGURE 3   Exercise Sample #1 (history)

This particular task, taken from an *Australian History* subject, requires students to prepare a summary of a secondary text – a book chapter written by an historian working in the field of indigenous history. Some guidelines are given concerning the form that this summary should take. Students are advised, for example, that they need to do more than provide 'simply a blow-by blow' account of the text, but should impose some structure on their summary (Line 5). The key critical elements mentioned here are: 'showing the main arguments' (L. 6); 'describing the most important evidence contained within the text (L. 6–7); and 'restating the author's main contention or thesis' (L. 7–8). A component that is clearly absent in the task is the need for students to offer any explicit evaluation of the text. This aspect of the task recalls the view expressed by a number of informants in the previous chapter regarding the key role of summary writing in academic work, and the need for students to appreciate how the accurate representation of ideas is a skill that precedes any move towards the evaluation of these ideas.

Sample 2: 'Critical analysis'

A second type of task was one focused on primary material – typically a document – and requiring students to provide an interpretation of this material. In the particular example cited here (Figure 4), taken from a modern history subject, *Contemporary Worlds*, students are required to select a document written by a major historical figure from the period (Wilson, Lenin, etc.) and to 'critically

---

Critical analysis

You are required to critically analyse one primary source document
5   from weeks 2 to 5 in your handbook (i.e. Condorcet, Wilson, Lenin, Himmler, Moseley, etc.).

In the critical analysis you should aim to:

10   – place your document in its historical context (who wrote it and when, and how does it reflect those times?)

– outline the author's argument (what are the author's main points and why was he/she writing?)

15   – suggest the author's motivation for writing the document (what 'agenda' does he or she seem to have; or what is the 'bias' of the piece; what does the document itself reveal about the author and his/her involvement in events?)

Contemporary Worlds HSY 1030

FIGURE 4   Exercise Sample #2 (history)

analyse' it (L. 3). Of particular interest in this task is how the idea of being 'critical' is conceived. The task rubric suggests that one element of this analysis is of a similar order to the previous exercise, that is, the requirement for students to 'outline the author's argument' (L. 11–12).

However, the task outlines additional ways in which students need to engage with the material; they are asked, for example, to 'place the document in [a broader] historical context' (L. 8–9), and also to give some account of the 'motivation' or 'agenda' that its author may have had for writing it (L. 14–16). Thus, we can see here the need for a more 'interpretative' and inferential reading, one that requires students to go beyond the text itself, and to make some connection with resources external to it. It may be recalled that such a reading, one requiring a sensitivity to context, was particularly emphasized by a number of historian informants in interview – including for example, Nell (history) who spoke of the need for students to 'go further into an historical document', and to have 'a go at working out its intentions'.

Sample 3: 'Evaluating historians'

Another type of history exercise was an additional one focused on secondary source material. It was noted that the first secondary source task considered (Figure 3) was adamant about students needing only to 'summarise' an historical argument ; that is, for them to be able to 'comprehend' a text, and to show their understanding of it. In this additional exercise type, students are required to go beyond demonstrating their understanding of a secondary text, and to offer some explicit evaluation of it. The rationale for the sample task shown below (Figure 5) taken from a *Renaissance History* subject, would seem to derive from the basic historiographical principle outlined at the beginning of the exercise – namely, that all historical writing is of its nature interpretative ('Historians have arguments, not simply facts' (L. 3–4)). In light of this statement, students are invited to consider the 'arguments' of two historians – in this case two differing 'positions' regarding historical factors behind the rise of the Renaissance – and to make a judgement about which of these interpretations they find 'the more convincing' (L. 3–5).

It is of interest that in this particular case, the task is explicitly described as one involving 'critical thinking' ('This evaluative exercise requires you to *think critically* about historical writing' (L. 7.)). The rubric then provides some explanation of what this might involve. It is stated, for example, that students should not just 'summarise' the texts in question, but seek to give an account of the authors' 'underlying points of view' (L. 9–10). Students are also invited to 'defend' or 'raise criticisms' of the positions presented, with the clear proviso that any evaluation advanced by them should be adequately supported ('you [must] supply an argument to support your case' (L. 12–13). It was noted above that the judgement that students ultimately need to make of the two texts is the

---

Exercise: Evaluating historians

5
Historians have arguments, not simply facts. Which of the two positions regarding the rise of the Renaissance – Lopez's or Goldthwaite's – do you find the more convincing? Why?

10
The evaluative exercise requires you to think critically about historical writing. This means that it must not be just a summary of what each author says. Rather you must show that you understand the underlying point of view being expressed, as well as the type of evidence presented to support this view. Do not be afraid to defend or raise criticism of either author, so long as you can supply an argument to support your case.

Renaissance Europe HSY 1020

FIGURE 5 Exercise Sample #3 (history)

extent to which they are 'convinced' by each of them (L. 5). Although the task rubric does not explicitly indicate on what basis students might arrive at such a judgement, the need for them to focus on the use of evidence in each article (L. 11) would suggest this as at least one evaluative criterion to be applied.

Sample 4: 'Supporting a case'

A final type of task identified in the corpus was one that had as its focus not the way other writers might frame their arguments, but rather how students might develop and support their *own* arguments. In the sample task below (Figure 6), it is explained that a key skill for history students in the 'developing of an argument or contention' is their ability to 'use relevant evidence to support a case' (L. 3–4). Thus, in this particular task, again from an *Australian History* subject, students are provided with a thesis to argue (in this case – alternative views expressed in the early twentieth century concerning Australia's perceived lack of 'national greatness'). The key elements of the task are for students to 'locate appropriate evidence' and to 'use this evidence' in support of the particular position they wish to argue (L. 5). As in the other tasks cited above, there is an emphasis here on students being able to 'summarise' source material, and also in this case to correctly cite and reference this material in accordance with the conventions of the discipline (L. 14–15).

Summary of 'critical' elements in history exercise tasks

The four sample tasks described above give a sense of some of the skills that it is thought necessary to develop in students commencing their studies in

---

Exercise: Supporting a case

In developing a **contention** or **argument**, one of the most important skills is using relevant evidence to support your case. In this exercise, you are
5   given a case to establish: you must locate appropriate documentary evidence from primary sources and use that evidence in writing. The case you are asked to argue is that: 'During the first decades of the twentieth century, some observers argued that women's selfishness was destroying Australia's chance for national greatness; others believed that the fault
10   lay with bad social conditions and lack of government support.'

Write 500 words arguing the case above and using specific examples from the documents to illustrate and explain points: you may use direct quotation, but you should also use short summaries of the evidence you
15   choose to present. All primary source material cited should be properly documented.

Australian History HSY 1040

Figure 6   Exercise Sample #4 (history)

history. Table 10 provides a summary of the specific terminology used in each task, according to the three categories of the analytical schema.

Each of the tasks can be seen to have a different configuration of elements. Drawing on these configurations, we can summarize the nature of each task thus:

- Task 1   Summary of argument in a secondary text (Reynolds/Mabo)
- Task 2   Analysis of content in a primary document (Wilson, Lenin, etc)
- Task 3   Evaluation of arguments of two secondary texts (rise of Renaissance – Lopez , Goldthwaite)
- Task 4   Development of own argument ('national greatness')

In the suite of tasks described here, we can see a strong, even systematic, connection with the way study and writing in history was characterized in the advice document considered earlier:

5.55   [*students need*] *to develop and defend an argument or contention by discussing and analyzing a range of appropriate evidence, and by critically assessing the interpretations of other historians* (L. 32).

Indeed, a link can be drawn with the various component skills indicated in this statement. Tasks 1 and 3, for example, would seem to be deliberately intended to develop the skills of 'critically assessing the interpretations of other historians'; Task 2 gives students practice in the 'analysis of appropriate evidence'; and

Table 10   Critical elements in history exercise tasks (by task #)

T A S K	OBJECT OF INQUIRY What type of entity is to be analysed?	PROCESS OF INQUIRY By which type of mental/ verbal process?	CONTENT OF INQUIRY By which analytical criteria/ categories?
#1	secondary text/chapter (*Henry Reynolds* – Age of Mabo)	reading/comprehend-ing/summarizing/	identification of main argument/most important evidence/main contention or thesis
#2	primary source docu-ment (*Condorcet, Wilson, Lenin, etc.*)	critically analysing	identification of document in historical context/author's arguments /author's motiva-tions/agendas
#3	arguments of two historians (*rise of Renaissance*)	evaluating positions/ supporting case	decide which more convinc-ing (*on basis of evidence*)
#4	own contention/argu-ment/documentary evi-dence (*Australia's lack of 'national greatness'*)	developing, supporting (*argument*)/locating, summarizing (*evidence*)	illustrate/explain main points of case

Task 4 is clearly aimed at the first of these components – 'the developing and defending of an argument'.

5.3.2 Philosophy tasks

In the advice protocol document for philosophy students described above, it was suggested that the activity of 'doing philosophy' can be reduced ultimately to two basic functions: exposition (that is, 'clarifying the meaning of texts or issues') and critical discussion ('making judgements about these texts or issues'). In the range of exercises set on the first-year programmes, there would appear to be a quite deliberate effort to develop students' abilities along these two lines. It is perhaps also significant that considerable emphasis appeared to be initially placed on the first of these functions – 'exposition'; that is, for stu-dents to be able to indicate in their work what a text is essentially about.

Sample 1: 'Popper'

The exercise type most obviously directed at the function of 'exposition' in the philosophy corpus of tasks was that which drew on a 'comprehension question' format. Thus, in the following sample task from a first-year unit (*Science, Religion and Witchcraft*), students are required to read an extended philosophical tract – a well-known text by Karl Popper, *Philosophy of Science: A Personal Report* (20 pages) – and to answer a number of specific questions about its content (Figure 7). The nature of the questions asked (What does X think ...? What is

---

Exercise: Popper

5   Read Karl Popper's 'Philosophy of Science: A Personal Report' ... Then answer the following questions *in your own words*, with one paragraph for each question.

i. Why do some scientists believe in induction? What answer does Popper give in Section VIII (Mention 'demarcation', and explain
10   very briefly what Popper means by this term?)

ii. The scientists have a reason for believing in induction: does Popper think this is a good reason? (Why, or why not?)

iii. In Section IX Popper describes the logical problem of induction
15   as a perceived class among three propositions (a), (b), and (c). Explain these three in your own words.

iv. What is Popper's response to suggestions that there is a clash among (a), (b), and (c)?

Introduction to Philosophy (Science, Religion and Witchcraft)
PHL 1010

FIGURE 7   Exercise Sample #1 (philosophy)

X's response ...? Explain what X means ...?) suggests that the intention here is to get students to engage very carefully with the details of the author's text, and to try to record as faithfully as possible their understanding of these. The persistent instruction in the task for students to 'use their own words' (L. 4; L. 16) is in line with comments made by a number informants concerning the need for students to be able to express their own understanding of the concepts presented without relying too heavily on the words of the author.

It is clear from the attributed structure of the four question items (i.e. with all containing a reference to the author, e.g. 'Popper's response' L. 18) that the purpose of this task is a strictly exegetical one, with no requirement for students to offer any evaluation of the material being considered, nor to advance their own views of the issues raised. The task bears some resemblance to the first of the history exercises discussed above, the 'secondary source summary' – where engagement with the assigned text was also restricted to an exposition of its contents (see Figure 3). The comprehension question format of the philosophy task suggests, however, a more guided and scaffolded approach to this content – a difference perhaps to be explained by the additional complexity of texts in this discipline area.

Sample 2: 'Identifying arguments'

Another type of essentially 'expository' task set in philosophy were ones that required a 'stand alone' summary of text material – as opposed to answers to a

> **Exercise: Identifying arguments**
>
> The passage below is an argument from Sigmund Freud's classic work
> *Civilization and its Discontents.* Outline the argument of the passage in
> 5   standard form (i.e. as a sequence of premises and conclusions). Feel free
> to paraphrase and to add unstated premises or conclusions if necessary.
>
> **Analyzing Arguments PHL 1030**

FIGURE 8   Exercise Sample #2 (philosophy)

series of comprehension questions (as in the Popper example above). What was
common in this type of format was the requirement that students summarize
material according to modes of analysis specific to the discipline. The most
common of these formats were tasks that required the analysis of a passage in
terms of its underlying argument structure – that is, as a relationship between
the various propositions of which it is comprised (premises and conclusions), as
seen in the following sample (Figure 8). In this sample task, from a subject specifically aimed at developing these skills (*Analyzing Arguments*), students are
required to 'outline the argument' contained in a passage from a work by Freud
(L. 4). It is of interest that in this case representing the content of the text
would appear to involve not only recording what is actually stated in the text,
but also identifying what is implicit or 'unstated' in it ('Feel free to ... add
unstated premises or conclusions if necessary' (L. 5–6)).

The nature of this exercise, particularly the suggestion that students see a text
as having a clearly identifiable argument (even one that may be incompletely
expressed by its author), provides some perspective on a controversy that
emerged in the interview data regarding the nature of texts and the types of
meanings that might emerge from a reading of them. It may be recalled that a
number of the philosophers saw one of the principal skills of reading to involve
'figuring out what a person is saying', or more specifically, as Eric suggested,
'identifying *the* argument contained in a block of normal English prose' (emphasis added). Such a conception of reading, it may be recalled, was at odds with an
alternative view – notably that held by those working in literary/cultural studies,
who questioned the idea of a text having an 'objective and 'unitary' meaning,
one capable of being identified through careful and conscientious reading. We
can perhaps see in the technique described in this particular exercise (i.e. the
analysis of a text as an argument structure) at least one basis on which the philosophers might claim that an objective reading of a text is possible.

Sample 3: 'Argument types'

Along with analysing 'blocks of normal English prose' as arguments, there were
additional tasks in the exercise corpus specifically designed to develop students'

Exercise: Argument types

5   Suppose you want to know whether or not it will rain, and ask a stranger who is sitting next to you on the bus. The stranger replies with the argument below. Read the argument, then answer the questions which follow:

Yes it's going to rain today. That's why my leg is aching.

10   i.   Write the argument in standard form and say what type of argument you think it is.[1]

ii.   How strong is the argument? In two or three lines explain why. In your assessment of the argument indicate whether its strength

15   depends on whether the prediction is true or not.

Introduction to Philosophy (Reason and Rationality) PHL 1010

FIGURE 9   Exercise Sample #3 (philosophy)

familiarity with the standard argument notation of premises and conclusions. Some of these typically required students not to engage with the extended texts of philosophers (such as Freud's work mentioned above), but rather with simple everyday arguments, such as the one shown in the sample above from a first-year unit – *Reason and Rationality* (Figure 9).

This sample task is also notable for requiring students to begin providing some evaluation of the material they are considering. Thus, in the second part of the question, they need to assess the 'strength of the argument' they have analysed, and also to 'explain' the basis on which such a judgement might be made (L. 12). It would appear that a task such as the one shown in Figure 9 has an important transitional role in the development of relevant philosophical skills; that is, students are introduced to what we have seen as the two archetypal functions in philosophy work ('exposition' and 'critical discussion'), but they have the opportunity here to work with these functions in relation to a manageable and accessible content.

Sample 4: 'Argument analysis'

An extension of the previous type of exercise (shown in Figure 9) is typically one that requires students to summarize and evaluate arguments as presented in the writings of established philosophers. An example of such a task is shown in Figure 10, where students are asked to provide an 'analysis' and 'evaluation' of the argument contained in short passages by one of two thinkers – Descartes or Berkeley (both approximately two pages long).

For the first part of the task, 'the analysis', students are asked to represent the structure of the argument in the now-familiar standard form (L. 7).

Exercise: Argument analysis

5

Consider the following passages by Descartes or Berkeley. Select one of these and provide a) an analysis of the argument contained in the passage b) an evaluation of the argument.

10

That is, for a) identify the premises and the conclusion of the argument; for b) say whether or not you think the argument is successful, then explain why by pointing out a flaw in one or more of the premises or in the structure of the argument. If you think the argument is successful, then consider an objection that someone might make to it and provide a reply to that objection.

Analyzing Arguments PHL 1030

Figure 10   Exercise Sample #4 (philosophy)

The rubric for the second part of the task, 'the evaluation', is notable for providing some detail about the way in which students should handle this function. Thus, it is explained that if students are inclined to view the argument negatively (that is, they decide that it is 'unsuccessful'), they should support this position on the basis of identifying either: i) problems in the premises of the argument, or ii) problems in the relationship between the argument's premises and conclusion; that is, its structure (L. 8–10). If, on the other hand, students have a positive view of the argument, they are advised to establish its 'success' by countering at least one possible 'objection' that might be mounted against it (L. 10–12).

These directives to students about how they should handle rhetorically the function of evaluation in the task recall some of the quite specific evaluative techniques mentioned both in the advice protocol document (Section 5.2.2) and also by some of the philosophy informants in interview, suggesting a degree of consensus about the nature of critical practices in the discipline. Thus, it will be recalled in the *Philosophy Writing Guide* that the optimal method suggested for indicating an argument's virtues was for students 'to defend the author against possible and/or actual criticisms'. Similarly, in interview, Henry and Jonathon discussed several standard critical routines that students in the discipline needed to be able to manage; namely, an ability to make judgements about the 'acceptability' of premises, and the 'validity' of an argument's overall structure.

Sample 5: 'Evaluating arguments'

A final type of task noted in the philosophy corpus was one that provided further extension of the 'exposition-critical discussion' format by requiring

---

Exercise: Evaluating arguments

Dawkins and Singer (Items 2.1 and 2.3 in the reading) argue for a common conclusion:

> *Our everyday morality rests on speciesist assumptions which cannot be defended.*

But their arguments are very different. Do each of the following:

i. In about 10 lines, outline Dawkins's argument, making it clear how the conclusion is supposed to be supported by the considerations he advances.

ii. In about 10 lines, outline Singer's argument, making it clear how the conclusion is supposed to be supported by the considerations he advances.

iii. Which of the two gives the more plausible argument for their conclusion? Why?

Introduction to Philosophy (Contemporary Moral Issues) PHL 1010

FIGURE 11   Exercise Sample #5 (philosophy)

students to write a comparative evaluation of two arguments. In the previous task (Figure 10), students were required to make an assessment of only a single argument.

Thus, in the sample task in Figure 11, students need to consider the texts of two writers, Richard Dawkins and Peter Singer, both writing here on the issue of animal rights. For the two texts, students are asked to prepare an 'outline' of the argument proposed in each, and then to decide which of the two arguments they find the more 'plausible'.

Summary of 'critical' elements in philosophy exercise tasks

Table 11 provides a summary of the specific terms used in each of the philosophy exercise tasks, according to the three categories of analysis. In the design of such tasks, we can see the intention to develop the abilities of students to handle the two basic functions that are identified as fundamental to the rhetoric of philosophy; namely, the 'exposition' and 'critical discussion' of arguments. (It is noted in passing that a range of seemingly synonymous terms were used in the tasks to denote each of these functions. Thus, 'exposition' is variously referred to as 'explaining', 'outlining' and 'analysing'; and critical discussion as 'evaluating' and 'assessing'.) Drawing on the more basic terms of 'exposition'

Table 11 Critical elements in philosophy exercise tasks (by task #)

T A S K	OBJECT OF INQUIRY What type of entity is to be analysed?	PROCESS OF INQUIRY By which type of mental/ verbal process?	CONTENT OF INQUIRY By which analytical criteria/ categories?
#1	philosopher's text (*Popper's 'Philosophy of Science: A Personal Report'*)	reading/answering questions/explaining	——
#2	philosopher's text (*argument from Freud's 'Civilization and its Discontents'*)	outlining/paraphrasing/ adding to text	identification of premises/ conclusions (*including unstated premises/conclusions*)
#3	everyday argument (*basis for prediction of rain*)	reading/writing argument/identifying type (*of argument*)	identification of premises/ conclusions
		assessing argument	strength of argument
#4	philosophers' texts (*arguments from Descartes or Berkeley*)	analysing	identification of premises/ conclusions
		evaluating – pointing out flaws – replying to objection	success of argument/ acceptability of premises/ structure of argument
#5	philosophers' texts (*arguments from Dawkins and Singer*)	outlining	how conclusion supported by considerations
		evaluating (comparing)	plausibility (*which more plausible?*)

and 'critical discussion', the structure of the five tasks considered can be characterized thus:

- Task 1   Exposition of details of argument in a philosopher's text (Popper)
- Task 2   Exposition of structure of argument in a philosopher's text (Freud)
- Task 3   Exposition of structure + critical discussion of an everyday argument
- Task 4   Exposition of structure + critical discussion of argument in philosophers' texts (Descartes or Berkeley)
- Task 5   Exposition of structure + critical discussion of arguments in two philosophers' texts (Dawkins and Singer)

In the structuring of these tasks, one notes what appears to be the staged development of students' critical capacities, with some tasks focusing exclusively on the more basic function of 'exposition', and other tasks combining both 'exposition' and 'critical discussion'. It was mentioned in interview that the purely 'expository' tasks tended to be set for students in the early stages of courses.

5.3.3 Literary/cultural studies tasks

In the analysis of tasks for the preceding two disciplines (history and philosophy) it was possible to trace certain correspondences between information provided in the protocol documents and the apparent pedagogical intent of many of the tasks assigned on these programmes. Thus, for example, it was noted in the history materials that a number of the tasks appeared to reflect the distinction drawn in that discipline between engagement with sources of a primary and secondary nature; in philosophy, the distinction between the functions of 'exposition' and 'critical discussion' appeared salient. For the tasks collected in the final discipline area, literary/cultural studies, locating an underlying coherence and unity of purpose was more difficult – no doubt due, in part, to the schismatic nature of literary/cultural studies in the faculty, and also, as we have seen, within the discipline more generally.

In the small corpus of tasks collected from a range of first-year literary/cultural studies subjects, the activities set for students were found to be of a diverse nature, and could be said to reflect the ecumenical view expressed about the field in one of the literature documents – namely, that there are 'many different legitimate ways of going about reading, describing, and analysing a literary text'. As we shall also see, the matter of what qualifies as a legitimate text for such 'readings' and 'analyses' is also subject to some variation. The following tasks were collected from a range of subjects including: *Reading Literature, Text and Context, Introduction to Cultural Studies.*

Sample 1: 'Short story exercise'

The first task – entitled *Short story exercise* – comes from the *Reading Literature* subject, from the more traditional literature stream in the faculty (Figure 12). In this task, students are asked to write a 'response' to one of several short stories written by two well-known Australian writers. The type of response required is given several designations in the rubric of the task, both bearing the term critical – namely, 'critical interpretation' (L. 3) and 'critical discussion' (L. 8). As a way of guiding students in the development of their particular 'interpretation' or 'discussion', a number of 'starter' questions about the two texts are provided, covering some of the literary elements we saw earlier in the protocol documents: narrative voice, characterization, theme and motif, metaphor and so on. A sample of these questions is shown as a footnote in Figure 12 below (L. 29–40).

One of the more notable features of this task's design concerns the advice given about how students might draw on this guide material. It is stressed to them that the questions provided about the stories are of a 'preliminary' nature only, and are merely intended to help students 'formulate' some initial ideas

---

Short Story Exercise

Topic: Write a critical interpretation of ONE of the following short stories:

5   Patrick White 'Being Kind to Titina'
       Olga Masters 'The Lang Women'

In this exercise you need to produce a properly presented critical discussion of the chosen story. We have suggested here some preliminary
10   questions to assist your reading and the formulating of your ideas about your chosen story*. You may use them or disregard them, but do not write a series of six answers as your response to the assignment. Instead, be sure to write an integrated, unified and single response, if necessary concentrating on just one or two of the starter questions, or on questions that you have devised yourself.

       In working out your answers always be ready to indicate, by quota-
15   tion or reference, some word, speech, image or passage in the story which supports your reading. Much of the meaning of a story lies in the detailed arrangement and interaction of words, images, phrases, voices, etc. It is worth looking at some passages closely to see how the
20   author is managing such detailing.

                                    Reading Literature ENH 1010

---

       * These starter questions refer to such elements as narrative voice, characterisa-
25   tion, theme, motif, metaphor, style, e.g.: (from *The Lang Women*).

       i.   *This story uses a third-person narrative voice. Through whose consciousness do we receive the story, and what effect does this point of view have on our response?*
       ii. *The title of the story brackets Jess, Carrie and Lucy together as the 'Lang Women'. Do these characters have anything in common apart from the family name?*
       iii. *Kerryn Goldsworthy remarks that female subjectivity and the treatment of poverty*
30   *are frequent themes in the work of Olga Masters. In this story how is poverty shown to impinge particularly on the lives of women?*
35   iv. *Would you agree that Olga Masters is both compassionate and unsentimental about her characters?*
       v.   *What is the cumulative effect of the story's references to clothing and washing?*
       vi. *Published in 1982, the story is set in 1930s Australia. Does it express nostalgia for that world, or satisfaction that it has passed away?*

FIGURE 12   Exercise Sample #1 (literary/cultural studies)

(L. 9–10). They are told that they may in fact disregard the questions altogether, and opt instead to take up other aspects of the text that they think are worth pursuing. The only stipulation amid all this open-endedness is that students not structure their work as a series of separate answers, but aim instead to 'write an integrated, unified and single response' to the story (L. 12–13).

In such an approach, it would appear that the critical routines here are of a less prescribed nature, with students invited to respond to the text (*object of inquiry*) in their own personal ways. This represents something of a contrast with many of the other tasks observed so far, where the nature of the critical engagement expected of students is laid out in quite systematic fashion – for example, in the history tasks, where students were given quite specific directives about the aspects of an historical document to comment on (Figure 4); or in the philosophy tasks, where the techniques for defending or criticizing a philosophical argument were clearly laid out (Figure 10).

One other feature worth noting in the task's design – perhaps the only part of it that qualifies as a clear prescription – is the requirement that students refer in their writing to specific instances of language from the selected story: quotations, dialogue, passages and the like. It is explained that one's apprehension of the meaning of a text is always dependent on engagement at this level of detail:

> 5.56   ... *always be ready to indicate, by quotation or reference, some word, speech, image or passage in the story which supports your reading. Much of the meaning of a story lies in the detailed arrangement and interaction of words, images, phrases, voices, etc. It is worth looking at some passages closely to see how the author is managing such detailing.*

Sample 2: 'Analysis of narrative structure'

The second task for analysis comes from a subject *Text and Context*, the core first-year subject in the alternative literature strand in the faculty, based in the Centre for Comparative Literature and Cultural Studies (Figure 13).

The 'comparative' paradigm suggested in the centre's title is immediately evident in this task, with students asked to consider a wide range of texts, all covering in some way the archetypal theme of 'the Fall'. It is noted that the term 'text' is used here in a more general way, with the task taking in both literary and visual genres, as well as texts of both a canonical and popular nature (Genesis, Milton's *Paradise Lost* and Goethe's *Faust*, and 'films or television programmes with which [students] are familiar' (L. 13)). In the design of this task, there are echoes of the more technical, structuralist mode of analysis outlined in the second of the literature protocol documents. The title of the task, for example, draws on the concept of structure (in this case 'narrative structure'), and the major activity prescribed for students is the 'drawing of a plan' for the various 'Fall' stories they need to consider.

The rubric contains one reference to the term 'critical', which is associated here with another key element in the task – the 'notion of intertextuality':

> 5.57   *Explain how the notion of intertextuality can assist one to arrive at a **critical** understanding of the cultural relationships between these texts* (L. 13-15).

Analysis of narrative structure

Part A: Draw a plan showing how the idea of the Fall is represented in *Genesis*. Who falls? Why do they fall? How do they fall? What is the outcome?

5   Choose either Milton's *Paradise Lost* or Goethe's *Faust*. Draw a similar plan. Who falls? Why do they fall? How do they fall? What is the outcome?

Explain how the notion of intertextuality relates to the two texts you
10   have considered.

Part B: Find examples of stories of the Fall in contemporary cultural texts (e.g. from films or television programmes with which you are familiar). Explain how the notion of intertextuality can assist one arrive at a
15   critical understanding of the cultural relationships between these texts.

Text and Context CLS 1010

FigURE 13   Exercise Sample #2 (literary/cultural studies)

Thus, we can see here in the design of this task, that students need to draw explicitly on a particular secondary notion ('intertextuality') as a basis for investigating the primary *object of inquiry* – the various 'Fall' stories. It is of interest that the idea of being critical in this instance appears not to involve making a judgement about this secondary material *per se* (e.g., to decide how much the notion is valid, plausible and so on, as we saw in the philosophy tasks, for example), but instead relates more to the idea of students being able to draw on this kind of theoretical material as the basis for their analyses. In the design of such a task, one sees the clear expression of a particular view of reading expressed in interview by several literary/cultural studies informants – namely, that any legitimate and critical reading of a text by definition needs to 'bring theoretical resources from outside the text to bear'.

Sample 3: 'Analysing a section of text'

A different type of literary/cultural studies task was one involving a focus not on a whole text or range of texts, but rather on the detail of a short text extract. In the task below (Figure 14), taken from an additional *Text and Context* subject, the extract for students to consider is a passage from a dramatic work – Ibsen's *Ghosts* (*object of inquiry*), and the *process* of engagement suggested to them is one of 'analysing'. As in the preceding task (Figure 13), this one also gives prominence to additional secondary material (referred to as 'ideas we have developed about communication and the functions of language' (L. 4–5)), which students are advised to draw on in the framing of this analysis.

Analysing a section of text

1. Analyse a short piece of dialogue between two characters in Ibsen's *Ghosts* which involves some distinctive language uses. You should use the **ideas** we have developed about communication and the functions of language (including 'speech acts', 'choice of codes', 'subtexts', 'noise', 'feedback').

5

2. Drawing on these ideas about communication, identify if the ways that you communicate change during the course of the day depending on your addressees, shared subcodes, contexts, noise, etc. Consider samples of your own talk during the day.

10

Text and Context CLS 1020

FIGURE 14   Exercise Sample #3 (literary/cultural studies)

In the discussion of the literary/cultural studies tasks so far, we have also noticed some variety in the type of texts thought to be worthy of study on a literature programme (*object of inquiry*). Thus, some tasks are focused on examples of 'high' culture texts (including short stories, poems and plays) and others on those of a popular nature (films or television programmes). This present sample is notable for bringing in a very different kind of 'text' – namely, the language that students produce in the context of their everyday social interactions:

> 5.58   *Drawing on these ideas about communication, identify if the ways that you communicate change during the course of the day depending on your addressees, shared subcodes, contexts, noise, etc. Consider samples of your own talk during the day* (L. 8–12).

Sample 4: 'Textual analysis'

In all of the preceding literary/cultural studies tasks, the main *object of inquiry* has been a primary text(s) (e.g. a short story) or some part of a text (e.g. a stretch of dialogue from a play). Present also in some of the tasks, as noted, has been an additional secondary entity that students have needed to consider. This was particularly the case in Sample #2 (Figure 13), where students needed also to be concerned with the theoretical notion of 'intertextuality', along with the texts they were to explore (the 'Fall' narratives). A final task sample taken from an additional subject offered in the Centre for Comparative Literature and Cultural Studies – *Introduction to Cultural Studies* – is notable for giving arguably greater prominence to the theoretical material than to the primary text (Figure 15). Thus, in the first part of the task, the focus is exclusively on a range of 'key

---

Textual analysis:

Write a short explanation of your understanding of any four of the following key **concepts** (you should give examples where appropriate to demonstrate your understanding)

5

　　a)　intertextuality
　　b)　paradigm and syntagm
　　c)　denotation and connotation
10　　d)　sign and signification
　　e)　narrative
　　f)　the spectacle
　　g)　transgression
15　　h)　commodity culture
　　i)　space and place

Select any two of the cultural texts* we have considered on the course so far this semester and provide an analysis of each. In each analysis, you should draw on one (or several) of the categories above that you find relevant to the material you are considering.

Introduction to Cultural Studies CLS 1040

*Texts include: *Frankenstein* (novel, film); *Heart of Darkness*, *Apocalypse Now*, *Alien Trilogy*, Madonna videos, Cyberpunk magazines.

FIGURE 15　　Exercise Sample #4 (literary/cultural studies)

concepts' from the field (e.g. *transgression, the spectacle*). Here students are asked to provide an 'explanation of [their] understanding' of a number of these concepts. In the second part of the task, these concepts are then to be used ('drawn on') as the basis for their 'analysis' of several primary texts from the course.

Like the first sample task we considered above – the short story exercise (Figure 12), this final sample is also quite open-ended in its prescriptions, with students given the freedom to choose both which primary texts they will consider, as well as which concepts they will draw on to develop the analysis:

5.59　*you should draw on one (or several) of the categories above that you find relevant to the material you are considering* (L. 18–19).

Thus, it would appear in both these examples that the judgement required of students is concerned arguably as much with deciding the means by which they will frame the analysis of the text as with the actual analysis itself. The key difference in the tasks would seem to lie in the extent to which this framing depends on the explicit use (and explication) of an *a priori* theoretical position.

Summary of 'critical' elements in literary/cultural studies exercise tasks

Table 12 provides a summary of the terms used in each of the literary/cultural studies exercise tasks.

Drawing on the terms in Table 12, the four literary/cultural studies exercise tasks can be characterized thus:

- Task 1   Interpretation of short story (Patrick White or Olga Masters)
- Task 2   Analysis of structure of narratives ('Fall' stories) + Discussion/ use of concept (intertextuality)
- Task 3   Analysis of dialogue (Ibsen/own) + Discussion/use of concept (communication theory)
- Task 4   Discussion/use of concept (various) + Analysis of texts (various)

Table 12   Critical elements in literary/cultural studies exercise tasks (by task #)

T A S K	OBJECT OF INQUIRY What type of entity is to be analysed?	PROCESS OF INQUIRY By which type of mental/ verbal process?	CONTENT OF INQUIRY By which analytical criteria/ categories?
#1	short story (*Patrick White, Olga Masters*)	critically discussing/critically interpreting/reading/formulating ideas/ devising (*own questions*)	identification of narrative voice/characterization/ theme /metaphor, etc.
	language of selected passages from story	looking/supporting (*your reading*)	identification of detailed arrangement and interaction of words, images, phrases, voices, etc.
#2	idea of 'Fall' in selected texts (*Genesis, Paradise Lost, Faust*)/ contemporary cultural texts (*films, television*)	drawing plan/ finding examples/	identification of narrative structure (*who/why/how/ outcome*)
	notion of intertextuality	explaining how	relationship between texts
#3	short piece of dialogue (*Ibsen's Ghosts*)/samples of own talk during the day	analysing/ identifying (*change*)/	identification of aspects of dialogue (*speech acts/choice of codes/subtexts/noise/feedback*)
	ideas about communication and functions of language	drawing on ideas /using	
#4	key concepts (*the spectacle, transgression, etc.*)	explaining concept/giving examples	ND
	cultural texts considered on the course	providing analysis/choosing relevant concepts	use of relevant concept in analysis

Emanating as they do from the two different literature strands in the faculty, it is difficult to identify any obvious connection between these tasks. They do, however, certainly have in common a focus on some literary/cultural text (or texts) as their principal *object of inquiry*; though, as we saw, the range of texts covered in these tasks constitutes a diverse and disparate collection.

The paradigmatic differences between the two literature streams in the faculty have been explored in different ways. One difference noted in these tasks is the distinctly different ways in which students are encouraged to view the nature of literary language. Thus, in the first task – the short story exercise from the traditional literature strand (Figure 12) – students are invited to look carefully at the details of language use in specific passages 'to see how *the author is managing* such detailing' (L. 19–20, emphasis added). Significantly, in the remaining tasks (all from the comparative strand), such evocations of authorial agency are entirely absent. Instead of students being encouraged to explore the relationship between an author and his/her text, the relevant relationship established in these other tasks is one between the text and other texts, as suggested, for example, in the key notion of 'intertextuality'.

As has been noted, it is the inclusion of secondary notions (such as 'intertextuality' 'transgression', etc.) that marks the major point of departure between the critical approaches of the two strands. Although the more traditional literature exercise shown in Figure 12 does include in its rubric a number of textual features that students might wish to consider in their analysis (in the form of 'starter questions'), these are of a more random nature, and are not suggestive of a clearly articulated analytical procedure.

5.3.4 Summary of exercise task analysis

The many different tasks presented in this section can be viewed as important apprenticing activities for students in the different discipline areas of the study. The element common in each is that they are all concerned in some way with showing students how to work with texts, though the nature of these 'texts', as well as the type of work that needs to be done with them, was found to vary a good deal.

A sense of these differences is captured in the variable use of one of the most frequently occurring terms in the rubric of these tasks – the keyword 'argument'. In the philosophy tasks, the term 'argument' was central, and in all instances referred to the *object of inquiry* of tasks; that is to say, in all cases, students needed to do something with an 'argument' – whether this was to provide a summary of it, an evaluation of it and so on. This was also the case for some of the history tasks, though a more important usage of the term 'argument' here was as a reference to what students themselves needed to produce – as in the last of the history tasks (Figure 6), which gave students practice in assembling evidence for the 'development and defense of their own argument'. The term 'argument' here might thus be thought of more as a *process* of inquiry than an *object*.

What was significant about the term's usage in literary/cultural studies was, in fact, how sparing it was. It is interesting to note that while the idea of 'argument' was central to the tasks in the other disciplines, in the literary/cultural studies tasks the notion appeared to have less relevance to what students needed to do in this discipline area – in both its guises. This variable usage is suggestive of some quite basic epistemological differences – which are explored in more detail in the next chapter in relation to arguably the most important pedagogical texts for students in undergraduate studies – the essay task.

5.4 Essay Tasks in the Three Disciplines

In the previous section, an analysis was made of the exercise tasks that were set in the three discipline areas. In this section, another type of pedagogic discourse is considered – the essay topic. While these two genres have certain features in common – both, for example, have the purpose of eliciting some form of written product – they can be distinguished in a number of ways. One is their relative importance as assessment activities on undergraduate programmes. The exercise task, as noted previously, usually constitutes a minor form of assessment, attracting a relatively low weighting in the overall marks awarded in the subjects; the essay, in contrast, is often the main assessment activity set for students on many courses. This is particularly true in the case of the humanities, where the essay continues to occupy a special place – described by Hounsell as that form within which students 'struggle to give meaning to their experience'. (1997: p. 106)

The two genres also differ in the nature of the written product they are designed to elicit. Exercise tasks, as we have seen, often have a quite clear and specific pedagogical purpose – principally one of scaffolding certain key skills thought necessary for effective participation in the particular discipline area. The essay as a genre has a more standalone quality about it and is usually conceived of as a type of writing less tied to the specific learning context in which it is set (Coulthard 1994). An example of this difference can be seen in the variable rubric used in these task types. Thus, in the exercise task, the activity prescribed often takes the form of a set of instructions to students, usually realized as a sequence of imperative forms (highlighted in the following samples, seen earlier in Section 5.3):

5.60 For this exercise, you need to **read** Henry Reynold's chapter in *In the Age of Mabo: Native title and historical tradition* and then **write** a 500 word summary

Extract from history exercise

5.61   **Consider** the following passages by Descartes or Berkeley. **Select** one
       of these and **provide** a) **an analysis** of the argument contained in the
       passage b) **[provide] an evaluation** of the argument.

Extract from philosophy exercise

5.62   **Write a short explanation** of your understanding of any <u>four</u> of the
       following key concepts ... **Select** any two of the cultural texts we have
       considered on the course so far this semester and **provide an analysis**
       of each.

Extract from literary/cultural studies exercise

For the essay task, the more common format is not as a set of instructions, but
as a question (or questions), as in the following sample topics from the same
disciplines:

5.63   **How should we understand** the legacy of Aboriginal dispossession in
       Australia?

History essay topic

5.64   **Is** religion the opium of the masses? If it is, **does it follow** that God
       does not exist, or that it is unreasonable to believe that God exists?

Philosophy essay topic

5.65   **To what extent** can *Nineteen Eighty-Four* be considered a science
       fiction text?

Literary/cultural studies essay topic

From these examples, we can see that the essay task is less focused on pedagogic
processes as such, and is concerned more with broad intellectual questions and
issues relevant to the specific discipline in which it is set. This feature means
that of the different types of textual data that have been considered in the
research, it is the essay tasks which afford the best access to a discipline's more
basic concerns, and which are ultimately most revealing of the type of critical
judgements that students need to make.

For this part of the analysis, a corpus of essay topics from the three discipline
areas was compiled. Topics were provided by the study's informants. The corpus
in each area consisted of around 50 topics with most (but not all) of those collected being taken from first-year undergraduate subjects. As with the previous
analyses of texts (documents and tasks), the approach used in this part of the
study was to focus on the essay topics as textual samples, and to draw on the

categories of analysis that have been used so far as a way of exploring both inter- and intrafield patterns of variation. Once again, the initial focus of this analysis was on the type of entity that students need principally to direct their thinking towards (i.e. *the object of inquiry*). Also, following the procedure from the previous sections, commentary from the interviews is introduced into the discussion in cases where this is able to shed additional light on the textual analysis.

5.4.1 History essay topics

The importance of essay writing in the School of Historical Studies has already been noted in the main document provided to students to guide their academic work in the school – the *History Essay Writing Guide*. In this, it was explained that of the different types of work that students need to produce in their studies in history, it is the essays they write that are the most substantive, because of 'the opportunity [they provide] to explore a particular issue or theme in depth'. This emphasis on essay writing as the principal intellectual activity for students was affirmed in the various history subjects from which the essay data were collected. The following, for example, is an account provided for students in the course outline for one particular history subject:

5.66 *The writing of essays is crucial in this subject. The term 'essay' comes from the French word 'essayer' meaning to try or to attempt. From this older form we get our terms 'assay' or 'test'. An essay therefore asks you to answer a question by constructing and testing an argument. You will be assessed on the quality of your attempt.*

Course outline document – *Renaissance Europe*

History: Principal object of inquiry

In the history exercise tasks we considered in Section 5.3.1, a distinction was noted between those tasks that required engagement with primary sources on the one hand, and with secondary sources on the other. It was concluded from these examples that the *objects of inquiry* in these tasks were mainly of a textual nature (e.g. a chapter written by an historian, a document produced by a major historical figure, variable interpretations of a particular historical period (see Figures 6–8)). The first pattern to note in the corpus of history essay topics is a shift away from these overtly textual entities to what might be termed 'real-world' entities, or phenomena. This contrast can be illustrated in the following examples (also quoted above). In this particular case, the real-world entity in question – 'aboriginal dispossession' – is what the historian Henry Reynolds has referred to as 'that indelible stain' on the nation's history (Reynolds 2001).

5.67   *Exercise task:*

[Write a summary] of **Henry Reynolds' chapter** in *In the Age of Mabo: Native title and historical tradition: past and present*

(*Object of inquiry* = text)

5.68   *Essay task:*

How should we understand the legacy of **Aboriginal dispossession** in Australia?

(*Object of inquiry* = real-world phenomenon)

This difference can be understood in terms of the distinctive purpose of essay writing as described in the *History Essay Writing Guide* – that is, to be able 'to explore a particular issue or theme in depth'. Thus, in the examples above, we see a shift away from a focus on a particular author's treatment of an historical phenomenon (#5.67) to the actual phenomenon itself (#5.68)

A survey of the essay tasks in the history corpus suggests that students need to engage with quite a variety of such phenomena in their history studies. The list shown in Figure 16 gives a flavour for the topics collected in this part of the study and also illustrates the range of historical phenomena with which students need to contend – classified loosely here as: 'states of affairs', 'activities', 'events', 'actions', 'policies', 'attitudes' and 'perceptions'.

This shift from the 'textual' to the 'real' seems a significant one, and is suggestive of the domain difference captured in the field of semantics between what are known as 'second- and third-order entities' (Lyons 1977). As John Lyons explains the schema, the primary category – first-order entities – refers to entities which exist in both time and space (i.e. physical objects or beings). Second-order entities are said to exist in time, but rather than *exist* in space they *take place* or *occur* within it; thus, taking in the types of entities noted in the topics above (events, processes, states of affairs and so on). Third-order entities, on the other hand, are said to be unobservable and have no spatio-temporal location, taking in the abstract textual realm of propositions, facts and so on. A similar distinction between these realms is described in Halliday's categories of 'phenomena' (taking in 'material' and 'behavioural' processes) and 'metaphenomena' (taking in 'verbal' and 'mental' processes), and for him is suggestive of quite different discourse worlds (Halliday 1994). Further discussion of this point is taken up in Chapter 6.

History: Principal processes of inquiry

The essay topic data was found to be less comprehensive in the information it provided about the second analytical category – the thinking *processes*. This can be related, to some extent, to the linguistic structure of essay topic rubric – which, as was noted previously, relies more on question forms than instruction

5.69

States of affairs

How were **women's status and lives** affected by their experience of the American Civil War?

American Civil War

5.70

Activities

What, besides aesthetic impulses, motivated the patrons of Renaissance culture to **commission works of art**?

Renaissance Europe

5.71

Events

How do you account for **the rise and fall of right-wing paramilitary organisations** in Australia during the 1930s?

Australian History

5.72

Actions

To what extent did the **government responses** to unemployment protests in the 1930s involve the repression of legitimate grievances?

Australian History

5.73

Policies

In assessing the **policies of Lyndon Johnson** with regard to Vietnam, some analysts see his personality as the key, while others argue the importance of his advisors. Which of these factors in your view had the greatest impact on Johnson's Vietnam policies?

The Vietnam War

5.74

Phenomena

In what ways has economic **globalisation** affected national governments?

Contemporary History

5.75

Attitudes

Was **prostitution** a more acceptable activity in 18th, 19th or 20th century in London?

Murder and Mayhem

5.76

Perceptions

Has what **terrorism** 'is' changed in recent years?

Contemporary History

FIGURE 16   Sample history essay topics (showing principal *objects of inquiry*)

forms. We saw, for example, in the previous analysis of 'exercise tasks' that many of the *processes* of thinking prescribed to students were to be found in the imperative verb forms used to frame task instructions (e.g. *provide an analysis* of X ; *critically evaluate* Y). In question-form topics, such process verbs are less prominent.

However, some information about mental *processes* is to be found in the data. The most abundant example from among the samples above is Sample #5.73 from the *Vietnam War* subject. This is shown again below with the relevant *processes* in bold.

> 5.77   In **assessing** the policies of Lyndon Johnson with regard to Vietnam, some analysts **see** his personality as the key, while others **argue** the importance of his advisors. Which of these factors in your **view** had the greatest impact on Johnson's Vietnam policies?
>
> *The Vietnam War*

The *process* in this example most directly related to the student is the final one – 'viewing' ('*Which of these factors in your* **view** ...?'), although the other processes shown in the introductory part of the topic ('assessing', 'seeing' and 'arguing') are also relevant. Among the other history topics shown in Figure 16, those that include process terms in their rubric are Samples #5.68 ('understand') and #5.71 ('account for'). Table 13 (Column 2) summarizes all process terms identified in the history corpus.

Table 13   Terminology used in main topic-type (history)

OBJECT OF INQUIRY What type of entity is to be analysed?	PROCESS OF INQUIRY By which type of mental/ verbal process?		CONTENT OF INQUIRY By which analytical criteria/ categories?
states of affairs (e.g. *women's lives/ 1960s*)	discuss	8	causation (e.g. *factor/reason*)
activities (e.g. *commissioning works of art/violent crime*)	view	3	
	see	3	
events (e.g. *rise of new right/ outbreak of WWI*)	argue	2	consequence (e.g. *legacy/ impact*)
actions (e.g. *responses to unemployment /attack on Pearl Harbor*)	assess	2	
	account	2	
policies (e.g. *Johnson & Vietnam War/ aboriginal dispossession*)	think	1	comparison (e.g. *similarity/ difference/change*)
	understand	1	
phenomena (e.g. *globalization / imperialism*)	compare	1	characterization (e.g. *democratic/ wise*)
attitudes (e.g. *to prostitution/to Kray brothers*)			
perceptions (e.g. *of terrorism*)			

These main processes – *discussing, viewing, seeing, arguing* and so on – are consistent with the emphasis noted in the history data overall on what is seen as the principal 'critical' activity for students in the discipline – namely, the development of a particular view about events in the past. Thus, it will be recalled that a number of historians in interview wished to emphasize the fundamentally 'constructive' nature of historical inquiry. Such a view, for example, was expressed by Edward, who suggested that one's critical engagement with sources (of the type we saw in the exercise tasks) needed to be concerned ultimately with the 'constructive' process of developing one's own coherent interpretation of events.

> 5.78 **EDWARD** (history): [Being critical in history] is concerned … with the sources and the way in which you use them. It's building on the sources, or organizing them in a particular way to construct a particular … picture of the past.

History: Principal content of inquiry

In Edward's account of what being critical in history fundamentally involves, there was further elaboration of the kinds of interpretations of the past that students may need to develop. In addition to his generic 'picture of the past', he suggests that such 'constructions' might also involve advancing views about the causes ('explanations') of events and their 'consequences'.

> 5.79 **EDWARD**: [students may also need to provide] an explanation about an event, or an explanation about what the consequences of an event are. [These are] sometimes referred to as the 'how, what, and why' kind of questions – the basic historical ones.

These particular characterizations of the way that students need to think about 'events' (or phenomena) take us into the third category of the analysis – the *content of inquiry*. For this category, the essay topics were found to be a rich source of information, and provide much insight into the discipline's more basic intellectual concerns. In the corpus, a number of broad question-types were identified, ones that largely overlap with the rough taxonomy suggested by Edward above. These have been labelled variously as 'causation', 'consequence', 'comparison' and 'characterization', and are discussed briefly in turn below (see also Table 13 above).

Question-type 1: Causation

The notion of causation has always been thought of as a pre-eminent concern for historians. E. H. Carr famously declared that 'the study of History is the study of causes' and that all historical arguments revolve ultimately around 'the question of the priority of causes' (1961: p. 87). This particular characterization of the discipline is reflected strongly in the corpus of history essay tasks. In the initial list of history topics shown in Figure 16, for example, a number are clearly concerned with judgements about the causes of phenomena. These are shown again below with highlighting of those linguistic elements in the topic denoting causality.

5.80   **How do you account** for the rise and fall of right-wing paramilitary organisations in Australia during the 1930s?

Australian History

5.81   **What**, besides aesthetic impulses, **motivated** the patrons of Renaissance culture to commission works of art?

Renaissance Europe

5.82   In assessing the policies of Lyndon Johnson with regard to Vietnam, some analysts see his personality as the key, while others argue the importance of his advisors. **Which of these factors** in your view had the greatest impact on Johnson's Vietnam polices?

The Vietnam War

In the overall history corpus, it was noticed that certain question structures appeared to be more favoured by some lecturers than others. Thus, in Samples #5.83 and #5.84 below, taken from the subject *Australian History*, agentive forms are used ('How do *you* account ...?'), whereas in Samples #5.85 and #5.86, taken from the subject *Murder and Mayhem*, questions are posed using the more standard (non-agentive) 'why' form.

5.83   **How do you account** for the rise in student activism in the 1960s and 1970s?

Australian History

5.84   **How do you account** for the success of Robert Menzies and the Liberal Party in the 1949 Federal Election?

Australian History

5.85   **Why** did the Bloody Code come into such force in the 18th Century, and then was largely abolished in the early part of the 19th century?

Murder and Mayhem

5.86 **Why** did violent crime in London appear to decline across the 18th and 19th centuries?

Murder and Mayhem

A final sample from the corpus (#5.87) is one that on the face of it looks to be more concerned with 'consequences' than causes. On closer inspection, however, we can see that the topic is oriented more towards antecedent than consequent events, (that is, whether the phenomenon of globalization is seen as a factor contributing to the rise of a particular political movement.)

5.87 To what extent should the rise of the new right be **seen as a consequence** of globalization?

Contemporary History

Question-type 2: Consequence

The obverse of 'cause-related' questions are those concerned not with the origins of events, but with their outcomes. The following are examples from the initial list of questions (Figure 16) that require students to make judgements about the consequences of events.

5.88 How should we understand the **legacy** of Aboriginal dispossession in Australia?

Australian History

5.89 How were women's status and lives **affected** by their experience of the American Civil War?

American Civil War

5.90 In what ways has economic globalization **affected** national governments?

Contemporary History

Several additional 'consequence' questions were noted in the history corpus. In Sample #5.91, taken from a classical history subject, *The Golden Age of Athens*, students need to consider the consequences of certain decisions made in war – in this case Athens' rejection of an armistice proposed by Sparta in a battle during the Peloponnesian War.

5.91   Following the capture of Pylos in 425, the Spartans sued for peace; the Athenians refused and this marked a turning point in the war (Thuc IV. 17 22). How would you have voted had the peace proposal been taken to a meeting of the Athenian ekkelesia and why? Do you think the Athenians made **a wise decision**?

The Golden Age of Athens

Also concerned with the wisdom of military decision-making, a last sample (#5.92) asks students to assess the 'impact' of John F. Kennedy's Vietnam policies.

5.92   In retrospect, JFK can be seen to have increased the American commitment in Vietnam. Many argue, however, that Kennedy would have resiled from extending the War. Examine the available evidence, including the views of Kennedy's contemporaries and the historians who have studied his presidency to assess the nature and **impact** of JFK's Vietnam policies.

The Vietnam War

This final topic is notable for providing a fair amount of detail about how students should go about developing a response to the topic presented. Thus, students are advised that as a basis for 'assessing the nature and impact of JFK's Vietnam policies', they will need to investigate a range of evidence from both primary and secondary sources (namely, the views both of Kennedy's contemporaries and of historians of his presidency). In such rubric, we see a quite explicit exemplification of the kernel information found in the *History Essay Writing Guide*, where the evidential basis for making claims about the past is outlined for students:

5.93   *you need to develop and defend [an] argument or contention by discussing and analyzing a range of appropriate evidence, and by critically assessing the interpretations of other historians*

Question-type 3: Comparison/change

A third category of 'real-world' question-types noted in the corpus took in topics dealing with issues of historical change (including comparison of the same or similar phenomena over different time periods). Examples from the initial list above (Figure 16) include the following:

5.94   Was prostitution a **more acceptable** activity in 18th, 19th or 20th century in London?

Murder and Mayhem

5.95   Has what terrorism 'is' **changed** in recent years?

Contemporary History

Other samples from the corpus were:

5.96   To what extent can the Japanese military regime in Indonesia be seen as **similar** to the Dutch colonial government?

Modern Asian History

5.97   **Compare** how female crime was perceived and dealt with in London in both the late 18th and late 20th centuries, and discuss reasons for any **change.**

Murder and Mayhem

It is noted that this final topic (#5.97) also requires students to engage with the central theme of causation ('discuss reasons for any change').

Question-type 4: Characterization

A final type of question identified in the history corpus was one that asked students to make judgements about particular phenomena with respect to some characteristic attributed to them. For example, the following question (#5.98) from the initial list of topics, asks students to decide how much the actions of a particular government should be seen as 'repressive' (and also how much the actions of a section of the citizenry as 'legitimate').

5.98   To what extent did the government responses to unemployment protests in the 1930s involve the **repression** of **legitimate** grievances?

Australian History

Other examples in the corpus are Samples #5.99 and #5.100 below. In Sample #5.99, students also need to make a judgement about government action (in this case the possible 'criminality' of government action in its prosecution of a war); in Sample #5.100, the judgement is concerned with the collective actions of a regime overall (how much these should be seen as 'democratic').

5.99   Among the several ways in which the term **war crime** can be defined is the following: 'Crimes against humanity which includes political, racial or religious persecution against any civilian population, either before or during a war'. How **much does this definition apply** to the Vietnam War in general or to any specific episode of the war?

The Vietnam War

5.100   How **democratic** do you consider the Athenian government to be in the time of Perikles?

The Golden Age of Athens

A feature of topics in this category is that the judgements asked of students are of an essentially normative nature, taking in criteria of 'legitimacy', 'criminality' and so on. It is also of interest that collectively these topic samples are mainly concerned with a theme of how power has been used (or abused) in different historical periods and episodes (the Great Depression, Vietnam War, etc.). Such a focus resonates strongly with the broadly ethical and activist view of critical thinking we saw expressed by a number of history informants. One of these was Nell, who was sure that the important 'critical' questions in the study of history always had a moral dimension to them:

5.101   **NELL** (history): It's not just asking questions about how did it happen, but how did it happen and is it a good thing.

Nell went on to suggest that in one's teaching, there was always an effort to 'set up certain values that [were then compared against] politics or history'. The sample questions in this latter category can be seen as a clear expression of this particular outlook.

History: Other topics

In the preceding sections, there has been an attempt to characterize the main type of questions set on undergraduate history programmes. This has been for the purpose of investigating the nature of the judgements that students are typically required to make in the main assessment activities they are set to complete. The archetypal structure of these questions can be summarized thus:

Object of inquiry: real-world phenomena (states of affairs, events, actions, etc)

Processes of inquiry: acts of interpretation (viewing, seeing, arguing, understanding, etc.)

Content of inquiry: thematic (causes, consequences, characterization, etc.)

While a clear majority of the questions contained in the corpus were consistent with this general structure, a number of other question-types were identified. These are commented on briefly below.

Text as object of inquiry

A contrasting type was one that required students to focus on secondary accounts of various historical phenomena (#5.102 and #5.103). Such topics, described by one informant as 'your standard historiographical essay', recall some of the history exercise samples shown earlier in the chapter.

5.102   On what evidence did Evans base his **view** that the Minoans were a peace-loving people? What evidence is there to counter that **assessment** and is it valid?

Minoans and Mycenaeans

5.103   Consider the **accounts** by Christopher Browning, Richard Breitman and Henry Friedlander about the origins of the Holocaust. Which of these three **interpretations** do you find the most persuasive and why?

Nations at War

Even though each of these topics above is concerned, as can be seen, with some 'real-world' phenomenon (i.e. the nature of Minoan culture; the Holocaust), what it is that students are asked to make their judgements about ultimately is not the phenomenon as such, but a particular textual account (or accounts) of it. In Sample #5.102, the evaluative criterion suggested is one of 'validity of evidence', and in Sample #5.103 it is 'persuasiveness'.

It is noted in passing that the structure of Samples #5.102 and #5.103 above is almost identical to the Exercise Sample #3 (Figure 5) considered earlier, where students were asked to adjudicate on rival interpretations of the Renaissance. We can see in examples such as these that while the types of assessment tasks considered in the research (i.e. exercise tasks and essay topics) are often of a qualitatively different order, there are instances where the two forms are not noticeably distinct.

Text versus real-world as objects of inquiry

Another topic-type identified in the history corpus was one that fits with neither the 'real-world' nor 'textual' categories considered so far, and which is notable for in a sense pitting these two realms against each other. Thus in Sample #5.104, which is concerned with the eighteenth century phenomenon of the highwayman (from the subject *Murder and Mayhem*), students need to assume a distinction between the way that the highwayman was represented in the literature of the time and the way he was in 'reality'. Sample #5.105 relies on a similar weighing of the 'textual' against the 'real', with students needing to judge the content of certain films about the Vietnam War against the actual 'reality of the War'.

5.104   How might we account for the differences between the **real 18th century highwaymen** and the **literary images of highwaymen?** Were these differences apparent to those living in the 18th century?

Murder and Mayhem

5.105   To what extent have **feature films** succeeded in representing the **reality of the Vietnam War?**

The Vietnam War

Evocations of the notion of the 'real' in topics such as these bring to mind an underlying tension evident in much of the discussion thus far – that is, between broadly realist notions of critique (as expressed by some informants) and the more phenomenological outlook held by others. For a number of the historians in the study, the idea of there being a 'reality' that exists independently of textual representations of it was thought to be one of the discipline's more basic tenets. Thus, Edward, in explaining the basis for topics like those above (# 5.104), was keen to point out that while the notion of 'historical fact' is not unproblematic in the discipline, it was essential, he thought, to be able to distinguish the 'actuality' of events from mere 'fictional' versions of them.

5.106   **EDWARD** (history): History is, above all, an empirical discipline. And even though there are difficulties with the idea of historical fact ... there is a core belief that in history we are dealing with something that actually happened. ... History is the telling of stories, but it is not a fiction.

A similar view was expressed earlier by Nigel, who insisted that one of his duties as an historian and as a history educator was always to seek to 'tell the truth' about events.

Such views, as we have seen, stand in contrast to the more phenomenological position expressed by a number of informants – in most instances, but not all, coming from the Centre of Comparative Literature. In discussing such matters, Brian, for example, explained how he needed to disavow his literature students of the idea that they could fall back on simple notions of the 'real' when dealing with the historical contexts of a literary work.

5.107   **BRIAN** (literary/cultural studies – comp.): [students] would like to rely on some sense of the contexts when they, say, read Milton – but [I tell them] the seventeenth century has gone. It's just not available as an immediate object of empirical study – we tell [students] all we can do is study text – historical text, historiographical texts – but they're still just texts ... they're archives.

Among the historians, the greatest affinity for this latter approach was expressed by Nell. She explained that over time her historical interests had tended more and more towards the textual – such that texts are studied not principally as a basis for constructing an accurate picture of the past, but rather as ends in themselves:

> 5.108   **NELL** (history): So the history I've become interested in is in a sense the history of certain genres, it's the cultural and textual dimension of things that interests me.

This interest in the textual *per se* is evident in the following essay topics set by Nell on her *Australian History* course, covering a range of genres (war diaries #5.109; recruitment notices #5.110; novels #5.111; and historical monographs #5.112).

> 5.109   Analyse a selection of **Australian prisoner of war writings** from World War 2. To what extent can they be described as 'embittered documents'?
>
> *Australian History*

> 5.110   Compare the strategies used in World War 1 **recruitment campaign notices** with **soldiers' descriptions** of their reasons for volunteering. Are there any differences you note? How can you account for these differences?
>
> *Australian History*

> 5.111   How does the **novel** *Come in Spinner* represent tensions on the home front in World War 2 in Australia?
>
> *Australian History*

> 5.112   Critically analyse the ways in which the mythology of Anzac is con-structed in the **historical writings** of CEW Bean.
>
> *Australian History*

The last of these topics (#5.112), requiring students to 'critically analyse' the war-time histories written by C. E. W. Bean, the official Australian historian of the First World War, suggests a rather different slant on historical writing from other examples seen in the corpus. The question here is not one of whether the text is thought to reflect accurately (or inaccurately) some underlying objective historical reality; rather it is how the text has contributed somehow to the construction of that reality.

5.4.2 Philosophy essay topics

As was seen in the history materials, studies in philosophy place a similar emphasis on the writing of essays. In the *Guide to Writing and Researching Philosophy Essays*, we saw a number of statements attesting to the importance of this mode of writing and thinking for students. In the following quotation from the guide, the centrality of the genre is asserted; it also suggests helpfully that there can be some 'pleasure' for students in the writing of such texts.

> 5.113   *If you have chosen to study Arts, it is likely that you will have a particular interest in – even a passion for – ideas and the variety of forms and genres in which ideas are expressed and explored. The argumentative or discursive formal academic essay is a key genre in the study of Philosophy, and one which can be a pleasure to read and to write.*

Philosophy: Principal object of inquiry

In its analysis of the essay questions that are typically set in philosophy, it was suggested in the *Philosophy Essay Guide* that questions could be divided into two broad categories: 'text-focused' topics (where students are asked 'to consider some particular philosopher's writing on some issue'); and 'issue- or problem-focused' topics (which are 'more directly about a particular philosophical issue, without reference to any particular philosopher's text'). The following topics were then presented as examples of the two different types:

> 5.114   *Text-focused topic*:
>
> Discuss critically David Hume's account of causation in Part III of Book I of his *A Treatise of Human Nature*

> 5.115   *Issue-focused topic*:
>
> What is scientific method?

In these samples, it can be seen that the first topic (#5.114) requires students to direct their thinking explicitly towards a text (in this case a particular passage contained within Hume's larger work); in the second (#5.115), the judgement, at least as it is framed in the task rubric, is concerned with a human activity (the practice of scientific method). The distinction would seem to approximate that which was evident among the history topics.

In the philosophy corpus, it is notable that a clear majority of topics (39 out of 56) were found to be of the former 'text-focused' type – a pattern which contrasts markedly with the findings for history. The following are examples of the dominant text-focused topics, with the textual element (and author) highlighted in each case (Figure 17). As was also the case in the exercise samples analysed earlier in the chapter, the main textual entity here that students need to consider is characterized as an 'argument'. Other terms used are 'claim' (#5.119) and 'conclusion' (#5.120). It is also noted that the rubric in each case

5.116   Provide a statement of **the argument of Aquinas' Third Way**. Do you think this is a persuasive **argument** for the existence of God?

God, Freedom and Evil

5.117   **Judith Jarvis Thomson argues** that even if we grant that embryos have a right to life, abortion should still be justifiable in some circumstances. Is she right? Outline and then critically evaluate her **argument**.

Contemporary Moral Issues

5.118   **Saussure argues** 'that initially the concept is nothing, that [it] is only a value determined by its relations to other similar values, and that without them the signification would not exist.' Explain what he means by this and critically assess his **arguments** for thinking this is the case.

Language, Truth and Power

5.119   'Religious ideas … are illusions, fulfilments of the oldest, strongest and most urgent wishes of mankind.' Why does **Freud say** this? What does he mean by this? Is his **claim** a valid one? Does it have any consequences of questions about the existence of God?

Philosophy of Religion

5.120   In **Euthydemus** and **Gorgias**, Plato's Socrates presents some rather astounding **conclusions** about the value of living justly and the power of wisdom. Should we as readers be convinced of the truth of Socrates' **conclusions** on the basis of the **arguments** presented? If not, where do the **arguments** go wrong?

Ethics

FIGURE 17   Sample philosophy essay topics (showing principal *object of inquiry*)

provides some encapsulation of the main content of the particular argument in question. Aquinas' argument (#5.116), for example, is summarized in a prepositional phrase ('argument for the existence of God') and Judith Jarvis Thomson's (#5.117) in a 'that' clause ('that abortion [is] justifiable in some circumstances').

All of the topics above direct students to engage critically with a particular text (e.g. Aquinas' Third Way, Freud's argument concerning the psychological basis of religious belief, etc). Some minor variations on this pattern were noted in the corpus. In the following examples (#5.121 and #5.122), the approach required is a comparative one, with students called upon to consider similarities and differences between two or more related texts.

5.121   Compare the **argument of St. Anselm's Proslogion** with the **arguments from Descartes' Fifth Meditation**. Do these **arguments** have exactly the same strengths and weaknesses?

God, Freedom and Evil

5.122   Contrast **Plato's theory of the tripartite soul** with **Freud's psychoanalytic theory**. Do both explain equally well, for example, the significance of myths?

Metaphysics

One other variant noted were tasks that set up an explicit debate or 'dialectic' between texts; that is, with one text presented as an initial proposal (for a set of ideas) and the second as a rejoinder (or objection) to these (#5.123 and #5.124). In these cases, students are typically asked to adjudicate in some way on the positions adopted by both the thinker and respondent.

5.123   **Walter Brown argues** that there is scientific evidence for a worldwide flood. What is your assessment of the evidence? Do you think that **Schadewald's arguments** provide compelling objections to the flood hypothesis?

Science, Religion and Witchcraft

5.124   What is **Duff's objection** to **Pascal's Wager**? Does it show that there is something wrong with **infinite decision theory**?

Philosophy of Religion

Sample #5.125 has a similar dialectic structure to those above, though in this case the position is not one held by an individual thinker, but by a general school of thought (i.e. 'utilitarianism').

5.125   How would utilitarians deal with the **criticism** that their **theory** would permit the punishment of the innocent?

Crime and Punishment

A final example among these variations is the following topic taken from a subject devoted to the writings of Sartre and de Beauvoir (#5.126). This example, which is arguably more complex in its requirements than the previous examples, is notable for including in its rubric both 'comparative' and 'dialectic' elements. Students are here asked to consider related texts written by these two thinkers (their independent accounts of 'an existentialist ethic'), and to then evaluate these texts in relation to the criticisms made by various 'commentators'.

5.126   At the end of ***Being and Nothingness***, Sartre promised the development of an existentialist ethic, and in ***Existentialism is a Humanism*** and ***The Ethics of Ambiguity*** both Sartre and de Beauvoir attempted a **sketch** of an existentialist ethic. **Many commentators** feel that these **sketches** were unsuccessful, and in the end it is impossible to ground a coherent ethical imperative in the ontology of *Being and Nothingness*. Do you agree?

Sartre and de Beauvoir

To conclude this section, a brief comment is made on the way that these textual entities are typically referred to in these tasks. As was noted in the topic samples considered above (Figure 17), the term 'argument' was used to characterize the types of texts that students need to consider. Such a pattern was also evident in the philosophy corpus overall. Table 14 (Column 1) shows the variety of terms used in task rubric to denote these text-focused entities in order of frequency.

Although a diverse group of terms is shown here (Column 1), upon analysis they can be reduced arguably to three categories – i) what might be loosely called a 'set of ideas' that have been proposed by a philosopher (or school of philosophy); ii) a criticism of these ideas made by another philosopher (or school); and iii) a response from the original philosopher to this criticism. The terms in Table 14 can be allocated to these categories thus:

i.   set of ideas – *argument, view, theory, account, claim, conclusion, contention, sketch, formulation, idea* and so on
ii.   criticism of ideas – *objection, criticism, critique, question*
iii. response to criticism – *reply*

Table 14   Terminology used in main topic-type (philosophy)

OBJECT OF INQUIRY What type of entity is to be analysed?		PROCESS OF INQUIRY By which type of mental/verbal process?		CONTENT OF INQUIRY By which analytical criteria/categories?	
argument	19	discuss (*critically discuss* = 4)	8	right	4
view	11	think		correct	3
objection	8	evaluate (*critically evaluate* = 4)	5	wrong	2
theory	4	explain	4	adequate	2
criticism/critique	5	assess (*critically assess* = 3)	4	compelling	2
account	2	refer	4	persuasive	2
claim	2	outline	3	reasonable	2
conclusion	2	agree	3	strong (*strength*)	2
contention	2		2	weak (*weakness*)	2
debate	2		2	valid	2
reply	2				
sketch	2				
Other: formulation, idea, evidence, interpretation, position, premise, question, suggestion, thesis		Other: compare, consider, defend (*a verdict*) examine, give (*an account*), justify (*a verdict*), provide (*a statement*), reconcile, see		Other: coherent, conclusive, convincing, effective, sound	

This patterning of terms is consistent with the dialectic account of argumentation emphasized in the *Philosophy Essay Guide* considered earlier – though on
the evidence of the essay topic data, the keywords 'argument' and 'objection'
might describe more precisely the nature of this dialectic than those used in the
guide – 'question' and 'response'.

>   5.127   *This dialectic of* **question** *and* **response** *is part of a tradition of thinking
>   – a great conversation – that dates back to the Ancient Greeks and has been a
>   fundamental influence in the development of the science, art, literature and
>   politics of Western civilization* (L. 31–34)

In a final sample to be considered in this section, Sample #5.128 (below) with
its heavily 'critically-laced' instruction – 'Critically discuss [Taylor's] criticism
[of Foucault]' gives a sense of the unending potential of this 'great conversation'. Indeed, if we take into account the fact that Foucault's original thesis on
'truth and power' was also a form of critique, we have a sequence here of at least
three 'critical' episodes.

>   5.128   What are **Charles Taylor's reasons** for thinking that **Foucault's posi-
>   tion** on truth and power is ultimately incoherent? Critically discuss
>   his **criticisms**
>
>   *Language, Truth and Power*

Philosophy: Principal processes of inquiry

For the *processes*, the data were generally consistent with the patterns noted in the philosophy exercise samples discussed in the preceding section; that is, for these processes to be mainly concerned with the 'exposition' and 'critical evaluation' of texts. Thus, in the following extracts from the samples shown in Figure 17, one notes a combination of 'expository' processes ('provide a statement', 'outline', 'explain') and 'evaluative' ones ('critically evaluate', 'critically assess'):

5.129 **Provide a statement** of the argument of Aquinas' Third Way ...

5.130 **Outline and then critically evaluate** [Judith Jarvis Thomson's abortion] argument

5.131 ... **Explain** what [Saussure] means by this and **critically assess** his arguments for thinking this is the case.

Table 14 (Column 2) shows *process* terms gathered from all the philosophy topics. The most frequently occurring verbs fitting with the function of 'exposition' were 'explain' and 'outline'; those with the second function of critique were 'discuss', 'evaluate' and 'assess'. It is interesting to note that these latter verbs were often collocated with the term critical, though not in all cases. Thus, in some questions, the instruction was 'to discuss', while at other times is was to 'critically discuss'. My philosophy informants reported no qualitative difference between these variants; the inclusion of the adverb, it was explained, was to emphasize to students that it was not sufficient for them to adopt a mainly – or exclusively – expository mode in their essays.

Philosophy: Principal content of inquiry

The analysis of the philosophy topics so far has seen an emphasis on the 'critical evaluation of arguments'. The data collected for this final category (*content of inquiry*) is generally reinforcing of the patterns observed in some of the previous philosophy sources; that is, for this form of evaluation to mainly involve the making of judgements about the 'success' or otherwise of such arguments. In the following examples, the different arguments to be considered are to be judged variously according to their *persuasiveness* (#5.132), *validity* (#5.133), *strengths/weaknesses* (#5.134) and *wrongness/rightness* (#5.135).

5.132 Provide a statement of the argument of Aquinas' Third Way. Do you think this is a **persuasive** argument for the existence of God?

God, Freedom and Evil

5.133   'Religious ideas ... are illusions, fulfilments of the oldest, strongest and most urgent wishes of mankind.' Why does Freud say this? What does he mean by this? Is his claim a **valid** one? Does it have any consequences of questions about the existence of God?

Philosophy of Religion

5.134   Compare the argument of St. Anselm's Proslogion with the arguments from Descartes' Fifth Meditation. Do these arguments have exactly the same **strengths** and **weaknesses**?

Science, Religion and Witchcraft

5.135   What is Duff's objection to Pascal's Wager? Does it show that there is something **wrong** with infinite decision theory?

Philosophy of Religion

The term used in the study to denote these types of judgements is 'epithetic' (Halliday 1994); that is, judgements that rely on the application of certain evaluative criteria. Other epithetic terms noted in the philosophy essay corpus, in addition to those above, were: *soundness, correctness, success, goodness, 'convincingness'* (Table 14: Column 3).

In interview, it was explained that some of these terms have quite specific meanings within the discipline. Lauren, for example, pointed out that a key distinction is often drawn in philosophy between the notions of 'truthfulness' and 'validity'. Truthfulness (or lack thereof), for example, is considered to be a property of statements (or premises) that typically go to make up an argument, whereas 'validity', strictly speaking, refers to the logical relationship that pertains between the premises and any conclusion drawn from these (regardless of the truth value of the premises). An additional term mentioned was 'soundness', which, Lauren explained, combines both notions. Thus, an 'argument is considered sound' if it satisfies both evaluative requirements – that is, its premises are thought to be true, and the conclusion drawn from these premises is thought to be 'valid'. Lauren pointed out that mastery of such terms – a challenge for many students studying in philosophy – is crucial for success in the discipline.

5.136   **LAUREN** (philosophy): These are fairly technical terms and can cause students difficulty. Often students use 'valid' to mean 'true'. For example, 'That's a valid fact'. But we use 'valid' as a term of appraisal of arguments. So an argument is valid if the conclusion follows on logically from the premises ... To be successful in the subject, students need to cumulatively absorb how this terminology works.

In the following topic (#5.137), which is concerned with Plato's account of Socrates' famous argument against pleasure (the *Gorgias*), a clear effort is made to have students properly distinguish some of these key criteria:

> 5.137 In Plato's *Gorgias*, Socrates provides three arguments for the conclusion that pleasure is not the good. Choose one of Socrates' three arguments and explain how it is supposed to work. What are the premises and how are they related? Is the argument **valid**? Is it **sound**?
>
> *Ethics*

However, while some of these terms have specific usages (and also prescribe specific critical routines), many of the other epithetic terms found in the corpus were of a more generic nature (e.g. 'persuasiveness', 'success', 'goodness', etc.). This slippage between these general evaluative terms and the semantically precise criteria of 'truthfulness' 'validity', 'soundness' and so on, was commented on by several philosophy informants. It was explained that while there are occasions in students' undergraduate training where it is useful to require them to apply the strict standards of argumentative validity, more often the approach is to leave it a little open as to how students might go about appraising the philosophical material presented to them. Eric, for example, summarized the basic approach as follows:

> 5.138 **ERIC** (philosophy): In philosophy, the judgements are primarily about arguments. That's really what we're asking [students] to render a verdict on usually. Is this a good argument or not? There are different ways of getting at that basic question.

Other philosophy topics

The main question-type set in philosophy – aptly summarized by Eric in his account above – can be represented as follows:

Object of inquiry: textual entities (arguments/objections, etc.)
Processes of inquiry: acts of evaluation (evaluate, assess, discuss, etc.)
Content of inquiry: epithetic (persuasion, validity, coherence, rightness, wrongness, etc.)

While a majority of the questions in the philosophy corpus were found to be consistent with this broad pattern, a number of other types were also identified. These are commented on briefly below.

Issue-focused questions

As was seen in the *Guide to Writing and Researching Philosophy Essays*, a distinction is drawn in the discipline between what are labelled 'text-focused' and 'issue-focused' topics. For this latter type of question, as the document explains, the judgement required of students, at least as framed in the essay rubric, is directed not so much at arguments of particular philosophers, but rather to some broad philosophical issue. Only a limited number of questions in the corpus were found to be of this type, with the following presented here as illustrative examples:

> 5.139   Must the punishment fit the crime?
>
> *Crime and Punishment*

> 5.140   Can human nature be adequately understood through the discovery of scientific laws?
>
> *Metaphysics*

> 5.141   Is religion merely a passing phase in the unfolding of history? If it were, would that show that God does not exist, or that it is unreasonable to believe that God exists?
>
> *Philosophy of Religion*

These questions are complex ones, taking in such difficult issues as the nature of justice (#5.139), ways of understanding human nature (#5.140) and the rational basis for religious belief (#5.141). On the face of it, they would seem to demand a rather more sophisticated form of judgement from students than was seen for the more common 'text-focused' topics above. In practice, however, it seems that the two topic-types may not be of such a different order. The reason for this was suggested in the *Guide* earlier; namely, that in responding to a particular philosophical issue, the usual practice in the discipline is to do this by engaging critically with certain key texts written on the issue. Thus, the *Guide* suggests that in responding to issue-focused topics (such as those shown in #5.139–5.141), the tack is often to adopt a 'dialectic' approach by 'setting up … a comparison of two or more [rival] accounts'.

This apparent convergence between 'text-focused' and 'issue-focused' questions was evident in a number of topics in the philosophy corpus. A number of topics, for example, were found to contain no direct reference to a particular philosopher, but upon analysis were clearly aimed at specific texts. For example, Sample #5.142, which is ostensibly concerned with the broad issue of religious belief, can be seen to refer manifestly to Marx's famous critique of religion outlined in his *Critique of Hegel's Philosophy of Right*.

> 5.142 Is religion the opium of the masses? If it is, does it follow that God does not exist, or that it is unreasonable to believe that God exists?
>
> *Philosophy of Religion*

Similarly, Sample #5.143, set on the *Contemporary Moral Issues* subject, can be recognized as an invitation to consider critically the 'animal liberationist' writings of philosophers such as Peter Singer. The epistemic entity ('view') in the topic rubric is understood, in this context, to refer to the 'view expressed by certain relevant philosophers'.

> 5.143 Critically evaluate the view that animals are entitled to at least some of the same basic rights as humans.
>
> *Contemporary Moral Issues*

In the corpus, it was also noted that certain unattributed 'issue-focused' questions were sometimes accompanied by a parallel attributed 'text-focused' question. Thus, in Samples #5.144 and #5.145 below, one notes how the philosophical issue in question ('the problem of evil') is given similar coverage within the two alternative formats.

> 5.144 Is the universe better because it has some evil in it than it would be if there were no evil? Do you think that an affirmative answer to this question can be used to provide an adequate solution to the 'problem of evil'?
>
> *God, Freedom and Evil*

> 5.145 Critically discuss **Mackie's formulation** of the 'problem of evil'.
>
> *God, Freedom and Evil*

In topics such as these, there is a clear convergence between the 'text-focused' and 'issue-focused' topics, with the former type seeming to be the dominant, unmarked form in the discipline. At the heart of such questions, as we have seen, is the need for students to 'render verdicts' on the arguments they are asked to consider.

Action-focused questions

Among these additional topic-types, there was one that appeared to fall outside the broad framework outlined above. These included questions framed not around a text or issue, but rather a specific 'real-world' scenario requiring some

practical resolution, as exemplified in Samples #5.146 and #5.147 from the field
of bioethics.

5.146   A patient tells you (a health professional) that he has genuine and
         informed desire to die, and asks you to assist him in carrying out
         his wish. How can you respond? How can ethical theories help to
         resolve this issue?

Ethical Issues in Health Care

5.147   Suppose you are a doctor and a patient of yours who has tested HIV
         positive refuses to disclose his diagnosis to his partner. What should
         you do? Would you be morally justified in informing the partner
         yourself? Which ethical principles will be most useful for you in deal-
         ing with this situation?

Ethical Issues in Health Care

In these samples, the principal judgement required (*content of inquiry*) is not
one of evaluating arguments *per se*, but rather one of deciding on a course of
action (i.e. how to respond professionally to the medical dilemmas described).
Accordingly, the philosophical arguments students need to consider (referred
to in the rubric to as 'ethical principles/theories') are conceived here not as
entities to be evaluated in their own right, but rather as heuristics that can provide some reasoned and principled basis for action.

The distinctive practical orientation of such questions was explained by Kim,
the convenor of the bioethics programme in the School of Philosophy. The
course, which is mainly aimed at students already employed in the health sector, was developed principally as a response to the increasing complexity of
work in this area.

5.148   **KIM** (philosophy): The students I have on my course are often health
         care professions. [In their work] they encounter numerous ethical
         issues everyday, not just one a day but perhaps ten, fifteen. So they
         often come to the course feeling very bewildered by all of this and
         wondering what on earth to do and how they can make decisions.

For Kim, the particular approach employed is not one of seeking to provide
answers to students, but rather to give them the philosophical tools which will
enable them to make decisions in a critically informed way.

5.149   **KIM**: I don't see our role as saying to [the students] this is what you
         have to do in the situation. The type of philosophy we teach seeks to

help them decide on, to understand and evaluate the frameworks and sets of principles so they can then decide in some critical way which they think are the most plausible and should be applied here.

Among the various disciplines (and sub-disciplines) considered in the study, this particular branch of philosophy – sometimes referred to as 'practical ethics' (Singer 1993) – appears, in some respects, to be distinctive. Whereas all the other areas investigated so far have been concerned arguably with judgements about knowledge *per se*, the focus here is more on how knowledge is to be applied – a contrast captured in the literature by the terms *episteme* (knowing that) and *techne* (knowing how) (Becher 1989: p. 15). The seemingly distinctive nature of the bioethics questions above, can thus be seen as further evidence of the diverse ways in which students need to be critical in the faculty. In the case of philosophy, the particular characteristics of this applied branch serve to undermine any impression we may of the discipline having a single and unified critical mode.

5.4.3 Literary/cultural studies essay topics

In the analyses of essay topics from the disciplines of history and philosophy, there was an attempt to identify in each case what might be called an 'archetypal question structure'. Although a number of important exceptions were noted in both disciplines, many of the questions in each of the two corpora were found to conform to broad archetypal patterns. In the history materials, the key to many questions was the requirement that students develop and present a view (or interpretation) about a particular real-world event; in philosophy, the principal task was found to involve the evaluation of (or 'rendering of verdicts on') the arguments of individual philosophers.

As might be expected from the data presented from the discipline so far, locating an archetypal question structure in the field of literary/cultural studies was a considerably less straightforward task. In line with the generally fissiparous nature of the field, a good deal of variation was observed in the essay topics collected for this final discipline area. Once again, at the heart of this variation would seem to be the extent to which notions of theory are present in task rubric, and how much the critical approach required of students is dependent on them making explicit use of such theory in their work.

Literary/cultural studies: Principal objects of inquiry

If one is able to posit any generalization about the essay topics in the literary/cultural studies corpus, it is that most have as their *object of inquiry* some literary or cultural text. Such an account of the discipline is, in fact, to be found in one of the protocol documents considered earlier (*Frequently asked questions: English literature*). While the document acknowledges the considerable diversity of approaches that can be adopted ('There are so many different legitimate ways of going about reading … and analysing a text', it states), the element common to virtually all approaches to literary criticism, it suggests, are the texts themselves:

> 5.150   *What is common to almost all approaches [to literature] nowadays is that they are in the end text-focused. That is, they don't feel comfortable in making assertions about anything unless they can back it up in some way through reference to text.*
>
> Frequently asked questions: English literature

Figure 18 (below) presents a sample of these strongly text-focused topics, taken from a range of subjects within the literary/cultural studies programme. As has already been noted, what qualifies as a literary text is much broader in some areas of the discipline than others. Thus, in the list below, it can be seen that in some topics the principal *object of inquiry* is an established work of literature (#5.151, #5.152 and #5.153); in others, students are asked to consider texts from distinctly non-literary genres, such as popular films (#5.155) and television programmes (#5.156). In some, but not all, of these samples, some characterization of the text in question is provided in the topic rubric; for example, *novel* (#5.151 and #5.152); *science fiction text, fictions* (#5.153); *American TV comedy series, film* (#5.156).

Table 15 (Column 1) below provides a summary of terms (and sample titles) identified under the *object of inquiry* category in the corpus as a whole. As can be seen, some of these *objects* are described according to specific genre designations (novels, poetry, film, film adaptations, etc.). A general, overarching term ('text') was also used, which, as the table shows, took in a broad range of materials – in fact any conceivable *object of inquiry* in the field (from biblical passages, to Shakespeare, to the title sequence of a popular television series). This 'text' designation, it was noted, was used only for the comparative literature materials. The origins of this usage can be traced to Barthes (1977), whose seminal tract, 'The work and the text', laid out a theoretical basis for distinguishing traditional genres of literature ('works') and cultural artefacts of all types ('texts'), creating in the process, it seems, a perfect democracy of literary forms.

Literary/cultural studies: Principal processes of inquiry

As it was with the history and philosophy corpora, the topics collected here do not provide abundant information about the types of thinking *processes* that underlie the work needed to be done by students. The following extracts, however (taken from the samples above), do provide some picture of the way that engagement with material is envisaged. A full list of related *processes* is shown in Table 15.

5.151   Mr Rochester describes in Vol 3 Chapter 1 of *Jane Eyre*, the circumstances in which he was married to Bertha Mason, and how he came to incarcerate her in the attic at Thornfield. What do we learn about him from this, and how far does **the novel** endorse his claim that he has acted for the best?

Reading Literature

5.152   In *Wide Sargasso Sea*, Antoinette remembers: 'Our garden was large and beautiful as the Bible – the tree of life grew there. But it had gone wild. The paths were grown and a smell of dead flowers mixed with the fresh living smell'.

Comment on the way in which descriptions of landscape and environment in the **novel** mark stages in the spiritual and psychological journey of the heroine.

Reading Literature

5.153   To what extent can *Nineteen Eighty-Four* be considered a **science fiction text**? Your answer will need to explore the novel's generic and intertextual contexts. (Your answer might also discuss early 20th century dystopian and utopian **fictions** by writers such as Zamyatin, Kapek, Huxley and Wells.)

Text and Context

5.154   Critically discuss the representation of the 'other' in Scepanovic's **Mouth Full of Earth**

Postmodernism and the Novel

5.155   Compare and contrast the different versions of the 'posthuman' in any of *RUR; Metropolis; Blade Runner, Simians, Cyborgs, and Women and Les particules élémentaires (Atomised)*.

Text and Context 2

5.156   In the 1960s, **two American TV comedy series** were produced about monstrous families, *The Munsters* and *The Addams Family*. A **film** based on the latter was produced in 1990s. How do these representations of 'monster families' intersect or disrupt the dominant ideology of the family values as represented/constructed in current family discourses of media and politics.

Introduction to Cultural Studies

Figure 18   Sample literary/cultural studies essay topics (showing principal *object of inquiry*)

Table 15 Terminology used in main topic-type (Literary/Cultural Studies)

OBJECT OF INQUIRY What type of entity is to be analysed?	PROCESS OF INQUIRY By which type of mental/ verbal process?		CONTENT OF INQUIRY By which analytical criteria/ categories?
novel (e.g. *Jane Eyre/Wide Sargasso Sea*)	discuss	5	stages of life*
	compare	3	fulfillment in life*
poem (e.g. *poetry of the Great War*)	contrast	3	motivation of character*
	explore	3	women's experience*
film (e.g. *The Belly of an Architect*)	comment on	2	spiritual journey*
	see	2	—
film adaptation (e.g. *The Sound of One Hand Clapping/ Apocalypse Now*)	show	1	versions of 'human'**
	characterize	1	versions of 'posthuman'**
	interpret	1	intertextual relations**
TV series (e.g. *The Munsters/ The Adams Family/Buffy, The Vampire Slayer*)	learn	1	metonymic meanings**
	be taught	1	suppression of referent**
	agree	1	concept of genre**
text (e.g. *Genesis/Midsummer Night's Dream/Ghosts/1984/ Kill Bill/title sequence in The Simpsons*)	value		postmodern nostalgia**
			narrative practices**
			mimetic/symbolic meaning**

* Categories from traditional literature strand
** Categories from comparative literature strand

5.157 **Comment on** the way in which descriptions of landscape and environment in the novel mark stages in the spiritual and psychological journey of the heroine.

Reading Literature

5.158 Your answer will need to **explore** the novel's generic and intertextual contexts. (Your answer might also **discuss** early 20th century dystopian and utopian fictions by writers such as Zamyatin, Kapek, Huxley and Wells.)

Text and Context

5.159 **Critically discuss** the representation of the 'other' in Scepanovic's *Mouth Full of Earth*.

Postmodernism and the Novel

5.160 **Compare and contrast** the different versions of the 'posthuman' in any of *RUR; Metropolis; Blade Runner, Simians, Cyborgs, and Women* and *Les particules élémentaires (Atomised)*.

Text and Context 2

These processes of *discussing, exploring, commenting on* and *comparing* from the essay rubric fit with some of the generic statements quoted earlier about the way it is suggested that students should engage with texts in the discipline:

5.161　*A literature essay should reveal what it is a student has come to* **understand** *about a text.*

> Frequently asked questions: English literature

5.162　*The meanings of a text are given life in each successive reader's* **exploration** *of it.*

> Introduction to the analysis of a literary text: Comparative literature

Literary/cultural studies: Principal content of inquiry

While it may be agreed that the fundamental task for students studying in the field of literary/cultural studies is to *explore* texts, and to express their *understanding* of them, what specific aspects of these texts should be explored (and what this understanding might consist of) remain highly contentious issues, as we have seen. As was noted earlier, one of the key points of divergence among the discipline's different critical traditions is the part that notions of the 'real' come to play in one's conception of text. Thus, it will be recalled that within more traditional approaches, connections between the world of the text and the world one inhabits as a reader are seen as crucial, and thought to lie at the heart of a critical outlook. As was explained, it is apprehensions of these connections that allow one both to relate empathetically to the characters portrayed in a literary work, and to feel some involvement in the moral issues and dilemmas they typically confront:

5.163　*The text gives you an opportunity to evaluate critically your own assumptions. The really worthwhile literature very rarely simplifies its moral positions; it usually shows awareness of the complexity of the issues being talked about and this will overlap with the world we live in.*

> Frequently asked questions: English literature

In the alternative literature strand, these putative connections between the textual and the real are thought to be far more problematic, and are, in fact, the subject of a good deal of theorizing within the discipline. We saw in the alternative advice document, for example, a very emphatic statement about the incommensurability of the two domains:

5.164   *The structure [of a] literary work ... does not relate to a reality outside itself. What the structure does is to incorporate a reality of its own, which is autonomous and separate from nature, life, the writer's biography, even history.*

Introduction to the analysis of a literary text

A similar – though somewhat more tempered – account was offered in interview by Brian, from the Centre for Comparative Literature and Cultural Studies. While Brian did not wish to insist on a fundamentally non-materialist view, held by some within the ranks of postmodernist thought, he was nonetheless sure that many aspects of the reality we perceive are in some sense 'textual':

5.165   **BRIAN** (literary/cultural studies – comp.): it's not that we [in CCLCS] are all postmodernists, but we are basically concerned with texts and we're interrogating texts which are artefacts that exist now ... I'm not saying there's nothing outside the text. There is a lot outside the text. But a lot of things are textualized that people don't realize.

In the essay topic data, it is in the *content of inquiry* that these different conceptions of literature are most evident, with topics from the more traditional stream relying on distinctly 'humanist' categories of interpretation such as *stages of life, motivation of character, women's experience* and those from the comparative stream drawing on a very different set of analytical categories; for example, *metonymic meanings, intertextual relations, suppression of referent, narrative structure* (Table 15). Examples from the corpus exemplifying the more 'humanist' approach are the following topics about the novel *Jane Eyre* from the subject *Reading Literature* (#5.166 and #5.167).

5.166   Mr Rochester describes in Vol 3 Chapter 1 of *Jane Eyre*, the circumstances in which he was married to Bertha Mason, and how he came to incarcerate her in the attic at Thornfield. What do we learn about him from this, and how far does the novel endorse his claim that he has acted for the best?

Reading Literature

5.167   *Jane Eyre* is presented as an autobiography, wherein a mature woman looks back over the stages and development of her life. What distinguishes the **stages of her life**, and what do they seem to teach us?

Reading Literature

In topics such as these, the aspect of the novel that students need to render judgements about is the actions and lives of the novel's characters – that is, Rochester's treatment of his wife (#5.166), and the stages and development of Jane's life (#5.167). We can see that in each topic the intention is to have students derive some form of moral and psychological instruction from the novel. For example, it is notable that the respective key verbs in the two topics are 'learn' ('what do we *learn* about Rochester'?) and 'teach' ('what do the stages in Jane's life ... *teach* us?').

An explicitly oppositional view to this approach, however, was advanced by several informants from comparative literature. In interview, Brian, for example, was keen to highlight a basic disjuncture he saw lying between topics such as these and those he would typically set on his programme:

> 5.168   **BRIAN** (literary/cultural studies – comp.): Such topics are quite dissimilar to what I would set. They don't actually alert students to the fact that what they are talking about is text. It's as if the characters are real people, and that what they say and do happens almost as if it were outside the novel. These are less theoretical questions – they don't problematize the idea that all that happens is in fact a construction.

Lois, also working within comparative literature, suggested similar contrasts. For her, to have students engage intimately with the lives and circumstances of characters in a literary work requires a distinctively different critical mode – what she called a 'psychological and ethical reasoning'.

> 5.169   **LOIS** (literary/cultural studies – comp.): So whereas the emphasis in the traditional literature essay, I would have thought, is on a type of psychological and ethical reasoning, the emphasis we have is on what we would call textual reasoning.

This contrasting 'textual reasoning', wherein texts are seen 'to incorporate their own separate reality', is evident in many of the topics collected in the corpus. In the topic below (#5.170), for example, about George Orwell's *Nineteen Eighty-Four*, it is apparent that the novel is not to be understood here in terms of how it might connect to some broader social and political reality, but rather how it relates to other texts.

> 5.170   To what extent can *Nineteen Eighty-Four* be considered a science fiction text? Your answer will need to explore the novel's **generic** and **intertextual** contexts. (Your answer might also discuss early 20th century dystopian and utopian fictions by writers such as Zamyatin, Kapek, Huxley and Wells.)
>
> *Text and Context*

The same framework is evident in the following topic (#5.171), one drawing on certain popular culture texts (TV comedy series – *The Munsters* and *The Addams Family*). It is of interest that while this particular topic alludes to a broader social context ('the dominant ideology of the family'), this context is conceived here as a fundamentally textual one (i.e. 'family discourses of media and politics').

5.171   In the 1960s, two American TV comedy series were produced about monstrous families, *The Munsters* and *The Addams Family*. A film based on the latter was produced in 1990s. How do these representations of **'monster families'** intersect or disrupt the dominant ideology of the family values as represented/constructed in current family discourses of media and politics.

Introduction to Cultural Studies

An important dimension of the 'textual reasoning' described by Lois (#5.171) is the role played by theory in 'coming to an understanding' of text. Brian also discussed the place of theory in literary studies, insisting that it was somehow the key to being 'critical' in the discipline:

5.172   **BRIAN** (literary/cultural studies – comp.): We stress that what [students] are doing in their essays is using – I mean, we're quite explicit about this – they're using theoretical notions to explore and to interrogate literary texts.

The following topics from Figure 18 (above, #5.173–5.175), exemplify such an approach. The particular theoretical notions that students need to draw on in their analyses are highlighted in each case. It is, in fact, conventional in the construction of such topics for the theoretical element to be indicated by inverted commas.

5.173   Critically discuss the representation of the **'other'** in Scepanovic's *Mouth Full of Earth*.

Postmodernism and the Novel

5.174   Compare and contrast the different versions of the **'posthuman'** in any of *RUR; Metropolis; Blade Runner, Simians, Cyborgs, and Women* and *Les particules élémentaires (Atomised)*.

Text and Context 2

5.175   To what extent can Peter Greenaway's film *The Belly of an Architect* be characterized as **'postmodern nostalgia'**?

Postmodernism and the Novel

The literary/cultural studies topics considered thus far have proven themselves resistant to any simple and straightforward analysis. This is due, in part no doubt, to the susceptibility all have to the varying influences and attractions of these rival literary paradigms. Amid this diversity, however, it is possible to distill some overall patterning in their construction. The single element common to all topics, as has been noted, is a focus on literary/cultural texts, however broadly or narrowly these are defined. It was noted further that the key task for students was to provide some form of 'interpretation' of such texts – though the nature of such interpretations (i.e. their 'thematic' content) was also found to differ widely. In the face of all this disparateness, a broad structure can nevertheless be summarized thus:

Object of inquiry: textual entities (novels, plays, films, television series, etc.)

Processes of inquiry: acts of interpretation (exploring, investigating, discussing, etc.)

Content of inquiry: thematic (aesthetic, moral, textual, etc.)

Other literary/cultural studies topics: Theory as principal object of inquiry

While topics described in the schema above (i.e. having a focus on a particular text or texts) were the most common in the corpus, in a number of other topics, one notes a clear de-emphasizing of the literary work, with a greater focus placed on the conceptual and theoretical element. This difference can be illustrated in the two sample topics below. In the structure of the first topic (discussed earlier, #5.176), the literary work (*Nineteen Eighty-Four*) is clearly salient. In terms of Halliday's functional grammar, this salience derives from the work being present in the rubric in 'thematic' (or initial) position (Halliday 1994: p. 58). By contrast, in Sample #5.177, the literary/cultural works (*Heart of Darkness, Apocalypse Now*) are positioned in the rubric as 'rheme', with arguably greater prominence given to the theoretical concepts ('modernism' and 'postmodernism').

> ### *Work-prominent topic:*

5.176   To what extent can ***Nineteen Eighty-Four*** be considered a science fiction text? Your answer will need to explore the novel's **generic** and **intertextual** contexts.

(Literary work as theme; Theory as rheme)

> ### *Theory-prominent topic:*

5.177   What is meant by the terms **'modernism'** and **'postmodernism'**. Show your understanding of these concepts through your analysis of aspects of ***Heart of Darkness*** and ***Apocalypse Now***.

(Theory as theme; Literary work as rheme;)

Other examples of topics within the literary/cultural studies corpus fitting this latter pattern were the following:

> 5.178   Discuss the **concept of genre** (and in particular the genre identified as 'ficto-criticism'), using J.M Coetzee's *Elizabeth Costello* as a reference. Does a text such as this represent a development of the novel, or should it be seen as a whole new genre?
>
> *Narrative Practices*

> 5.179   **Violence in postmodern texts**. Is it mimetic or symbolic? Discuss this concept with reference to Tarantino's *Kill Bill Vol 1*.
>
> *Postmodernism and the Novel*

> 5.180   What is **'liquid modernity'** and how useful is it as concept? Use the phenomenon of reality television to assess the strengths and weaknesses of this concept.
>
> *Introduction to cultural studies*

Thus, it can be seen in such topics that the task for students is to first elaborate on the concept and then investigate how it might be exemplified in a literary work.

In other topic samples (#5.181 and #5.182), there is even greater de-emphasizing of the literary work, with the theoretical concept itself prescribed (e.g. Derrida's trace; narrative theory), and students given a choice about which literary texts they will draw on to exemplify the concept in question.

> 5.181   What is a **'trace'** in **Derrida's sense**? Show your understanding of the **concept** by giving an example from a work of fiction in which Derrida's trace is transformed into plot. (You may wish to refer to Spivak's introduction to Derrida's *Of Grammatology*).
>
> *Postmodernism and the Novel*

> 5.182   **Narrative theory** shows that 'telling it as it is' is an illusion: narrating competently requires us to make ruthless selections, to shape the material available to us through ethical choices and to bring stories to specifically weighted conclusions. Consider elements of this claim in relation to two of the texts studied in this unit.
>
> *Narrative Practices*

Finally, there were topics in the literary/cultural studies corpus where the literary work is seen to disappear from the task rubric altogether – though such an absence would not necessarily preclude students from referring to works in their written responses. In Sample #5.183, students are asked to evaluate Roland Barthes' famous pronouncement on the idea of authorship in literary criticism; in Samples #5.184 and #5.185, Frederic Jameson's particular characterization of 'postmodernism' is to be assessed. It is of interest that these final three questions with their focus on the evaluation of certain theoretical positions have much in common with many of the topics seen in the philosophy corpus.

> 5.183   Reports of the death of the author tend to be greatly exaggerated. Discuss
>
> *Text and Content 2*

> 5.184   Frederic Jameson describes 'postmodernism' as 'the cultural logic of late capitalism'. To what extent do you agree with this assessment? Give reasons for your answer.
>
> *Text and Content 2*

> 5.185   Why does Simon During disagree with Frederic Jameson's theory of postmodernism? Is he right?
>
> *Postmodernism and the Novel*

The importance of theory in literary criticism was asserted by a number of informants, as we have seen. In keeping with the generally disputational tendencies within the discipline, others from the more traditional literature strand in the faculty were keen to express their disdain for such an approach. Lending some credence to the patterns observed above (#5.183–5.185), Quentin (literary/cultural studies – Eng.) suggested, somewhat ruefully, that in a highly theoretical approach, interest in the discipline's most basic concern – the literary work itself – could sometimes be lost altogether.

> 5.186   **QUENTIN** (literary/cultural studies – Eng.): I'm not sure how much some of my colleagues are actually interested in literature anymore … [In the types of questions they set] it's a bit like putting a work of literature through a theory machine and seeing what comes out the other end. … [The interest seems more in] documenting the machine than the literature.

It is interesting to note that those about whom such reservations were expressed (the more theory-oriented 'colleagues') also admitted their own concerns about studying literature exclusively in this way. Brian, for example, perhaps the strongest advocate for a theoretically informed approach, thought that while such an approach was necessary, it was also important that students be allowed to experience literature in some personal and spontaneous way:

> 5.187   **BRIAN** (literary/cultural studies – comp.): But I have to say ... we are worried, we don't want to destroy [students] enjoyment, which sometimes people say you do. Once you've taken [literary works] apart and analysed them into boxes the fun is gone, whereas of course being overwhelmed by the text, which is how the Leavisites wanted you to be, is close to the experience of the first time you read a novel.

Lois described the challenge in similar terms, noting that the theoretical methods employed within the centre could be at odds with the more personal approaches to literature that students were used to from their secondary education.

> 5.188   **LOIS** (literary/cultural studies – comp.): The difficulty is in teaching literature the way students usually learned to love literature at school, that is by using it as an opportunity to share personal responses ... So the challenge is to draw them into a more rigorous and scholarly way of working with literature without dampening their delight in the process of reading.

Reflecting on the types of theoretical questions typically set for students in the Centre for Comparative Literature, Lois went on to acknowledge the criticisms made by those working within more 'humanist' paradigms, noting that these more theoretically oriented approaches risked descending into an excessive 'formalism', and becoming increasingly irrelevant to students' lives outside the confines of the department.

> 5.189   **LOIS** (literary/cultural studies – comp.): So you can understand the impatience of more old-fashioned humanist literary scholars. If they see a question like that [they say] 'Well, who cares? I mean, that's so formalistic.' So the danger with this approach is that it heads off in the direction of a kind of highly professionalized formalism in which case you're left with the question, 'Well, so what? How is this developing the student as a citizen or as a member of society?' I have some sympathy with the kind of humanist objection to the formalism.

It is not the place here to adjudicate on these methodological dilemmas, nor to suggest allegiances to any of the positions that have been outlined. Perhaps, the significance of the concessionary remarks made by the 'critical theorists' above is indeed the 'critical' tenor they bring to discussions about their own preferred approach. In acknowledging the limitations of a highly theoretical literary criticism – one that is elsewhere valorized – there is the suggestion that there can be no impeccable 'critical' mode, and that every method of its nature has the potential both to open up certain perspectives on the object being considered, while at the same time closing others down.

5.4.4 Summary of essay topic analysis

In the preceding sections, a large number of essay topics have been considered. The analysis of each corpus has made it possible to identify a distinct archetypal structure for each of the three discipline areas, one that in each case is suggestive of a distinctive type of critical thinking. However, this is not to suggest that what has been uncovered in this process is some essential form of critique for each of the three areas. Indeed, the picture was far from being so simple, with a range of tasks emerging in each area that resisted ready allocation to the various patterns identified. The implications of these findings, and of those from the investigation as a whole, are now addressed in the remaining two chapters.

Chapter 6

Critical Thinking: So What Is It?

6.1 Introduction

The investigation described thus far has sought to explore the meanings of critical thinking in the university in different disciplinary contexts. This has been done by inquiring into the conceptions of critical thinking held by academics as articulated by them in interview, and also by looking in detail at some of the key documents used by these academics in their teaching. In its description of the findings of this investigation, the study has been concerned with the drawing of many different comparisons. Central to these have been comparisons concerning the notion of disciplinarity – that is to say, how ideas and practices of critical thinking might vary and overlap across the three discipline areas we have considered. This interdisciplinary dimension of the study was the chief focus of the analysis in the preceding chapter.

But, there have been additional comparisons that have found their way into the discussion. For example, attention has been paid to the variations within individual discipline areas, focusing on differences between sub-disciplines within a field, and also (in some cases) between individual academics working on the same programme. A final type of comparison, one that has loomed over much of the research, is what might be called extra-disciplinary comparison. In this dimension of the study, there has been an effort to see how understandings of critical thinking held by the study's informants correspond to those whose perspective lies, in a sense, outside the disciplines; that is, the thinkers and educationists associated with the general critical thinking movement – Robert Ennis (1992), Peter Facione (1990), Tim van Gelder (2001) and others. In the present chapter, the intention is to try to make some sense of the study's different comparative strands and to try to bring the various – and at times desultory – threads together into some coherent whole. This will be done by returning to the questions that were posed at the beginning of the investigation, and trying to propose some answers to them; namely:

i. What does 'critical thinking' seem to mean to individual academics teaching in different disciplines within the university?

ii. In what ways, and to what extent, can we say that there are disciplinary variations in these meanings of critical thinking?
iii. What implications do the answers to i) and ii) have for the teaching of critical thinking in the university?

6.2 Conceptions of Critical Thinking

The first issue to address is the broad definitional question. It will be recalled from the earlier discussion that one of the key motivations for the study was the problem of the 'ineffability' of critical thinking. Thus, in the earlier discussion of the literature, it was suggested that while critical thinking is thought to play an integral role in contemporary higher education, the problem is that academics' understandings of the notion tend to be somewhat inchoate, and that they are often unable to convey to students what is meant by the term. For a number of writers (Atkinson 1997; Fox 1994; Resnick 1987), this apparent inability arises from the notion being so fundamental and deep-rooted in the thinking and practices of academics – a part of their professional *habitus* – that apprehensions of criticality are often limited only to the recognition of instances when they occur:

> we become aware that although we cannot define it exactly, we can recognize higher order thinking when we see it. (Resnick 1987: p. 2–3)

In the interview data, a number of examples of this definitional uncertainty were evident. It was suggested by one informant, for example, that the term was notoriously difficult to 'nail down' and was 'probably going to turn out to be a very broad diverse set of things'. For another informant, the term had a certain 'wonder' about it for the way 'you [could] make it mean almost anything'. The same lack of precision was also detectable at times in some of the documents considered in the study. Thus, in the history protocol document for example (discussed in Chapter 5) it was noted that although students were enjoined frequently to adopt the right 'critical' approach in their studies ('to write *critical* and clear arguments', 'to be *critical* of the interpretations of historians', 'to generally read *critically*'), missing from this particular counsel was any attempt to explain to students what exactly this might involve.

But, while one can point to examples in the data where the notion was left vague or undescribed, claims in the literature about the inability of academics to give substance to the term are not borne out in the study's findings. Indeed, as was seen, many of those surveyed had much to say on the subject, and when asked, were able to offer quite cogent accounts of what the quality might involve. One informant, for example, was sure critical thinking meant thinking about something in an evaluative way and thinking about the ways in which it might be *valid*, or *invalid*; for another, it meant not just *accepting* what you have, but asking questions about it; and for yet another, it was *challenging* the assumptions that underlie accepted knowledge.

Many of the documents analysed in the study were also found to contain the same kind of clarifying statements. The philosophy protocol document, for example, featured a quite elaborate discourse on what 'critical evaluation' in a philosophy essay might involve, with the suggestion that the form this critique takes is likely to vary depending on whether the *object* of one's evaluation is a philosophical text or philosophical issue. Similarly, among the exercise tasks, a fair amount of explication of the term was provided for students – as in the following rubric from one of the history tasks:

6.01   *The evaluative exercise requires you to* **think critically** *about historical writing. This means that it must not be just a summary of what each author says. Rather you must show that you understand the underlying point of view being expressed, as well as the type of evidence presented to support this view* (emphasis added).

It is worth pausing for a moment to consider why this should be the case – that is, why most of those interviewed were able to articulate so readily some coherent understanding of the term. Part of the answer may lie in the nature of the disciplines considered in the investigation. The study confined itself to investigating certain humanities disciplines, and it may be the case that the term has a more immediate resonance for academics in these fields than for those in other parts of the university. Indeed, a number of examples were seen in the data where the term was central to the intellectual outlook of the particular discipline concerned. Thus, for literary/cultural studies, the term 'criticism' is used to denote the general activity of scholars in this field – 'literary *criticism*'; and in one of the strands of this discipline, the word describes a major theoretical paradigm relied on by scholars – '*critical* theory'. The term's centrality was also noted in philosophy, where one of the subjects taught within the programme in fact used the designation '*critical* thinking'.

One can speculate, however, about a broader explanation – that some of the changes that have occurred in higher education in recent decades appear to have lead academics to become more aware of educational practices, and also to be more aware of the needs of some of the student cohorts they teach. As pointed out earlier, the shift from a small elite system to a burgeoning mass one has meant, among other things, that assumptions once made about the types of knowledge and skills possessed by commencing students can no longer be relied on in the framing of a course of study (Bauldauf 1996). The imperatives of these changes – along with greater accountability pressures felt generally by institutions and staff – have been responsible, some suggest, for the emergence in recent years of a distinct 'discourse of education' within university teaching (Ryan, Dearn and Fraser 2002). This discourse, which takes in such notions as 'objectives, 'outcomes', attributes', 'evaluation', 'quality' and so on, can be seen as a new type of *habitus* for the contemporary academic – albeit one not always wholeheartedly embraced by them. It is therefore possible to see these more articulate understandings expressed by the study's informants as a manifestation of these larger social and educational processes. On this point, it is of interest to note that one informant (Nell) talked about her understandings of 'critical thinking' being fashioned largely out of discussions she had with colleagues about the development of an 'education plan' for the faculty.

What then is to be said about these academics' conceptions of critical thinking? The first point to note is that while the study's informants could readily engage with the notion, there was in fact a good deal of variety in the descriptions offered. This was particularly the case with the interview data, where a number of different definitional strands, or themes, were seen to emerge. For some informants, critical thinking was mainly thought of as sceptical thinking, with students always needing to bring a circumspect attitude to the ideas and beliefs they are introduced to. For others, it was a more creative attribute, one that enabled students to say new and potentially interesting things about the various objects of their study. At a minimalist level, most were in agreement that critical thinking involved the making of judgements in some way, although the way that such judgements were characterized varied a good deal. Of particular interest in the data here was the variety of spatial metaphors that were used. Thus, in some instances, the desired form of judgement was seen as a type of 'cutting down' (e.g. *deconstructing* or *being a sharp knife*); in others it was a 'building up' (e.g. *putting together* or *assembling*); and yet in others, a lateral kind of movement (e.g. *moving sideways*, or *heading in a different direction*).

Not only would we say that there was variety in the descriptions offered, but also that some of these were of a conflicting nature. Thus in the data – both in the interviews and in the documents – we saw the playing out of a number of controversies, ones which seemed to arise not only out of the different epistemological underpinnings of the disciplines investigated, but also from the particular beliefs and worldviews of individual informants. Among these controversies were questions concerning the extent to which critical thinking should be thought of as a fundamentally rational mode; whether a critical engagement with knowledge invariably takes in individual subjectivities; how much theory has a role to play; and finally, whether being a critical thinker necessarily involves engaging with the world in some ethical and activist way.

The findings of the study suggest that our term needs to be thought of as being both a polysemous and contested one, and confirms the view of Resnick that thinking skills in the academy seem 'to resist the precise forms of definition associated with other kinds of educational objectives' (1987: p. 3). Even the philosophers in the study, who were the ones most wedded to the idea of a precise and universal definition, found it difficult to sustain such a position. This is evident in the following commentary made by the philosopher in the study who was arguably the most committed to the universalist idea:

6.02 **JONATHON** (philosophy): There is a sense that … all intellectual work is engagement with a rational project, it is not surprising that it is a commonality.

In his commentary, however, this assertion was followed by a qualification:

but of course I am coming from a view according to which what we mostly think of as critical thinking is similar and universal.

There is an interesting paradox in these statements. On the one hand, critical thinking is seen as 'a commonality', and as 'similar and universal'; but on the other, it is conceded that this is only a particular 'view'. Such a concession, while commendably ecumenical in its outlook, immediately suggests a plurality of views and undermines any claims to a single critical method.

6.3 Comparisons with The Critical Thinking Movement

The idea of critical thinking being a 'single and universal' ability – as noted above – has been a key article of faith for many in the critical thinking movement. Thus, out of this movement have emerged a number of systematic accounts of critical thinking. The generic accounts proposed by this movement, both in the form of core definitions (Ennis 1987; Paul 1996; van Gelder 2001) and of taxonomic lists of constitutive skills (Ennis 1987; Facione 1990), have been significant for the influence they have exerted over education policy and practice. While this has been the case for some time in the US (Atkinson 1997), such ideas have been felt increasingly in debates in Australian and British higher education – especially around the notion of graduate attributes, and recent proposals for the generic testing of such attributes (Australian Council of Education Research 2001; Department of Education Science and Training 2003).

An important question for the study is how much correspondence there is between these generic, 'extra-disciplinary' understandings of critical thinking and the various disciplinary-based understandings to emerge out of the research. In exploring this type of comparison, reference is made again to the taxonomy of Robert Ennis (see Figure 19), which, as noted previously, has been arguably the most influential among the generic accounts on offer (Norris 1992; Australian Council of Educational Research 2001).

In such a collection of 'abilities', it is certainly possible to detect a number of similarities with those identified in the study's interviews and documents.

1. grasping the meaning of statements
2. judging whether there is ambiguity in a line of reasoning
3. judging whether certain statements contradict one another
4. judging whether a conclusion necessarily follows
5. judging whether a statement is specific enough
6. judging whether a statement is actually the application of a certain principle
7. judging whether an observation statement is reliable
8. judging whether an inductive conclusion is warranted
9. judging whether the problem has been identified
10. judging whether something is an assumption
11. judging whether a definition is adequate
12. judging whether a statement by an alleged authority is acceptable

FIGURE 19   Taxonomy of critical thinking abilities (Ennis 1987)

The key *process* in Ennis's account is adamantly one of 'judgement', which, as noted, was arguably the principal theme to emerge from the interviews. This motif is very much in line with many of the working definitions that were proffered by informants – for example, the view of one who suggested that critical thinking 'always means judgement and the making of distinctions of some kind'; or another who thought it was essentially about the 'rendering of verdicts' on ideas.

Clear correspondences can also be detected in some of the individual abilities outlined in Ennis's list. A number of these, for example, evoke the sceptical outlook emphasized by many informants, including ability #7 ('judging whether an observation statement is reliable'); and ability #12 ('judging whether a statement by an alleged authority is acceptable'). This last attribute, in particular, has a strong resonance with many of the accounts offered by informants. Indeed the use of the term 'acceptable' (and variants 'accepting', 'accept' and 'accepted') was a feature of the talk of a number of informants on this subject:

6.03   **LAUREN** (philosophy): Well, I suppose that … critical thinking is not just *accepting* what somebody tells you.

6.04   **MICHAEL** (history): it's about getting [students] to think 'well, just because this guy writes it in a book it's not something you have to *accept*'.

Such a view was expressed even by informants from the comparative literature area – a field sometimes accused, as we saw, of not always being as 'critical' of some of its more favoured thinkers and theories as it might be:

6.05   **LOIS** (literary/cultural studies – comp.): students – indeed not only students – will often be tempted to … adopt [certain fashionable theories] as the new Bible and it then becomes the truth. ... [and] you then get this phenomenon of the theory being *accepted* without question.

But while some important commonalities are to found in the two domains, there is much that is not covered in a generic account such as that given by Ennis. One element noticeably absent, for example, is the more 'constructive' version of critical thinking, thought by some informants to be just as important as any permanently sceptical outlook. For these informants, this was an important counterbalance to a mainly negatively evaluative approach, affording students the opportunities to build on knowledge in some way – for example, to put together an individual 'interpretation' of a text, or to 'view' an historical event in an interesting, even original, way.

Also missing in the generic account of Ennis – or at least greatly simplified in it – is the idea of critical thinking as the 'sensitive' reading of texts, another of the major themes to emerge from the data. In Ennis's assembly of skills, acts of reading are largely covered in the first of his putative abilities ('grasping the meaning of statements'). Such a formulation suggests a very literalist view of reading, where the essential purpose is to identify the key propositional content contained within a text. While this version of reading was affirmed by some informants (and was also evident in the structuring of a number of assignment tasks), also present in the data were a range of very different, even adversative, accounts. For many of the historians, for example, a 'critical' reading of a text was one which was not focused on the text alone, but informed by some knowledge of the context in which it was produced. For the comparative literature academics, such a reading was one to which other textual resources – especially 'theoretical resources' – are brought to bear.

Arguably the most important idea to emerge from the study is the notion that what one directs (or is required to direct) their thinking towards (the *object of inquiry*) is ultimately determinative of the nature of the thinking that needs to be done, and that different types of these objects invariably require different types of thinking. It is in the *objects of inquiry* in generic schemata such as Ennis's (Figure 19) that one can get a sense of the rather 'particular' form of critical thinking that is being proposed. Thus, among the skill items listed, we have the following entities:

1. ... statements ...
2. ... line of reasoning ...
3. ... certain statements ...
4. ... conclusion ...
5. ... a statement ...
6. ... a statement ...
7. ... observation statement ...
8. ... inductive conclusion ...

9. ... the problem ...
10. ... something ...
11. ... a definition ...
12. ... a statement ...

The first thing to be said about these *objects* is that they are all of a textual nature, and one might go further and say that they denote a particular type of textuality – one concerned with the propositional dimension of texts (e.g. statements, conclusions and so on). Absent from the schema is some of the other types of *objects* evidently in the study – for example, texts that are of interest for their aesthetic qualities, or actions and events that are to be judged for their moral or ethical content.

Not only are the entities in Ennis's schema of a particular type, but they are also suggestive of a particular 'logistic' form of engagement. This can be seen in the types of evaluative criteria (*content of inquiry*) evoked in his schema – 'ambiguity', 'contradiction', 'adequacy', 'validity' and so on. Such a conception of critical thinking – that is, one founded upon a mainly rationalist view of knowledge – has been the object of some quite pointed criticism within educational circles. For some (e.g. Walters 1994; Clinchy 1994), to conceive of critical thinking in this way is to exclude, and indeed to marginalize, other more 'empathic' modes of thought. It is significant that a number of informants in the study were keen to make the same point, and to suggest that methods of logic, while facilitative of critical thought in some contexts, could in fact be an obstacle to it if relied upon in others.

Of the various disciplines considered in the research, the generic accounts clearly have most in common with that version of critical thinking to emerge from the philosophy data. In this discipline (or at least in its particular incarnation at University X), as noted, the principal task for students in many of the assignments set was to make judgements about the adequacy, or otherwise, of various 'arguments' covered in their courses. This evaluative element was also strongly emphasized by the philosophers in interview. In the other disciplines, while there were certainly occasions where a similar kind of evaluative mode was also required (for example in adjudicating on different historical interpretations of the Renaissance, or on the value of a particular theorist's take on 'postmodernism'), such tasks, it was noted, were often directed at texts of a more secondary nature, and thus, constituted a less central role in the critical routines of these other disciplines.

The study's findings suggest therefore, that one needs to be wary (indeed 'sceptical') of the 'generic' definitions advanced by the critical thinking movement, and to see these as offering only a limited account of the ability in question. While one would not want to suggest that it is wrong to have students learn about such skills, it would seem a mistake to see these as a comprehensive and robust foundation for the many different types of contexts and tasks students will encounter in their studies. A much more serious concern, however, is the suggestion that a generic account (such as Ennis's) could be seen by education authorities as an adequate synopsis of the many and diverse modes and activities of an undergraduate education, and in turn for this to be used as the basis for the testing of students' thinking abilities at the end of their studies. The dangers of such a proposal lie not only in the inadequacy of this type of test construct, but also in the potential that such testing has – through the processes of test washback – to have a constraining effect on academic curricula across the university (Clerehan, Chanock and Moore 2004). Cautioning against such generic trends, Barnett suggests that 'to prescribe a particular and overarching framework of thought is to impose an iron cage and to emasculate ... academic inquiry' (2001: p. 5).

6.4 Interfield Comparisons

If one is to reject any single generic conception of critical thinking, the question then is how much it should be thought of as a field-specific quality. It will be recalled in the earlier discussion (Chapter 2) that this is very much the view of certain thinkers who hold to a specifist position. Thus, Stephen Toulmin has argued that arguments and ideas in one field need to be judged only 'by standards appropriate to that field' (1958: p. 32). John McPeck expresses a similar view, suggesting that 'certain principles of reasoning' which apply in one discipline area (e.g. law) do not necessarily have applicability in another (e.g. ethics) (1981 p.72).

In the study's investigation of different disciplines, an important question has been this interfield issue; that is, whether one can say with any certainty that the critical thinking in Discipline A (say history) is of a fundamentally similar or different order to that in Discipline B (say philosophy) or in C (say literary/cultural studies). The clearest suggestion in the study of any distinctive disciplinary modes of thinking emerged from the analysis of the essay topic data in Chapter 5. In this part of the study, it will be recalled, an effort was made to identify the main question-types in the three discipline areas according to our three categories of analysis (the *object*, *process*, and *content of inquiry*). The resulting archetypal structure to emerge for each discipline is reproduced in Figure 20 below.

This particular analytical schema would seem a useful basis for drawing some 'broad brush' distinctions between the disciplines. It shows, for example, how study in history is distinguishable from the other two disciplines by having as its principal *object of inquiry* the domain of the 'real' (states of affairs, actions, phenomena), in contrast to the fundamental textual interests of philosophy and of literary/cultural studies, though the nature of the texts in these latter two disciplines is often very divergent. Similarly, philosophy can be seen to differ from history and literary/cultural studies by requiring a fundamentally 'evaluative'

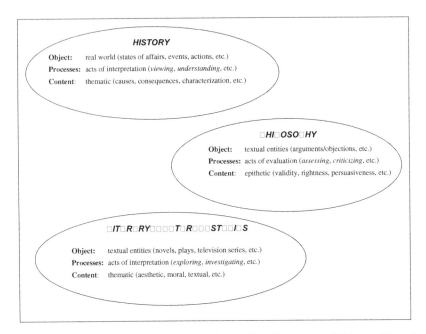

FIGURE 20 Principal question-types in three discipline areas (object of inquiry; process of inquiry; content of inquiry)

(as opposed to an 'interpretative') approach to its subject matter (usually the 'arguments' contained within philosophical texts). Literary/cultural studies can be distinguished from the other two disciplines for the considerable variety of 'interpretative' approaches that can be applied to its texts, including 'aesthetic', 'moral' and 'textual' perspectives. It is findings such as these that leads one to conclude that the critical modes operating in these particular disciplines are somehow of a distinctive and disparate nature.

But while it is possible to point to certain archetypal question structures within the disciplines, one needs to be careful about adopting too reductionist a view here. Significantly, it will be recalled that for each discipline area a fair number of essay questions were found to fall outside these patterns. It is of interest that among these non-typical cases, a degree of convergence would seem to exist between the disciplines, so that the questions set in one discipline can resemble, in many respects, those set in another. This phenomenon can be seen in the question pairings shown below (Figures 21.1, 21.2 and 21.3), where in each case the sample question from Discipline A is largely congruent with the archetypal structure from Discipline B. Thus, in the first pairing, for example (Figure 21.1), we can see that the literary/cultural studies topic – here requiring students to analyse and evaluate one critic's objections (During's) to another's theory (Jameson's) – resembles in many respects the archetypal structure from philosophy, as exemplified in the *Pascal* topic shown below it.

6.06   **A: *Literary/cultural studies non-archetypal sample:***

Why does Simon During disagree with Frederic Jameson's theory of postmodernism? Is he right?

6.07   **B: *Philosophy archetype:***

What is Duff's objection to Pascal's Wager? Does it show that there is something wrong with infinite decision theory?

Object: textual entities (arguments/objections, etc.)

Processes: acts of evaluation (*assessing, criticizing*, etc.)

Content: epithetic (validity, rightness, persuasiveness, etc.)

FIGURE **21.1**   Sample topics – literary/cultural studies as philosophy?

6.08   **A: *Philosophy non-archetypal sample:***

What do you think was Plato's purpose in writing the *Gorgias*?

B: *History archetype:*

6.09   What (besides aesthetic impulses) motivated the patrons of Renaissance culture to commission works of art?

Object: real world (states of affairs, events, actions, etc.)

Processes: acts of interpretation (*viewing, understanding*, etc.)

Content: thematic (causes, consequences, characterization, etc.)

FIGURE **21.2**   Sample topics – philosophy as history?

6.10   **A: *History non-archetypal sample:***

To what extent can Australian prisoner of war writings from World War II be described as 'embittered' documents?

B: *Literary/cultural studies archetype:*

6.11

To what extent can Peter Greenaway's film *The Belly of an Architect* be characterized as 'postmodern nostalgia'?

Object: textual entities (novels, plays, television series, etc.)

Processes: acts of interpretation (*exploring, investigating*, etc.)

Content: thematic (aesthetic, moral, textual, etc.)

FIGURE **21.3**   Sample topics – History as literary/cultural studies?

Similarly in 21.2A, which is a philosophy question, students are not required to 'evaluate' the arguments contained in these works of Plato, as was the pattern in many tasks in the philosophy corpus, but instead to offer an 'interpretation' of the purpose Plato might have had for writing them at the time. The question is notable for being framed in past tense (What *was* Plato's purpose ...?) as opposed to the predominant use of the 'universal present' found in most philosophy questions in the corpus (e.g. #6.07 above: *Is* there something wrong with ...?). Judgements such as this one about Plato's text, concerned as it is with the motive for a particular historical act, is arguably more of a piece with our history archetype, as exemplified in the accompanying sample from Renaissance history (#6.09).

In a final pairing of topics (Figure 21.3), we can see that the history topic (#6.10) is not concerned with a 'real-world' entity as such, but rather a strongly textual one (an archive of prisoner of war writings). Furthermore, the interpretative mode that students need to bring to these texts appears a distinctly literary one (i.e. deciding how much these documents express an 'embitteredness'). In this way, the topic has much in common with the structure that has been proposed for literary/cultural studies, as exemplified in the accompanying *Greenaway* topic (#6.11).

The findings summarized above, which show variation but also some overlap among the disciplines, return us to a key issue raised in the review section in Chapter 3 – that is, how one might sensibly deal with the notion of disciplinarity, and how much it should be viewed as the underlying source of the variation we have seen. This issue is not only important as a way of understanding the nature of critical thinking, but also for the implications it has for the ways in which students are taught about these matters.

The more conventional line of thinking, as noted previously, is that despite some admitted blurring at the edges, individual disciplines need to be thought of as embodying quite separate and distinctive intellectual cultures. It was noted earlier that such a view is a foundational one within the 'disciplinary discourses' movement, where the cultures of the disciplines are held to be discrete structures, marked by 'strong boundaries', defining:

> variations in knowledge, structures and norms of inquiry, different vocabularies and discourses. (Candlin, Bhatia and Hyland 1997: p. 25)

In the data, the strongest evidence of distinctive community discourses at work was to be found in the protocol documents collected for the analysis – or at least in some of them. It will be recalled that for two of the disciplines – history and philosophy – a collective effort went into producing these documents, one aimed at guiding students in appropriate modes of thinking and writing in these respective fields. Significantly, a feature of these accounts was to show how the modes to be adopted in each area were distinctive somehow from those in other parts of the faculty. Thus, the philosophy document led off by suggesting that students should think of studying and writing in philosophy as something quite distinct from their experience of studying in 'more common school subjects such as literature and history'. The history document, in turn, sought to distinguish those skills 'particular' to the study of history ('analysing different forms of source material, using different kinds of evidence', etc.) from other more general skills required in the faculty at large. In these examples, we see not only an affirmation of the 'disciplinary discourses' view, but also a desire on the part of each of these disciplines to have their students understand these issues in 'separatist' terms.

The exceptional case, however, was the third discipline area – literary/cultural studies. The details of this case cannot be ignored, and they prevent one from falling too easily into any simple discipline-based account of differences. It will be recalled that not only was there no single account of the discipline on offer to students, but that in the two different literature documents identified, quite divergent – and at times incompatible – critical approaches were proposed. Indeed in one of these documents, a deliberate effort was made to draw attention to these differences, with a contrasting of an 'older *critical* approach', and a preferred 'structural approach'. Thus, in this instance, the significant cultural divide was seen to run not between broad discipline areas, but between rival paradigms within the same field.

A further confounding element was the lack of a collectively authored document from the comparative literature strand in the faculty's literature offerings. It may be recalled that the relevant document – entitled *Introduction to the analysis of a literary text* – was not the product of any joint enterprise from within the programme, but in fact constituted the favoured theoretical approach of an individual academic. On this point, it was suggested by a colleague on the comparative literature programme that – as a consequence of the great diversity of approaches and theoretical positions characteristic of the field – the prospect of being able to present a plausible single and consensual account was unlikely.

These examples from the literature data serve to undermine a conception of disciplines as distinct and unified structures, and as ones that can be relied upon to predict appropriate modes of engagement. As Lave and Wenger suggest, to hold to such a view is to misunderstand the dynamic nature of communities:

> Given the complex, differentiated nature of communities it seems important not to reduce a community of practice to a … uniform or univocal 'centre' or to a linear notion of skills acquisition. There is no place in a community of practice designated 'the periphery', and most emphatically it has no single core or centre. (1981: p. 36)

Understandings such of these have lead to a more dynamic – and one would say more nuanced – view of disciplinarity. We saw earlier Geertz's rejection of the idea of relying on disciplinary rubrics as simple 'borders-and-territories map of modern intellectual life' (1983: p. 7). Such a view is confirmed by Tony Becher in his extensive ethnographic work on the disciplines, where he concludes that the differences that play out within an individual discipline area can often be more telling and profound than those between them. Becher goes on to suggest that a greater understanding of disciplinary cultures is to be gained from 'attending to the diverse natures of the schisms which separate like from like' (1981: p. 116).

For a number of scholars, the nature of such 'schisms' and differences are best understood in terms of competing paradigms and ideologies (e.g. Taylor 2000; 1993), as was vividly seen in much of the literary/cultural studies data. For others, variety and conflict within disciplines can also be traced to more local, socially interactive forces. Sue Starfield, for example, in her study of academics' perceptions of student work in a university department, found that the diversity of views could be traced not so much to the different intellectual affiliations of staff, but what she calls 'the dense web of social, political and historical forces which shape every interaction' (2001: p. 135). In the department that Starfield investigated, the forces in question related to such factors as the status, gender and ethnicity of staff, which were somehow decisive in determining how discursive norms were established. Dynamics of this kind were not explored in any detail in the present investigation, although a hint of such forces was noted – as, for example, in the way that gender seemed to have some bearing on how informants across the disciplines viewed the place of 'logic and rationality' in students' emerging critical repertoires.

In coming to grips with the complex intellectual landscape of the academy, Paul Prior suggests that we need to abandon a conception of disciplines as 'definable abstract structures' and instead to see them as 'multiple, heterogeneous networks', shaped by such diverse factors as the 'object of study, methodologies, theories, institutional sites and roles, personal relationships and so on' (1998: p. 16). Indeed, such a view of disciplines would seem to accord very much with the way they are experienced by students in their studies, where the totality of their educational experience is measured by the contingencies and idiosyncrasies of the assortment of subjects and units they study along the way – some difficult, some easy; some with a strong theoretical orientation, some without; some taught in an inspiring way, some less so; some where the critical thinking expected of students is made clear, and some where it remains fully a mystery. Bazerman speaks of disciplinary knowledge being shaped by 'the mangle of practice and lamination of experience' (1998: p. vii) – and so we would say of the educational experiences of our students.

6.5 Critical Thinking and Family Resemblances

Where, then, does all this leave 'critical thinking'? What, out of the many comparisons that have been made in the study, are we able to say ultimately about this elusive notion? The study's findings compel one to conclude that it is not a generic ability; and while some overarching patterns can be identified in each of the three discipline areas considered, one is also reluctant to say that it is at heart a discipline-based quality. Indeed, to assert that there is an essential discipline-based mode of thinking is also to impose a generic definition on matters – albeit at a lower level within the academic hierarchy. So where does this leave us? Are we then forced into rejecting all generality, and to have to admit that 'critical thinking' is somehow different and distinct in all of the situations and contexts with which our students must contend? Indeed, is the suggestion made by one of the study's informants – that the term seems to be able to mean almost anything one wants it to – ultimately the position that we must adopt?

Such a conclusion, of course, is not a tenable one, and it would be a serious failing of the investigation to concede to this kind of semantic relativity. Such a conclusion is to be avoided partly for educational reasons. The term's overwhelming importance in contemporary education, and also its capacity to confound – even to debilitate – students means that the definitional challenge cannot be shirked, and that some form of generality must be attempted. However, there are also good philosophical reasons for rejecting this kind of 'meaning indeterminacy' (Medina 2005). In the discussion of these matters in the earlier review of literature, it was suggested that while it may indeed be folly to hope to be able to locate any single core of meaning of a term, one needs to assume that there is a coherence to be found (Wittgenstein 1961). Wittgenstein, as was noted previously, insists on the polysemy of language, such that any single term will typically denote a range of phenomena. But such phenomena, he goes on to explain, do not exist in some arbitrary relationship with one another, but rather need to be seen as connected in different and complex ways.

> I am saying that these phenomena have no one thing in common which makes us use the same word for all – but that they are related to one another in many different ways. (1958a: p. 31)

Wittgenstein's famous example, as described earlier, is the term 'game' and the variety of instances that fall under this category – 'board-games, card-games, ball-games, Olympic games, and so on'. Such instantiations, in all their variety, cannot be thought of as being united by some common Platonic element – their intrinsic 'gameness', but instead constitute what Wittgenstein calls a 'complicated network of similarities', ones that sometimes overlap, sometimes criss-cross and other times drop out and disappear altogether. The expression Wittgenstein uses to characterize such a network is 'family resemblances'.

> I can think of no better expression to characterize these similarities than family resemblances; for the various resemblances between members of a family: build, features, colour of eyes, gait, temperament etc. etc. overlap and criss-cross in the same way – and I shall say games form a family. (1958a: p. 31)

And so, like the category of 'games', the many different instances of critical thinking that have been observed in the study might also be thought of in the same familial terms. Such a conception of meaning suggests that the definitional task before us then is not to look for any core of meaning, or as Lave and Wenger suggest 'to reduce a community of practice to a … uniform or univocal center'; rather it is to try to give an account of a 'complex network of similarities', and to say which type of 'resemblances' might give this network its particular shape and substance.

6.6 Dimensions of Critical Thinking – A Proposal

In what follows I propose a list of categories, rather in the manner of the list of family traits which Wittgenstein suggests can be used to describe 'resemblances' in a family (i.e. 'build, features, colour of eyes, gait, temperament, etc. etc.'). Wittgenstein's use of a double 'etc.' in his list suggests the impossibility of proposing any impeccable and exhaustive list for whatever domain is being considered. This is also true for the list below (Figure 22). The categories presented – what I have termed 'dimensions of difference' – are an attempt to capture in some conceptual way the many overlaps and contrasts that have emerged from the study's findings. The list is composed of a number of contrasting terms ('text internal vs. text external'; 'objectivist vs. subjectivist', etc.). Each of these pairings needs to be understood not as a simple duality – either one quality or the other – but rather as end points on a continuum, so that some ideas and practices may relate more to the extreme ends on the continuum, and others more to the centre. What the different aggregations of these categories is intended to show is the complex warp and weft of critical thinking practices

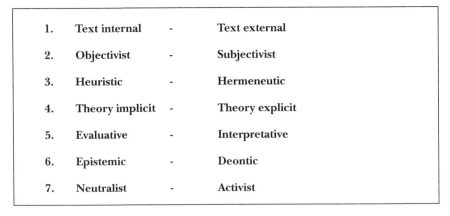

1.	Text internal	-	Text external
2.	Objectivist	-	Subjectivist
3.	Heuristic	-	Hermeneutic
4.	Theory implicit	-	Theory explicit
5.	Evaluative	-	Interpretative
6.	Epistemic	-	Deontic
7.	Neutralist	-	Activist

FIGURE 22   Dimensions of difference in critical thinking beliefs and practices

that have been observed across the disciplines of the study, and 'how they are related to one another in many different ways'.

6.6.1 Text internal – Text external

The first dimension is arguably the most important, and relates to the central idea running through much of the study – that the nature of one's thinking is indivisible from the object to which that thinking is directed. On this point, among the *objects of inquiry* seen in the data, a distinction can be drawn between those of a textual nature and those relating more to some real-world entity. Among the disciplines studied, virtually all the philosophy and literary/cultural studies materials were oriented towards the former, whereas much of the history materials were directed to the latter.

But this is not to suggest that disciplines can be simply divided along the lines of a textual-phenomenal binary. It can be argued that study in all academic disciplines is of its nature textually based – in the sense that the principal access to knowledge of all kinds in the academy is necessarily through texts of different kinds (Horowitz 1986). The issue then is whether – in the manner in which thinking tasks are conceived – the texts themselves are made the principal *object of inquiry* (text internal), or whether their function is more one of being the basis (or part of the basis) upon which inquiry into some real-world phenomenon is pursued. I have used the term 'text external' for this latter configuration, in the sense that one uses the text to look outward to some external realm. The distinction being proposed can be demonstrated in the following two topics taken from the history data (#6.12 and #6.13). Thus, while both cover the same general content area (understandings of the nature of the Athenian state in the time of Perikles), Sample A requires that judgements be made principally about actions and events, whereas Sample B requires that judgements be made about texts.

6.12 How **democratic** do you consider the Athenian government to be in the time of Perikles?

Sample A: Text external

6.13 How reliable do you think Thucydides is as an historian?

Sample B: Text internal

Not only is variety in these objects suggestive of different modes of thinking, but also of quite different patterns of language use; that is to say, to write about actions and events (e.g. those of a government) implies a different kind of discourse than writing about ideas and words (e.g. those of an historian). This difference is given some coverage in Halliday's *Functional Grammar*, where a

distinction is drawn between what he terms 'phenomenal' and 'metaphenom-
enal' discourses – the former constituted mainly by material and behavioural
processes, and the latter by verbal and mental processes (1994: p. 249). There
are also implications here for the type of citation patterns likely to be used in
the referencing of texts in a piece of work; that is, whether references are likely
to be more of an 'integral' (text internal) or 'non-integral' (text external) form
(Swales 1990: p. 153), as shown below:

Thucydides argued that Perikles …   (integral, text internal ref-
                                           erence)

Perikles was thought (by Thucydides) to be…   (non-integral, text exter-
                                           nal reference)

To understand the place that texts have in a discipline (or a particular subject in
a discipline) is clearly a central issue for students. This is important not only for
students to be able to grasp what it is that they need to direct their critical
thoughts towards, but also to have a broad understanding of the basic epistemological frame with which they are dealing. The study suggests that these are complex issues, and ones that should not necessarily be assumed to be understood.

6.6.2 Objectivist – Subjectivist

This second dimension also relates to variations in the *objects of inquiry*, but in
this case seeks to account for the status accorded to the thinking self in acts of
critique. The contrast drawn here is between broadly 'objectivist' and 'subjectivist' conceptions of knowledge. This difference was strongly evident in some of
the rival epistemological accounts enunciated by informants from philosophy
and literary/cultural studies. Thus, one of the philosophers described the
underlying objectivist view held by many in his department thus:

6.14   **ERIC** (philosophy) This is a department strongly in the Anglo-analytic
       tradition of philosophy, which is relatively untouched by post-structur-
       alist theory, and postmodernism. … The starting assumption [for us]
       is that there can be a sort of accurate representation of the world that
       is *independent of how we perceive it* (emphasis added).

The contrasting view from within the literary/cultural studies was a 'subjectivist' phenomenological position:

6.15   **NORA** (literary/cultural studies): Phenomenology is about represen-
       tation of reality. Reality can only be represented. It cannot exist for us
       in the raw … *it's not directly accessible to us* (emphasis added).

This basic difference of outlook was found to play out in different ways in the data. In the controversies about what a critical reading might entail, for example, one view (mainly expressed by the philosophers) was that students needed always to seek the objective meaning of a text; for others, such meanings are necessarily contingent, and always shaped by individual subjectivities. According to this latter view, an important part of being critical is to develop awareness of one's 'particular perceptual and conceptual apparatus', and to recognize how this affects the way that all is apprehended in the world. For Bob Hodge, such a contrast is captured in the distinction that can be drawn between a modernist stance of 'self-effacement' and a postmodernist one of 'self-reflexivity'. (1995: p. 42)

However, such differences about the role of self were not found to divide simply along disciplinary lines. In the literary/cultural studies data, we saw instances of more humanist approaches to literature where an important reason given for studying texts was the opportunity this afforded students 'to evaluate critically [their] own assumptions and experiences' (see #5.40). In contrast to this were more formalist approaches (outlined, for example, in the second protocol document), where a focus on the objective analysis of 'textual structures,' rendered individual biographies – those of both author and reader – largely irrelevant to the critique. (#5.45)

The question of where the individual thinking self fits within disciplinary discourse is often a very important one for students. It underlies, for example, the difficult issue of whether individual life experiences have, in fact, any evidential status in one's engagement with a subject, and whether it is valid to refer to these. An even more pressing issue is the types of identity students are entitled to construct for themselves in their writing – what in the literature is sometimes referred to as 'discursive voice' (Ivanic and Simpson 1992). This kind of ontological difficulty, as was suggested earlier, manifests itself in that most fraught of questions, one that seems, at times, to baffle academics as much as it does students; that is, whether in academic discourse one is entitled to invoke that most basic expression of individual cognition – 'I think'.

In his reflections on changes in the humanities over the last decades, Robert Pascoe suggests that the 'individual thinker' has assumed greater status within the disciplines, and that there has been a progressive shift away from objectivist paradigms towards more subjectivist ones:

Earlier generations of students [in the Humanities and Social Sciences] had regarded their education as a means of understanding and controlling an external environment. Now, this education [is] as much a pathway to understanding oneself and one's social class and ethnic situation. (2002: p. 11)

This may be true, though one would not want to suggest that this shift has been by any means a complete one. The study's findings suggest that students in the course of their studies are likely to encounter quite varying understandings about the place attributed to the self in the practices of critical thinking, and that these may indeed be matters that need some explaining to them.

6.6.3 Heuristic – Hermeneutic

This dimension is concerned with the nature of critical *processes*, and whether these processes are stipulated in advance as a type of protocol to be followed, or whether they are left relatively open for students, and are to be decided upon in relation to the specific material being considered. The former process-type is designated 'heuristic' in the schema, and the latter 'hermeneutic'. Instances of more heuristic processes were most clearly present in some of the philosophy materials, where, for example, the specific techniques for analysing and evaluating an argument were explicitly outlined (e.g. Figure 10). As one philosophy informant suggested, the fundamentals of learning how to be critical in philosophy (or at least the mainly Anglo-analytical variety taught at University X) are principally concerned with developing the techniques of argument analysis and applying the notion of 'argumentative validity'.

The prescribing of this kind of tight heuristic approach, however, was not the exclusive preserve of the 'analytics' in the School of Philosophy. Examples were also seen in some of the work set in literary/cultural studies, particularly by those who favoured more structuralist approaches to textual analysis. Such an example was the following exercise task which required students to draw on a particular technique as a basis for recognizing patterns of narrative structure (Figure 13).

> 6.16   ***Part A:*** Draw a plan showing how the idea of the Fall is represented in Genesis. Who falls? Why do they fall? How do they fall? What is the outcome?

Other tasks in the data, by contrast, were of a much more open-ended nature. Thus, a very different type of 'instruction' issued to students was a task set in the traditional literature strand, where students were given a range of 'starter' questions to help them shape their critique of a short story, but also told they were at liberty 'to disregard' these entirely and to pursue whatever was of interest to them in the text (see Figure 12). The same looser, hermeneutic mode was also sometimes evident in the other literary/cultural studies strand, where in a number of tasks students were asked to select a cultural text and then to write an analysis by drawing on whichever theoretical concept (or concepts) they 'thought relevant' (see Figure 15). As has been suggested, critical judgements in these contexts would seem to be as much about deciding how the critique is to be pursued, as they are with any conclusions to be drawn about the object itself.

This 'heuristic – hermeneutic' trope captures, in part, the varying attitudes expressed by informants about the place of 'rationality' and 'logic' in critical thinking – whether this should be thought of as a prescribed, and also circumscribed, analytical mode, or whether a looser and more empathic one. In the data, such a distinction was not only noted between the preferred approaches of the informants, but also suggested in the different approaches to learning adopted by students, as explained in the previously quoted comment from one the history informants:

6.17   **EDWARD** (history): there are [students] who it would seem are born with particular kinds of approaches to the world ... some are interested in logical progressions in what we might call linear logic. Other [students] are interested in more natural kinds of connections and associations. And those who make these associations between things make accomplished art critics, for instance, but may or may not be as good at some of the other types of critical activities we have been talking about.

6.6.4 Theory implicit – Theory explicit

The previous dimension touches on the role of theory in critical processes. Theory as an idea has loomed large in the study, and, as has been seen, was the subject of a fair amount of debate and disputation among informants. For some, the bringing of a theoretical frame to material was seen as an indispensable part of being critical. On the other side were those who showed at best a wariness towards theory, and at worst an outright hostility to it – the latter attitude expressed most vividly by one informant from the traditional literature strand who saw the progressive 'theoretization' of literary studies over the last decades as largely a disaster for the discipline (#5.186).

This is not to suggest, however, that the dimension being considered here is a simple contrast between fields of study that rely on theory and those that are largely a-theoretical or even anti-theoretical. A more plausible contrast is how 'explicitly' or 'implicitly' a theory appears to operate in a field. On this point, the economist John Maynard Keynes once suggested that those of his fellow economists who disliked theory, or claimed to get along better without it, were simply in the grip of an older theory (cited in Eagleton 1996). Such a view was in fact echoed by one of the literary/cultural studies informants in the study:

6.18   **BRIAN** (literary/cultural studies): I think ... you can't make sense of anything without theorizing. Everybody theorizes. People who say they don't believe in theory, it just means they're not aware of it.

In line with this view, it was the opinion of this informant that the anti-theory literary critics in the faculty were largely Leavisite in their orientation, and the anti-theory philosophers were mainly empiricist.

In the data, we saw a number of instances where students were required to be explicitly theoretical. While this was particularly the case in the comparative literature material, examples of theoretical explicitness were also evident in other quarters – for example, in a number of essay tasks set in a bioethics subject which required students to draw on 'relevant ethical theories' as a basis for resolving certain medical dilemmas (#5.146 and #5.147). In contrast, in other tasks, no explication or justification for the approach seemed to be required, nor even necessary – for example, in the use of the arguably theoretical notion of 'argumentative validity' in the analysis of philosophical texts (Figure 10).

These contrasting situations – one in which the theoretical position requires explication, and one in which it does not – can be related to Bourdieu's notions of *doxa*. Bourdieu suggests that it is the nature of established orders (in our case established disciplines) to produce what he calls the 'naturalization of their own arbitrariness' (1977: p.164). Thus for Bourdieu, a 'doxic' culture is one in which the 'established cosmological and political order is perceived not as arbitrary [...] but as a self-evident and natural order', and as one which literally 'goes without saying' (p.166). Bourdieu's category of 'opinion', on the other hand, is the sphere of that which is contestable, and notably that which is discussed.

Given that it is the nature of study in a discipline to see the world through a particular 'prism', the issue then for students is whether they need to describe the prism along the way, or whether they may in fact proceed as if there was no prism there at all. For those discipline areas that are more 'heterodoxic' in nature (as, for example, literary/cultural studies), this kind of explication appears to be essential; for others, where the critical routines have become more or less 'naturalized' (as, for example, in analytical philosophy), it is not. These are cultural issues ultimately for students, and ones that may require some explaining to them.

6.6.5 Evaluative – Interpretative

The fifth dimension of the schema is concerned with the types of judgements that students need to make about different types of *object of inquiry*. This dimension, perhaps more than any other, goes to the heart of what being critical is – that is, it is concerned with the substance of the critiques that students need to make. The two main categories to emerge from the study, as we have seen, are 'evaluation' (the making of some definitive judgement about the *value* of a text or phenomenon), and 'interpretation' (providing some commentary about the *nature* of these texts or phenomena). While it was found that each of the discipline areas tended to favour one mode over the other as the dominant unmarked form, instances of the alternative mode were also found to be present to some degree, as in the following examples from literary/cultural studies corpus.

6.19   Compare and contrast the different versions of the 'human' in any of Genesis, *Paradise Lost* and

> **Sample A: Interpretative (dominant, unmarked mode in literary/cultural studies)**

6.20   Barthes' reports of the death of the author tend to be greatly exaggerated. Discuss.

> **Sample B: Evaluative (alternative, marked mode in literary/cultural studies)**

An important issue for students in managing these two broad modes is knowing about the bases on which the critique is to be developed. Thus, if one is required to be evaluative, the question is by which *criteria* these evaluations might be made. Similarly, if one is required to be interpretative, at issue is the *categories* (or *themes*) that one might draw on as a basis upon which to build the interpretation. In Sample #6.19, the relevant interpretative *theme* is the notion of the 'human'; in Sample #6.20 the evaluative *criterion* is (after Wilde) one of 'overstatement'.

It is interesting to note that in the materials collected for the study, very few academic tasks seemed to combine both modes. One notable exception was the following essay topic from literary/cultural studies:

6.21   What is 'liquid modernity' and how can it be used to understand the phenomenon of reality television? How useful ultimately do you find this concept?

We can see in this topic that in one part, students need to draw on the concept of 'liquid modernity' (Baumann) as a basis on which to *interpret* the 'phenomenon of reality television'; and in the other part, to take this concept and *evaluate* its 'usefulness' as an interpretative category. The different components of this task can be summarized thus:

OBJECT OF INQUIRY What type of entity is to be analysed?	PROCESS OF INQUIRY By which type of mental/verbal process?	CONTENT OF INQUIRY By which analytical criteria/categories?
phenomenon of reality television	interpretation	liquid modernity
concept of liquid modernity	evaluation	usefulness

The study has not considered in any way the relative ease or difficulty of the critical tasks set for students; it may be the case, however, that the critical thinking required for this 'hybrid form' is of a more sophisticated type.

6.6.6 Epistemic – Deontic

This sixth dimension is one that probes the difference between an 'epistemic' and a 'deontic' rhetoric. These terms, which derive from traditional semantics, attempt to capture a difference between thinking that is oriented towards reflection, and that which is oriented towards action. An epistemic clause, as Rodney Huddleston explains, has the status of a proposition; it asserts whether something is true, partly true, false and so on. A deontic clause, in contrast, has the character of an action: 'what is at issue is not whether something is true or not, but whether something is going to be done' (1982:168).

The difference in rhetorical modes being suggested here can be illustrated in the following two topics from the philosophy data, which cover in different formats basic issues of the right to life and death.

6.22   Judith Jarvis Thomson argues that even if we grant that embryos have a right to life, abortion should still be justifiable in some circumstances. Is she right? Outline and then critically evaluate her argument.

Contemporary Moral Issues; #E.2.4.1

Sample A: Epistemic

6.23   A patient tells you (a health professional) that he has genuine and informed desire to die, and asks you to assist him in carrying out his wish. How can you respond? How can ethical theories help to resolve this issue?

Ethical Issues in Health Care; #E.2.10.1

Sample B: Deontic

Whereas in the first sample, the task for students is to make a judgement about a set of propositions, as framed in the epistemic clause – *Is she [Jarvis Thomson] right?*; in Sample B, the judgement has more the 'character of an action', framed in the deontic clause – *how can you respond?*

In the university, differences such as these find expression in the broad division drawn between the pure and applied disciplines (Becher 1989). The particular humanities disciplines that have been investigated in the study all come arguably within the ambit of the 'pure', and thus, most of the forms of critique that have been encountered have been of an epistemic nature – that is to say, forms of commentary. The one exception noted however, has been that sub-branch of philosophy – practical or applied ethics (the source of the second topic), whose main intellectual concerns, as we have seen, are to explore the basis by which various professional and personal dilemmas might be resolved (#5.148 and #5.149). In the realm of the 'applied' generally, the main outcome of critical processes is not commentary, but rather action, or as Becher describes it: 'protocols and procedures, whose functions are judged mainly in pragmatic and utilitarian terms' (p. 16).

For students, it may be that these different realms of knowledge – the epistemic and deontic – need to be delineated in some way in order for them to have an appreciation of these contrasting purposes. Indeed, the influence of neo-liberal discourses in higher education in recent decades (Frow 1992), marked in part by the progressive encroachment of the applied into the pure, suggests that this may also be a distinction that needs to be insisted upon.

6.6.7 Neutralist – Activist

The final category is concerned with a different type of practice, one evoked by that specialist variant of the term – 'praxis', and which refers to consciously activist, (or engagée) notions of critique. As mentioned, the origins of this type of critique can be located, among other places, in Marx's famous 'thesis' concerning the purposes of learning and scholarship: 'Philosophers have hitherto only interpreted the world in various ways; [however] the point is to change it' (Thesis 11: 'Theses on Feuerbach', 1845). In educational theory, it has found expression in the critical pedagogies of such writers as Friere (1970), Giroux (1988), and Shor (1987). In the study, the clearest expression of this version of critique was to be found in the accounts of certain informants who saw the ultimate goal of education as the directing of one's critical thoughts towards society, and especially to focus this critique on social structures and practices thought to be oppressive and unjust in some way. In the rival view, such an approach was dismissed as a form of 'ideological correctness', and as one that severely circumscribed the possibility of an open and genuine critique.

This particular use of the term 'criticism' is a complex one, and, as noted earlier, is prone to certain conundrums and paradoxes. Thus, a number of informants saw an ever-present danger in certain well-known and established critiques in their field – ones that they themselves were inclined towards – becoming entrenched as orthodoxies, and being accepted by students in some unthinking way. Perhaps the worst manifestation of this kind of 'conventionalizing of critique' was the practice, reported by one informant, of students seeking to tailor their responses to fit with the perceived ideological preferences of their teachers.

Such concerns about this activist view of critique are common in the literature. They are there, for example, in Henry Widdowson's (1996; 1997) famous
critique of Norman Fairclough's Critical Discourse Analysis. While Widdowson
is generally sympathetic towards the social mission of CDA, his concern is that
as a result of the 'conviction and commitment' that guides its methods, the
analyses that are produced have a tendency to be presented as final and definitive ones. Thus, for Widdowson, the 'authority' that informs such an approach
often turns out to be a form of authoritarianism, one that can close down – perhaps inadvertently – the possibilities for discussion and debate (1996: p. 171).
As Burbules and Berk note, there is a danger in the area of education that these
kinds of pedagogies can end up 'crossing a threshold between teaching criticality and simple indoctrinati[on]'. (1999: p. 9)

For informants in the study, the antidote to these kinds of tendencies was
'always to be up front with students', as one informant termed it, about one's
particular ideological or theoretical orientations, and to allow these to be seen
also as legitimate objects of critique. One also saw some reassurance in a rubric
observed in some of the essay topic data – 'critically discussing the critiques', a
formulation which would seem to guarantee what was referred to in one of the
documents as the 'great conversation' of critical inquiry.

6.7 Conclusion

The different 'critical thinking' dimensions outlined in the preceding sections
are intended to capture the diversity of practices found in the study, and to
show how they can be thought of as a 'family of resemblances'. The schema is
also designed to show how the practices of a particular discipline (or sub-discipline, or even subject within a sub-discipline) might be understood in terms of
specific configurations of these terms. To take just one example, certain aspects

1.	**Text internal**	–	Text external
2.	**Objectivist**	–	Subjectivist
3.	**Heuristic**	–	Hermeneutic
4.	**Theory implicit**	–	Theory explicit
5.	**Evaluative**	–	Interpretative
6.	**Epistemic**	–	Deontic
7.	**Neutralist**	–	Activist

FIGURE 23   Clustering of categories for studies in philosophy

of the thinking required in philosophy, or at least in the Anglo-analytical variety taught principally at University X, would seem to fit broadly with the profile of categories shown on the left side of the schema (Figure 23). For other disciplines (and sub-disciplines), quite different clusterings of categories would seem to apply.

Chapter 7

Conclusions and Implications for Teaching

The question of how critical thinking is best taught to students has been one of the main motivations for the present investigation. As has been suggested throughout the study, to devise ways in which the idea of critical thinking can be coherently conveyed to students is not only an interesting challenge in itself, but, given the concept's ubiquity in current educational debates, also a pedagogical imperative. As Ronald Barnett (2000) suggests, in a time when universities have become particularly vocal about the goals and aspirations they have for their students, it is important that any rhetoric concerning qualities such as critical thinking be supported by a genuine pedagogical effort. Before discussing the study's teaching implications, it is worth returning briefly to current views about how critical thinking is best taught, and to see what consequences the study's findings might have for these.

7.1 Generic Skills and Disciplinary Discourses Revisited

As was noted in the early discussion of the literature (Chapter 2), ideas about the teaching of critical thinking have tended to coalesce around two dominant, and largely contrary approaches: i) the generic critical skills approach, and ii) the specificist disciplinary discourses approach. To take the generic approach first, the key to devising a thinking skills curricula, it is suggested, is to 'distill' the thinking that is characteristic of all manner of fields, and to establish what is core and common to them all. The guiding axiom in such an approach, as outlined by its main champion Robert Ennis, can be stated thus:

> Although not every principle [of critical thinking] applies in every field, there is a common core of basic principles that apply in most fields. (1987: p. 31)

In relation to the present study, we can represent this presumptive relationship between core and field in the diagram shown in Figure 24.

In the findings of the study, it is possible – if one is pushed – to identify some single common elements that might fit within this overlapping core shown in Figure 24. However, the complexity of relations evident in our fields – both between and within them – makes one unhopeful that such a reduction can

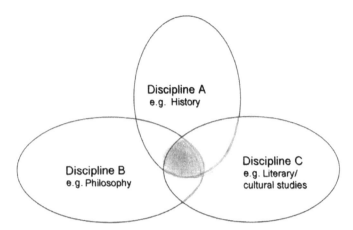

FIGURE 24 Underlying model of field relations in general 'critical thinking' approach

produce anything particularly substantive. On this point, one is inclined to agree with John McPeck who suggests that the kind of curriculum generated from such a design is unlikely to go much beyond certain 'obvious' skills, and scarcely qualify as a legitimate course of study in its own right:

> I [do] believe there are in fact some very limited general thinking skills ... however, these skills offer little to get excited about ... [Indeed] the more general they are, the more trivially obvious they are – for example, not contradicting oneself, not believing everything one hears and so forth. Conversely, the truly useful skills tend to be limited to specific domains or narrower uses of application. (1992: p.202)

The limitations of such a pedagogy – one based on some abstracted and generic notion of skill – is a common theme among certain educationists (see for example, Ramsden 1985; Taylor 2000). The problems of such an approach are well articulated by Tony Dudley-Evans (2002) in his comments on a different kind of 'generic pedagogy' – the teaching of genres of academic writing. In the following quotation, the relevance of Dudley-Evans's observations to the present investigation can be grasped if we substitute the term 'thinking' for 'writing':

> There is a particular danger in any kind of genre teaching: the *writing* teacher may find the teaching of a generalized set of moves a straightforward and popular method that may lead to a certain comfortable isolation from the actual discipline. The risk is that such an approach will not confront many of the day-to-day problems students encounter when *writing* the actual genres required by the department. As always in English for Specific

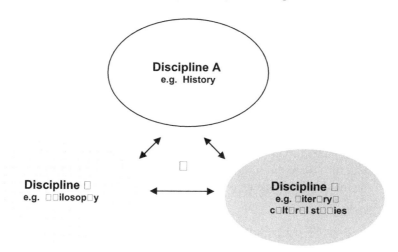

FIGURE 25 Underlying model of field relations in 'disciplinary discourses' model

Purposes work, there is a need to find out what the actual problems are and come up with innovative solutions rather than settle for accepted procedures. (Dudley-Evans 2002: p. 235)

The other main approach – the disciplinary discourses view – allows no 'comfortable isolation' from the actual disciplines, and in fact seeks a full immersion in them. In the stronger versions of this approach, the underlying view is not only that 'the truly useful skills are limited to specific disciplinary domains', but that such skills are in fact 'unique' to each, making the possibility of transfer unlikely (Hyland 2000). Hyland explains the position thus:

... while academic knowledge is frequently represented in style guides and in [generalist] university enhancement courses as attending to transferable skills, students actually have to readjust to each discipline they encounter. (2000: p. 145)

Such an approach, which seeks to teach the unique ways a discipline has of 'identifying issues, asking questions ... and presenting arguments' (Hyland, 2000: p. 145), suggests a largely discrete and 'separatist' model of disciplinary knowledge, as represented in Figure 25.

The findings of the study suggest that such a model is, at once, both too particularist and too generalist. It is too particularist for its lack of attention to certain commonalities (or 'resemblances') that clearly exist across different domains. The overgeneralization relates to the tendency we have seen to essentialize individual disciplines, and to impose upon students a rather idealized – and ultimately simplistic – account of the thinking and writing required in their different areas of study.

The two approaches – the generic and the discipline-specific – thus suffer from different problems. The first wants to have it that in learning to be an effective thinker, the differences between the disciplines are ultimately unimportant; in the second, the differences are seen to be so all-encompassing as to be almost impossible to negotiate. The over-application of each approach is liable to produce different types of consequences. In imposing a generic model of thinking on students, the risk is that their thinking will lack nuance and that they will come to rely on a template approach to the diverse problems and issues they confront; in insisting on different and distinct disciplinary modes of thinking, the risk is that students will become insular, and lack the ability – and also the instincts – to engage effectively with those from other fields.

7.2 An Alternative Pedagogy – Transdisciplinarity

One type of metaphor relied on in the study has been a geographical one. The conduct of the research, as we have seen, has involved exploring different territories in the faculty (both geographical and intellectual ones), with journeys made to different departments, different floors and different offices in search of the precious critical thinking grail. These various spaces, as the study found, were redolent with meaning. On certain floors, critical thinking was strongly associated with a 'robust sense of reality', on another this 'reality' was permanently problematic; in some offices, 'theory' was greatly prized and seen as the key to a critical outlook, in others it was viewed as, at best, an encumbrance.

And yet amid the variety of beliefs and practices, and in the tensions and conflicts evident in these different spaces, one felt that all residing there were connected in some way by a common sense of purpose and language. On this point, it is significant that no-one involved in the study rejected the term 'critical' as something not absolutely central to their work and worldview. Thus, rather than think of the building as housing a series of separate and detached communities, the study draws us into seeing it as a larger connected entity – a faculty. The main part of the study was thus concerned with trying to make sense of the different areas traversed in the building – both to understand them as individual sites, and also as ones connected inextricably to one another[1]

The experience for students – or at least students studying on undergraduate programmes – can be thought of in the same geographical terms. In the course of their degrees, which usually take in a variety of major and minor studies, students need to negotiate a range of disciplinary and sub-disciplinary cultures, and to try to interact in some meaningful way with the different communities with which they come in contact. The materials collected for the study have shown that some dedicated effort is made to help orient students towards individual 'sites of learning'. However, in the way that undergraduate education is conceived, it seems that not a great deal of attention is given to this broader, connected landscape, nor is much opportunity given for students to think about how their learning might be part of a larger whole. This seems to be not only true of studies in the arts and humanities, but in other types of undergraduate degrees as well.

This apparent lack of coherence and wholeness in students' experience of higher education has been a concern for education commentators for some time. The social critic Alan Bloom, writing at a time when changes in higher education were first gathering pace in the late 1980s, was trenchant about what he saw as the increasing fragmentation of university learning. For Bloom, academics, under the pressures of competition and specialization, were fast losing any sense of themselves as part of a shared and common enterprise, and instead were cast more and more in the role of partisan advocates for their own particular disciplinary offerings. 'Carnival barkers' is Bloom's dismissive description:

> Most professors are specialists, concerned only with their own fields, interested in the advancement of those fields in their own terms ... They have been entirely emancipated from the old structure of the university, which at least helped to indicate that they are incomplete, only parts of an unexamined and undiscovered whole. So the student must navigate among a collection of carnival barkers, each trying to lure him to a particular sideshow. (1987: p. 339)

Though expressing the idea in considerably more temperate terms, Barnett sees the situation several decades later as essentially unchanged:

> The university has become either a place for producing specialised technical capacities, or largely an amorphous institution, the character of its internal life lacking any kind of clarity. (2001: p. 3)

Barnett rues this state of affairs, which he feels makes it 'neither easy nor even possible for lecturers and students working in different fields to find any points of contact' in what they do. (Barnett 2001: p. 3)

One does not want to overstate the case, but we might see in the idea of critical thinking, a possible way in which some degree of clarity and coherence might be returned to the practices of teaching and learning in the academy. The type of pedagogy that is proposed from the study is a transdisciplinary one – one which assumes a diversity of understandings and practices of critique (different types of *habitus*), and which in turn seeks ways to encourage students to explore and try to make sense of the diversity they encounter. We might see such a pedagogy having two distinct parts to it.

In the first part, there is a need to find ways in which the habitus of 'critical thinking' in individual disciplines and sub-disciplines might be made more comprehensible to students – what Bourdieu refers to as 'the naming of the principles which generate its properties and judgements' (1984: p. 110). The categories of difference that have been proposed in the schema (see Figure 22) might be thought of as at least one account of such principles, and which might help to give some substance to what Bourdieu terms the 'tacit' and 'misrecognised' (Bourdieu 1977). One would not want to suggest, however, that such 'principles' merely require articulation and explication in order to allow students access to the mysteries of the disciplines. The pedagogy one envisages is of the type rooted in situated action – what Lave and Wenger (1991), for example, have described as 'legitimate peripheral participation'. The 'participation' we have seen in the study has mainly been in the form of the various academic tasks set for student, and it is in the context of work on such tasks that any talk about such principles is likely to have most value.

The other part of the proposed pedagogy is one in which students are encouraged to see connections between the different communities of their study. What is probably necessary in the first instance in pursuing such an approach is for academics to seek to rediscover themselves as 'parts of a larger whole'. Kay Harman suggests that this can only come about through better and more empathic understandings across the disciplines, and in particular an understanding of what might inhere their differences.

> Plans to reconstruct higher education that are based on … interdisciplinary linkages have little chance of success if the bases of the differences are not well understood. (1990: p. 52)

Thus, as part of a transdisciplinary pedagogy, one needs to envisage an approach where students and staff alike are more engaged in activity that crosses Geertz's (1983) 'borders-and-territories map of modern intellectual life', and which seeks to discover or rediscover 'points of contact'. Such an outlook might be encouraged through the setting of work that has this specific transdisciplinary purpose. The following is an imaginary assignment task, one, which in the way that undergraduate study is presently structured, is difficult to imagine being enacted (Figure 26). It is one however, that seeks to capture in a practical way many of the ideas about 'critical thinking' being proposed ultimately in this work.

7.3 Further Research and Thoughts

There are several areas of research that might be worth pursuing from the present investigation. One concerns the possible changing conceptions of critique. The approach that has been adopted in the present study has been a synchronic one; that is to say, it provides an account of the term 'critical' at just one point

---

An imaginary assignment task

At University X, it is claimed that students will develop, among other things, the ability to **think critically**.

Think about several subjects you have completed over the last semester.

In what ways (if at all), do you think work in these subjects has helped you to develop your abilities as a **critical thinker**? How would you describe the type of **critical thinking** you needed to develop in each case? Did this seem to be the same, or was it different in some sense? Is it somehow easier being **critical** in one subject than another?

In what ways (if at all), do you think these **critical capacities** might have relevance to your life (e.g. as a student, as a worker, as a citizen, etc.)?

Does University X, in your judgement, make good its claim that it teaches students to be **critical**?

FIGURE 26   Imaginary assignment task

in time. This time was the mid 2000s when the data were collected, and it is fair to say that they reflect a particular moment (and a particular place) in the development of the humanities and in higher education generally. We saw, for example in the accounts of many informants, the pervasive influence of a postmodernist outlook – for some a theoretical position to be enthusiastically embraced, and for others, one to be obdurately resisted.

Some five years on, it may be that certain particulars of the study are not as relevant as they were in the mid 2000s. On the hold of postmodernism on the academy, some commentators are beginning to suggest that the period of high theory, and of a mainly textually based view of knowledge, is now distinctly on the wane. Such a view is evident, for example, in the title of one of Terry Eagleton's (2003) more recent works – *After Theory*. It is hard to say whether new paradigms are already beginning to take shape, although the appearance on the intellectual landscape in recent times of some new types of critique – 'critical realism' and 'eco-criticism' – are suggestive of a return to a more phenomenally based outlook (Hart 2004). Indeed, the very serious problems that the natural environment now poses for humanity compel us to recognize that much does in fact 'exist beyond the text' – and it will be interesting in the days ahead to chart the effect that these rude intrusions from the material world have on notions of critique in the academy. The research has suggested that we need to think of 'critical thinking' as having a diversity of meanings; equally, these meanings need to be seen as dynamic and subject to change.

Another area that needs to be researched – and which in fact exists as a serious gap in the present study – is the matter of how students themselves apprehend the idea of being critical. The decision to focus only on academics' conceptions was a deliberate one, arising from the study's principal interest in exploring the epistemological dimensions of critical thinking. However, there is much that needs to be learnt about students' engagement with the idea of critical thinking. Some of the questions that need to be asked are suggested in the imaginary assignment task outlined above (Figure 26), though there are certainly others. What, for example, amid all the term's use and publicity, do students actually understand by 'critical thinking'? How effectively are they able to negotiate different types of critique, and how much do these differences need to be articulated in some explicit way to them? Is the idea of being critical actually as oppressive to students as the study has implied?

One other question – perhaps the most important in the current climate of higher education in Australia and elsewhere – is whether these issues actually matter all that much to students nowadays. I suggested above that in the period since the data were collected, one has a sense of gathering change in the overall intellectual climate. Another area of change has been in the general conditions of study and work that prevail in universities, where managerial processes of restructure and reform appear to have become even more intense in the last half decade. It is hard to feel anything but pessimism about such changes, especially for the effect they appear to be having on students. Indeed, a term now frequently invoked to characterize students' experience of tertiary study is 'disengagement' (MacInnis 2002), a phenomenon associated with declining student attendance at campuses and in classes, a perfunctory attitude brought to assessment work, and an increasingly instrumentalist and pragmatic view of the value of a higher education. While some commentators attribute these developments mainly to the increasing financial pressures felt by students (MacInnes 2002), for others they are the inevitable outcome of an increasingly market-driven system, where universities are run more and more along business lines, and where students are encouraged more and more to think upon their experiences of learning in terms of the levels of customer satisfaction attained (Marginson 2000).

In such an environment, one now criticized in almost equal measure by academics from the traditional right as well as the left (see Saunders 2006; Davies 2003)[2], it will be interesting to chart the progress of critique – to see whether, as a concept, it manages to retain any meaning and power for students, or whether increasingly it will be seen as just another 'skills box to be ticked and certified' in the overall 'educational package' delivered to them (Taylor 2000). The less-than-sanguine state of higher education currently in much of the English-speaking world gives one pause to think that the future of critique may be bound up somehow in students recognizing that some of their best critical thoughts might profitably be directed at the university system itself, and at the increasingly diminished education that many now seem to be receiving.

7.4 Final Remarks: Critical Thinking Defined?

This book began with an account of Raymond Williams' encounter with what he called new and difficult words. Williams' response to this experience was to write his famous work *Keywords* – his attempt to make sense of that shared, but 'imperfect' vocabulary which lies at the heart of 'our discussions of the most central processes of our common life' (1976: p.12). But, Williams' purpose in compiling his inventory of terms was not to try to get a fix on their meaning – to offer up some final consensual definition for each; indeed, his purpose was something like the opposite – to explore the complexity of these terms, and to recognize that there is always an element of struggle in making them comprehensible, both to oneself and to others.

I quote Williams at some length in these final pages, for his insights about words and their difficulties have much relevance to all that has been discussed previously. In terms rather similar to Wittgenstein, Williams suggests that any process which seeks to clarify the meanings of difficult words (such as we have seen among some within the critical thinking movement) is unlikely to help resolve confusions:

> I do not share the optimism, or the theories which underlie it ... which suppose that clarification of difficult words would help in the resolution of disputes conducted in their terms and [which are] often visibly confused by them. (p. 20)

Instead of seeking to 'purify the dialect of the tribe', an expression borrowed from Eliot, Williams suggests we need to see these imprecisions and uncertainties as matters of 'contemporary substance', and as 'variations' to be insisted upon.

> It is not only that nobody can 'purify the dialect of the tribe', nor only that anyone who really knows himself to be a member of a society knows better than to want, in those terms, to try. It is also that the variations and confusions of meaning are not just faults in a system, or errors of feedback, or deficiencies of education. They are in many cases, in my terms, historical and contemporary substance. Indeed they are often variations to be insisted upon, just because they embody different experiences and readings of experience, and this will continue to be true in active relationships and conflicts, over and above the clarifying exercises of scholars or committees. What can really be contributed is not resolution, but perhaps at times that extra edge of consciousness. (p. 21)

Thus, in the act of trying to understand and appreciate these 'varieties of tradition and experience', what might emerge, Williams suggests, is an 'extra edge of consciousness'. This evocative expression, which suggests a mainly empathic view of knowledge and of its creators and purveyors, may be as good a definition as any for the difficult term we have been considering in all the preceding pages. Indeed, in trying to make sense of 'critical thinking', and in working out how it might be best taught, it may be that it is above all this quality – 'an extra edge of consciousness' – that we should hope to encourage in our students, and also in ourselves, and in the world generally, in spite of the many challenges that we all face.

Notes

Chapter 2

[1] The CT acronym is avoided in this work.
[2] See also Burbules and Berk (1999) for an extended discussion of the differences between these two traditions.

Chapter 3

[1] The Department of Linguistics had, at the time, a strong sociolinguistic orientation which saw limited commonality of interest with the largely theoretical linguistic orientations of the philosophers.

Chapter 7

[1] In this way, the research site was different from the one investigated in Swales's (1998) university building study. Whereas Swales's building was inhabited by three distinct and unrelated departments, whose co-occupancy was largely an historical accident, we need to think of the building in the present study as housing a diverse but integrated community.
[2] As critiques go, it is hard to find a more devastating one than that contained in Coetzee's novel *Diary of a Bad Year*. In the novel, Coetzee's alter-ego protagonist argues that the transformation of universities into 'business enterprises' is now so complete that the time may have come for us to give up on them as places of learning altogether, and take the activity somewhere else (2006: p.31).

Bibliography

Atkinson, D. (1997), 'A critical approach to critical thinking in TESOL', *TESOL Quarterly*, 31/1: 71–94.

Audi, R. (1999), *The Cambridge Dictionary of Philosophy*, 2nd edn (Cambridge: Cambridge University Press).

Australian Academy of the Humanities (1999), *Knowing Ourselves and Others: The Humanities in Australia into the 21st Century* (Canberra: Australian Government Printing Service).

Australian Council of Education Research (2001), *Graduate Skills Assessment*. < http://www.acer.edu.au/unitest/index.html > accessed 11 August 2006.

Australian Higher Education Council (1992), *Higher Education: Achieving Quality* (Canberra: NBEET/AGPS).

Baldauf, R. (1996), 'Tertiary literacy policies: Needs and practice', in Z. Golebiowski, ed., *Policy and Practice of Tertiary Literacy: Selected proceedings of the First National Conference on Tertiary Literacy: Research and Practice Vol. II* (Melbourne: Victoria), 1–19.

Ballard, B., and Clanchy, J. (1988), 'Literacy in the university: An anthropological approach', in G. Taylor, B. Ballard, V. Beasley, H. Bock, J. Clanchy and P. Nightingale, eds, *Literacy by Degrees* (Buckingham: The Society for Research into Higher Education and Open University).

—(1991), *Teaching Students from Overseas: A Brief Guide to Lecturers and Supervisors* (Malaysia: Longman).

—(1995), 'Generic skills in the context of higher education', *Higher Education Research and Development*, 14/2: 155–166.

Barnett, R. (2000), *The Limits of Competence: Knowledge, Higher Education and Society* (Buckingham: The Society for Research into Higher Education and Open University).

—(2001), 'Recovering an academic community – above but not beyond', in R. Barnett, ed., *Academic Community: Discourse or Discord?* (London: Jessica Kingsley), 3–19.

—(2004), 'Learning for an unknown future', *Higher Education Research and Development*, 23/3: 248–260.

Baron, J., and Sternberg, R. (1987), 'Introduction', in J. Baron and R. Sternberg, eds, *Teaching Thinking Skills* (New York: W.H. Freeman), 1–6.

Barthes, R. (1977), *Image – Music – Text* (Glasgow: Fontana).

Baumann, Z. (1992), *Intimations of Postmodernity* (London: Routledge).

Bazerman, C. (1988), *Shaping Written Knowledge* (Madison: University of Wisconsin Press).

—(1998), Editor's introduction in P. Prior, *Writing/Disciplinarity: A Sociohistoric Account of Literate Activity in the Academy* (Malwah, NJ: Lawrence Erlbaum).

Becher, T (1981), 'Towards a definition of disciplinary cultures', *Studies in Higher Education*, 6/2: 109–122.

—(1989), *Academic Tribes and Territories: Intellectual Inquiry and the Cultures of Disciplines* (Milton Keynes: Open University Press).

Benesch, S. (2001), *Critical English for Academic Purposes* (New Jersey: Lawrence Erlbaum).

Berkenkotter, C., and Huckin, T. (1995), *Genre Knowledge in Disciplinary Communication: Cognition/Culture/Power* (Hillsdale, NJ: Lawrence Erlbaum).

Black, M. (1946), *Critical Thinking* (Englewood Cliffs, NJ: Prentice-Hall).

Blatz, C. (1992), 'Contextual limits on reasoning and testing for critical thinking', in S. P. Norris, ed., *The Generalizability of Critical Thinking: Multiple Perspectives on an Educational Ideal* (New York: Teachers College Press), 206–222.

Blair, A. (1992), 'The generalizability of critical thinking: The evaluation of sources', in S. P. Norris, ed., *The Generalizability of Critical Thinking: Multiple Perspectives on an Educational Ideal* (New York: Teachers College Press), 125–137.

Bloom, A. (1987), *The Closing of the American Mind: How Higher Education has Failed Democracy and Impoverished the Souls of Today's Students* (New York: Simon and Schuster).

Bloom, H. (1994), *The Western Canon: The Books and School of the Ages* (New York: Harcourt Brace).

Bourdieu, P. (1977), *Outline of a Theory of Practice*, trans. R. Nice (Cambridge: Cambridge University Press).

—(1984), *Distinction: A Social Critique of the Judgement of Taste*, trans. R. Nice (Cambridge, MA: Harvard University Press).

Bowen, J. (1972a), *A History of Western Education Vol. 1 The Ancient World: Orient and Mediterranean* (London: Methuen).

—(1972b), *A History of Western Education Vol. 3 The Modern West: Europe and the New World* (London: Methuen).

Burbules, N., and Berk, R. (1999), 'Critical thinking and critical pedagogy: Relations, differences and limits', in T. Popkewitz and L. Fendler, eds, *Critical Theories in Education* (New York: Routledge), 1–20.

Candlin, C. (1998), 'Researching writing in the academy: Participants, texts, processes and practices', in C. Candlin and G. Plum, eds, *Researching Academic Literacies* (Sydney: Macquarie University).

Candlin, C., Bhatia, V., and Hyland, K. (1997), *Academic Communication in Disciplinary Communities* (Hong Kong: Department of English, City University of Hong Kong).

Cannadine, D. (2001), *What is History Now?* (London: Palgrave Macmillan).

Capossela, T. (1993), 'What is critical writing?', in T. Capossela, ed., *The Critical Writing Workshop: Designing Writing Assignments to Foster Critical Thinking* (Portsmouth, NH: Heinemann), 1–10.

Carr, E. H. (1961), *What is History?* (London: MacMillan).

Chanock, K. (2000), 'Comments on essays: Do students understand what tutors write?', *Teaching in Higher Education*, 5/1: 95–105.

—(2005), 'John Grierson keynote: Critiquing and reflecting', *Proceedings of Eighth Biennial Language and Academic Skills Conference* (Australian National University).

Clendinnen, I. (2006), *The History Question: Who Owns the Past?* (Melbourne: Black Inc).

Clerehan, R, Chanock, K., and Moore, T. (2004), 'Shaping university teaching towards measurement for accountability: Problems of the graduate skills assessment test', *Australian University Review*, 47/1: 22–29.

Clinchy, B. (1994), 'On critical thinking and connected knowing', in K. S. Walters, ed., *Rethinking Reason: New Perspectives on Critical Thinking* (Albany, NY: SUNY Press), 33–42.

Coady, T. (1998), 'New things under the sun', in J. Bigelow, ed., *Our Cultural Heritage* (Canberra: The Australian Academy of the Humanities), 27–42.

Coetzee, J. M. (1999), *Disgrace* (London: Vintage).

—(2006), *Diary of Bad Year* (Melbourne: Text).

Coulthard, M. (1994), 'On analysing and evaluating written text', in M. Coulthard, ed., *Advances in Written Text Analysis* (London: Routledge), 1–11.

Critchley, S. (2001), *Continental Philosophy: A Very Short Introduction* (Oxford: Oxford University Press).

D'Angelo, E. (1971), *The Teaching of Critical Thinking* (Amsterdam: Gruner).

Davies, B. (2003), 'Death to critique and dissent? The politics and practices of new mangerialism and of evidence-based practice', *Gender and Education*, 15/1: 91–103.

Davies, W. M. (2006). 'An infusion approach to critical thinking: Moore on the critical thinking debate'. Higher Education Research and Development 25/3: 243–246.

Delanty, G. (2001), *Challenging Knowledge: The University in the Knowledge Society* (Buckingham: The Society for Research into Higher Education and Open University).

Derrida, J. (1967), *Of Grammatology* (Baltimore: John Hopkins Press).

Descartes, R (1965), *Discourse on Method* (Indiana: Bobbs-Merrill).

Dewey, J. (1933), *How We Think* (Boston: D.C. Heath).

Dudley-Evans, T. (2002), 'The teaching of the academic essay: Is a genre approach possible?', in A. M. Johns, ed., *Genre in the Classroom: Multiple Perspectives* (New Jersey: Lawrence Erlbaum), 225–35.

Eagleton, T. (1996), *Literary Theory*, 2nd edn (Oxford: Blackwell).

—(2003), *After Theory* (London: Allen Lane).

Edmonds, D., and Eidinow, J. (2001), *Wittgenstein's Poker: The Story of a Ten-Minute Argument Between Two Great Philosophers* (London: Faber and Faber).

Ennis, R. (1962), 'A concept of critical thinking', *Harvard Educational Review*, 32/1: 81–111.

—(1987), 'A taxonomy of critical thinking abilities and dispositions', in J. Baron and R. Sternberg, eds, *Teaching Thinking Skills* (New York: W.H. Freeman), 9–26.

—(1992a), 'The degree to which critical thinking is subject specific: Clarification and needed research', in S. P. Norris, ed., *The Generalizability of Critical Thinking: Multiple Perspectives on an Educational Ideal* (New York: Teachers College Press), 21–37.

—(1992b), 'Critical thinking: What is it?' *Philosophy of Education Society.* < http://www.ed.uiuc.edu/EPS/PES-yearbook/92_docs/Ennis.htm > accessed 22 October 2010.

—(2001), 'An outline of goals for a critical thinking curriculum and its assessment'.
< http://facultyed.uiuc.edu/rhennis/outlinegoalsctcurassess3.htm > accessed
22 October 2002.

Entwistle, N., Pery, K., and Nisbett, J. (1971), *Educational Objectives and Academic Performance in Higher Education* (Lancaster: University of Lancaster, Department of
Educational Research).

Evans, R. (2005), 'What is history?', in H. Swain, ed., *Big Questions in History*
(London: Jonathon Cape), 3–7.

Facione, P. (1990), *Critical Thinking: A Statement of Expert Consensus for Purposes of Educational Assessment and Instruction* (Millibrae, CA: The California Academic Press).

Fairclough, N. (1985), 'Critical and descriptive goals of discourse analysis', *Journal
of Pragmatics* 9: 739–63.

—(1996), 'A reply to Henry Widdowson's "Discourse analysis: A critical view"',
Language and Literature, 5/1: 49–56.

Foucault, M. (1970), *The Order of Things* (London: Tavistock).

—(1980), *Power/Knowledge: Selected Interviews and Other Writings, 1972–1977*, ed.
C. Gordon (New York: Pantheon Books).

Fox, H. (1994), *Listening to the World: Cultural Issues in Academic Writing* (Urbana:
National Council of Teachers of English).

Franklin, J. (2003), *Corrupting the Youth: A History of Philosophy in Australia* (Sydney:
Macleay Press).

Freire, P. (1970), *Pedagogy of the Oppressed* (New York: Seabury).

Frow, J. (1992), 'Beyond the disciplines: Cultural studies', in K. Ruthven, ed., *Beyond
the Disciplines: The New Humanities* (Canberra: The Australian Academy of the
Humanities), 22–28.

Gadamer, H. G. (1975), *Truth and Method* (London: Sheed and Ward).

Gardner, H. (1985), *The Minds New Science: A History of the Cognitive Revolution* (New
York: Basic Books).

Gellin, A. (2003), 'The effect of undergraduate student involvement on critical
thinking: A meta-analysis of the literature', *Journal of College Student Development*,
44/6: 746–762.

Geertz, C. (1973), *Interpretations of Cultures* (New York: Basic Books).

—(1983), *Local Knowledge* (New York: Basic Books).

Giroux, H. (1988), *Teachers as Intellectuals: Towards a Critical Pedagogy of Learning*
(South Hadley, MA: Bergin Garvey).

Glaser, R. (1984), 'Education and thinking: The role of knowledge', *American
Psychologist*, 39/2: 93–104.

Green, K. (1999), 'A plague on both your houses', *The Monist*, 82/2: 278–303.

Grosz, E. (1989), *Sexual Subversions* (St. Leonards: Allen and Unwin).

Haines, S. (2006), 'There's more to study than politics', *The Australian* 9/06/08.

Halliday, M. A. K. (1994), *An Introduction to Functional Grammar*, 2nd edn (London:
Edward Arnold).

Hamersley, J. (1996), *On the Foundation of Critical Discourse Analysis* (Centre for
Language in Education Occasional Papers: Southampton Centre for Language
in Education).

Harman, K. (1990), 'Culture and conflict in academic organizations', *Journal of
Educational Administration*, 27/3: 30–54.

Harney, M. (1992), 'The contemporary European tradition in Australia', in J. Srzednicki and D. Wood, eds, *Essays in Philosophy in Australia* (Dordecht: Kluwer), 125–151.

Hart, K. (2004), *Postmodernism: A Guide* (Oxford: One World).

Harvard Committee (1945), *General Education in a Free Society* (Cambridge, MA: Harvard University Press).

Hirsch, E. D. (1987), *Cultural Literacy* (New York: Houghton Mifflin).

Hodge, B. (1995), 'Monstrous knowledge: Doing PhDs in the new humanities', *Australian Universities Review*, 38/2: 35–45.

Hoggart, R. (1970), *The Uses of Literacy* (Oxford: Oxford University Press).

Horowitz, D. (1986), 'What professors actually require of students: Academic tasks for the ESL classroom', *TESOL Quarterly*, 20: 445–62.

Hounsell, D. (1997), 'Contrasting conceptions of essay writing', in D. Hounsell and N. Entwistle, eds, *The experience of learning* (Edinburgh: Scottish Academic Press).

Huddleston, R. (1982), *Introduction to the Grammar of English* (Cambridge: Cambridge University Press).

Humphries, R. (1999), 'Analytic and continental: The division in philosophy', *The Monist*, 82/2: 253–277.

Hyland, K. (2000), *Disciplinary Discourse: Social Interactions in Academic Writing* (London: Longman).

Ivanic, R., and Simpson, J. (1992), 'Who's who in academic writing?', in N. Fairclough, ed, *Critical Language Awareness* (Harlow: Longman), 144–73.

Johnson, R. H. (1992), 'The problem of defining critical thinking', in S. P. Norris, ed, *The Generalizability of Critical Thinking: Multiple Perspectives on an Educational Ideal* (New York: Teachers College Press), 21–37.

Kuhn, D. (1991), *The Skills of Argument* (Cambridge: Cambridge University Press).

Kuhn, T. (1962), *The Structure of Scientific Revolutions* (Chicago: University of Chicago Press).

Lave, J., and Wenger, E. (1991), *Situated Learning: Legitimate Peripheral Participation* (Cambridge: Cambridge University Press).

Leavis, F. R. (1948), *The Great Tradition* (London: Chatto and Windus).

Le Doeuff, M. (1980), 'Women and philosophy', *Radical Philosophy*, 17: 2–12.

Lipman, M. (1988), 'Critical thinking: What can it be?', *Analytic Teaching*, 8: 5–12.

—(1991), *Thinking in Education* (Cambridge: Cambridge University Press).

Lyons, J. (1977), *Semantics Vol. 2* (Cambridge University Press: Cambridge).

MacDonald, S. P. (1994), *Professional Academic Writing in the Humanities and Social Sciences* (Carbondale and Edwardsville: Southern Illinois University Press).

McInnis, C. (2002), 'Signs of disengagement', in J. Enders and O. Fulton, eds, *Higher Education in a Globalizing World* (Dordecht: Kluwer), 175–189.

Macintyre, S. (2003), *The History Wars* (Melbourne: Melbourne University Press).

McPeck, J. (1981), *Critical Thinking and Education* (New York: St. Martin's Press).

—(1990), *Teaching Critical Thinking: Dialogue and Dialectic* (New York: Routledge).

—(1992), 'Thoughts on subject specificity', in S. P. Norris, ed, *The Generalizability of Critical Thinking: Multiple Perspectives on an Educational Ideal* (New York: Teachers College Press), 198–205.

Marginson, S., and Considine, M. (2000), *The Enterprise University: Power, Governance and Reinvention in Australia* (Cambridge University Press: Cambridge).

Marton, F. (1988), 'Phenomenography: Exploring different conceptions of reality', in D. M. Fetterman, ed, *Qualitative Approaches to Evaluation in Education: The Silent Revolution* (New York: Praeger), 176–205.

Marx, K. (1845/1977). 'Theses on Feuerbach', in D. Mclellan, ed, *Karl Marx: Selected Writings* (Oxford: Oxford University Press).

Medina, J. (2005), *Language: Key Concepts in Philosophy* (New York: Continuum).

Milner A., and Browitt, J. (2002), *Contemporary Cultural Theory*, 3rd edn (Crows Nest, NSW: Allen and Unwin).

Mishler, E. G. (1980), 'Comments on symposium on adults conceptions of reality', paper presented at *American Educational Research Association*, Boston, April 7–11.

Moore, T. (2004), 'The critical thinking debate: How general are general thinking skills?' *Higher Education Research and Development*, 23/1: 3–18.

Montaigne, M. (1956), 'Of the education of children', in Donald M. Frame, ed, *Complete Works of Montaigne* (Stanford), 106–31.

Nelson, C., Treichler, P., and Grossberg, L. (1992), 'Cultural studies: An introduction', in L. Grossberg, C. Nelson and P. Treichler, eds, *Cultural Studies* (New York: Routledge).

Newman, J. H. (1980), *The Idea of a University* (London: Yale University Press).

Nightingale, V. (1998), 'Crisis in the humanities', in J. Bigelow, ed, *Our Cultural Heritage* (Canberra: The Australian Academy of the Humanities), 89–112.

Norris, S. P. (1992), 'Introduction: The generalizability question', in S. P. Norris, ed, *The Generalizability of Critical Thinking: Multiple Perspectives on an Educational Ideal* (New York: Teachers College Press), 21–37.

Nickerson, R. (1994), 'The teaching of thinking and problem solving', in R. Sternberg, ed, *Thinking and Problem Solving* (New York: Academic Press), 409–449.

Odell, L., Goswami, D., and Herrington, A. (1983), 'The discourse-based interview: A procedure for exploring the tacit knowledge of writers in nonacademic settings', in P. Mosenthal, L. Tamor and S. Walmsley, eds, *Research on Writing: Principles and Methods* (New York: Longman), 221–236.

Pascoe, R. (2002), 'An Australian perspective on the humanities', *Arts and Humanities in Higher Education*, 2/1: 7–22.

Pascoe, R., MacIntyre, S., and Ainley, J. (2003), *The Lettered Country: Learning Outcomes and Curriculum Development in the Bachelor of Arts, Humanities and Social Sciences* (Canberra: Commonwealth of Australia).

Paul, R. (1989), 'Critical thinking in North America: A new theory of knowledge learning and literacy', *Argumentation*, 3: 197–235.

—(1996), *A Draft Statement of Principles*, National Council for Excellence in Critical Thinking. < www.criticalthinking.org.ncet.html > accessed 22 October 2002.

Phillips, V., and Bond, C. (2004), 'Undergraduates' experience of critical thinking', *Higher Education Research and Development*, 23/3: 277–294.

Piaget, J. (1967), 'Language and thought from the genetic point of view', in D. Elkind, ed, *Psychological Studies* (New York: Random House), 88–99.

Price, H. (2004), 'Letter to the editor', *Times Literary Supplement*, 24 June 2004.

Prior, P. (1998), *Writing/Disciplinarity: A Sociohistoric Account of Literate Activity in the Academy* (Malwah, New Jersey: Lawrence Erlbaum).

Ramsden, P. (1985), 'Alternatives to learning skills', *Proceedings of the Sixth Annual Australasian Tertiary Studies Skills Conference*, Adelaide.

—(1992), *Learning to Teach in Higher Education* (London: Routledge).

Resnick, L. (1987), *Education and Learning to Think* (Washington, DC: National Academy Press).

Reynolds, H. (2001), *An Indelible Stain: The Question of Genocide in Australia's History* (Ringwood: Penguin).

Rubinstein, W. (2006), 'The culture wars down under: Keith Windschuttle, the aborigines and the left', *Social Affairs Unit.* < http://www.socialaffairsunit.org. uk/archives/001055 > accessed 23 October 2008.

Ruthven, K. (1992), 'Introduction', in K. Ruthven, ed, *Beyond the Disciplines: The New Humanities* (Canberra: The Australian Academy of the Humanities), vii–ix.

Ryan, Y., Dearn, J., and Fraser, K. (2002), *Investigation into the Provision of Professional Development for University Teaching in Australia* (Canberra: Department of Education, Science and Training).

Saunders, M. (2006), 'The madness and malady of managerialism', *Quadrant,* 424: 9–17.

Shor, I (1987), *Critical teaching and everyday life* (Chicago: The University of Chicago Press).

Siegel, H. (1988), *Educating Reason: Rationality, Critical Thinking and Education* (New York: Routledge).

Siegler, R., and Richards. D. (1982), 'The development of intelligence', in R. Sternberg, ed, *Handbook of Human Intelligence* (Cambridge: Cambridge University Press), 897–971.

Singer, P. (1993), *Practical ethics,* 2nd edn (Cambridge University Press: Cambridge).

Solomon, R. (1988), *Continental Philosophy since 1750: The Rise and Fall of Self* (Oxford: Oxford University Press).

Starfield, S. (2001), '"I'll go with the group": Rethinking discourse community in EAP', in J. Flowerdew and M. Peacock, eds, *Research perspectives on English for Academic Purposes* (Cambridge: Cambridge University Press), 132–47.

Sternberg, R. (1987) 'Introduction', in Baron, J. and R. Sternberg, eds, *Teaching thinking skills* (New York: W.H. Freeman), 1–6.

Swain, H. (2005), 'What is History?: Commentary', in H. Swain, ed, *Big Questions in History* (London: Jonathon Cape), 8–12.

Swales, J. (1990), *Genre Analysis: English in Academic and Research Settings* (Cambridge: Cambridge University Press).

—(1998), *Other Floors, Other Voices: A Textography of a Small University Building* (Mahway, N.J: Lawrence Erlbaum Associates).

—(2008), Personal communication, Comments made on original manuscript.

Tapper, J. (2004), 'Students perception of how critical thinking is embedded in a degree programme', *Higher Education Research and Development,* 23/2: 199–222

Taylor, G. (1993), 'A theory of practice: Hermeneutical understanding', *Higher Research and Development,* 12/1: 59–72.

—(2000), 'The generic and the disciplined: Can universal and particular be reconciled?' in G. Crosling, T. Moore and S. Vance, eds, *The Learning Dimension. Proceedings of the Third National Language and Academic Skills Conference* (Melbourne: Monash University).

Toulmin, S. (1958), *The Uses of Argument* (Cambridge: Cambridge University Press).

—(1972), *Human Understanding Vol. 1* (Oxford: Clarendon Press).

—(1995), 'Foreword', in R. F. Goodman and W. Fisher, eds, *Rethinking Knowledge: Reflections across the Disciplines* (Albany: SUNY), i–v.

Tsui, L. (2000), 'Effects of campus culture on students' critical thinking', *Review of Higher Education*, 23/4: 421–441.

—(2002), 'Fostering critical thinking through effective pedagogy: Evidence from four institutional case studies', *Journal of Higher Education*, 73/6: 740–63.

University X (2001), *Leading the way* (Clayton: University X).

van Gelder, T. (2000), 'Learning to reason: A reasonable approach', in C. Davis, T. van Gelder and R. Wales, eds, *Cognitive Science in Australia, 2000: Proceedings of the Fifth Australasian Cognitive Science Society Conference*, Adelaide.

—(2001), 'Improving critical thinking using educational technology'. *Proceedings of Fourth ASCILITE Conference*, Melbourne.

Vygostky, L. (1962), *Thought and Language* (Cambridge, Mass: MIT Press).

Waite, S. and Davis, B. (2006), 'Collaboration as a basis for critical thinking in undergraduate research', *Journal of Further and Higher education Research*, 30/4: 405–19.

Walters, K.S. (1994), 'Introduction: Beyond logicism in critical thinking', in K. S. Walters, ed, *Rethinking Reason: New Perspectives on Critical Thinking* (Albany, NY: SUNY Press), 33–42.

Wheeler, T. (1986), 'Indeterminacy of French translation: Derrida and Davidson', in E. LePore, ed, *Truth and Interpretation: Perspectives on the Philosophy of Donald Davidson* (London: Blackwell).

White, H. (1995), 'Response to Arthur Marwick', *Journal of Contemporary History*, 30/2: 233–246.

Widdowson, H. (1995), 'Discourse analysis: A critical view'. *Language and Literature*, 4/3: 157–172.

—(1996), 'Reply to Fairclough: Discourse and interpretation: Conjectures and refutations', *Language and Literature*, 5/1: 57–69.

Williams, R. (1976), *Keywords* (London: Collins).

Windschuttle, K. (1994), *The Killing of History* (Sydney: Macleay Press).

Wittgenstein, L. (1958a), *Philosophical Investigations*, 2nd edn (Oxford: Basil Blackwell).

—(1958b), *The Blue and Brown Books* (Oxford: Basil Blackwell).

—(1961), *Tractatus Logico-Philosophicus* (London: Routledge and Kegan Paul).

Zamel, V. (1997), 'Toward a model of transculturation', *TESOL Quarterly*, 31/2: 341–351.

Index

CPSIA information can be obtained at www.ICGtesting.com
Printed in the USA
LVOW01s1053210713

343870LV00002B/62/P